ALSO BY MARK DANNER

Stripping Bare the Body

The Secret Way to War

Torture and Truth

The Road to Illegitimacy

The Massacre at El Mozote

SPIRAL

TRAPPED *in the* FOREVER WAR

. . . . .

MARK DANNER

SIMON & SCHUSTER
New York London Toronto Sydney New Delhi

Simon & Schuster
1230 Avenue of the Americas
New York, NY 10020

Portions of the Introduction and Part One previously appeared in different form in the *New York Review of Books*.

Excerpt from "Tortures" from *View with a Grain of Sand: Selected Poems by Wisława Szymborska*, translated from the Polish by Stanisław Barańczak and Clare Cavanagh. Copyright © 1995 by Houghton Mifflin Harcourt. Copyright © 1976 by Czytelnik, Warszawa. Reprinted by permission of Houghton Mifflin Harcourt. All rights reserved.

First Simon & Schuster hardcover edition June 2016

SIMON & SCHUSTER and colophon are registered trademarks of Simon & Schuster, Inc.

For information about special discounts for bulk purchases, please contact Simon & Schuster Special Sales at 1-866-506-1949 or business@simonandschuster.com.

The Simon & Schuster Speakers Bureau can bring authors to your live event. For more information, or to book an event, contact the Simon & Schuster Speakers Bureau at 1-866-248-3049 or visit our website at www.simonspeakers.com.

Interior design by Lewelin Polanco

Manufactured in the United States of America

10 9 8 7 6 5 4 3 2 1

Library of Congress Cataloging-in-Publication Data
Names: Danner, Mark, 1958- author.
Title: Spiral : trapped in the forever war / Mark Danner.
Description: New York : Simon & Schuster, 2016. | Includes index.
Identifiers: LCCN 2016000732 (print) | LCCN 2016014476 (ebook) | ISBN
    9781476747767 (hardback) | ISBN 9781476747774 (trade paperback) | ISBN
    9781476747781 (ebook)
Subjects: LCSH: United States--History, Military--21st century. | United
    States--Military policy--21st century | War on Terrorism,
    2001-2009--Political aspects--United States. |
    Terrorism--Prevention--History--21st century. | United States--Foreign
    relations--21st century. | Military history, Modern--21st century. | World
    politics--21st century. | BISAC: POLITICAL SCIENCE / Government / General.
    | HISTORY / United States / 21st Century. | LAW / Military.
Classification: LCC E897 .D36 2016 (print) | LCC E897 (ebook) | DDC
    355.00973--dc23
LC record available at http://lccn.loc.gov/2016000732

ISBN 978-1-4767-4776-7
ISBN 978-1-4767-4778-1 (ebook)

For Robert J. Cox

Spiral: a curve that emanates from a central point, getting
progressively farther away . . .

CONTENTS

SPIRAL

INTRODUCTION

We must define the nature and scope of this struggle, or else it will define us.

—President Barack Obama, May 23, 2013

America must move off a permanent war footing.

—President Barack Obama, January 28, 2014

I came upon the half-destroyed truck atop a highway overpass outside Fallujah, the cab shot to hell, the trailer bloodstained and propped up at a crazy angle on its blown tires. On the highway below a great black burn scarred the concrete and over it a rust-red slash, the soot and blood marking the spot where, earlier that day in October 2003, the insurgents had used a cheap remote control to ignite barrels of concealed explosives just as the U.S. armored patrol rumbled by, killing one paratrooper, wounding several. Insurgents, hidden in houses nearby, followed with bursts from their AK-47s.

The Americans promptly dismounted and with their M16s and M4s began pouring lead into everything they could see, starting with the truck that happened to be passing on the highway above, eviscerating the unfortunate driver, and then fired into the houses. How many Iraqis had the troops killed and wounded? The more the better, as far as insurgent leaders were concerned. "The point is to get the Americans to fire back," the commanding general of the 82nd Airborne told me the next day, "and hopefully the bad guys'll get some Iraqi casualties out of that and they can publicize that." By week's end scores of family and close friends of those killed and wounded would join the insurgents, for honor demanded they kill Americans to wipe away family shame.

American firepower plus Iraqi deaths equals more insurgents: an axiom in the strategy of provocation. Provoke your enemy to kill civilians and thereby call to battle the sleeping population. You have no army? Use the aggression of the occupiers to help raise one of your own. In Iraq, insurgents have used that strategy to grow and prosper, recognizing the characteristic American quickness to react with overwhelming firepower as their best friend. Across continents, al Qaeda used it as well, blowing up towers in New York to create an indelible recruiting poster for the worldwide cause while provoking self-defeating responses. Lure the Americans into Afghanistan, where they'll sink into the quagmire that had trapped their superpower rival two decades before.

Such was Osama bin Laden's strategy. Could he have dared dream that the Americans would prove so cooperative as to invade Iraq as well? Like a celestial slot machine daily pouring forth its golden bounty, the September 11 attacks had led the administration of President George W. Bush not only to an assault on Afghanistan but, scarcely a year later, to a wonderfully telegenic invasion of a major Muslim country. To an attack by a small insurgent group that called for Muslims to rise up and throw off American oppression, the United States had responded by dispatching 150,000 Americans to oppress Muslims. Now the tiny Islamic fringe movement could point to television screens as American tanks rumbled down the streets of an Arab capital, as American soldiers rousted Muslims from their beds, threw them to the ground, placed unclean boots on their backs: as they stripped them and tortured them at the notorious Abu Ghraib prison, as they had hooded them and forced them to their knees at Guantánamo.

Abu Ghraib did for the Iraqi insurgents what Guantánamo had done for al Qaeda, embodying in powerful images their arguments about who Americans were, what they did to Muslims, why

they must be defeated. A dozen years later the Islamic State, malign
stepchild of that insurgency, carries the argument forward with its
signature image: a young American in orange kneeling in the dust
in a desolate landscape, a knife held to his throat by a masked figure in black who declaims into the camera until the moment when
the music rises and he brings his knife into play . . . To Western au-
diences the scene says barbarism, savagery, terror. To many young
Muslims it says oppression, torture, hypocrisy, the orange jumpsuit
calling to mind other prisoners, shackled, blindfolded, ear-muffed,
kneeling under the merciless tropical sun. Contrary to the American president who insists that Guantánamo is "not who we are," to
these viewers Guantánamo is precisely who we are because it is what
we have done: Imprison Muslims and hold them indefinitely without trial. Invade and occupy Muslim countries. Torture prisoners.
Assassinate with drones.

· · · · ·

As you read these words, the United States will have been at war for at least
fourteen years, making the "war on terror" by far the longest in the
country's history. The war began the week after the attacks of September 11, 2001, when Congress passed, and President Bush signed,
the Authorization for Use of Military Force. There is no telling when
it might end. Though President Barack Obama has withdrawn most
American troops from the shooting wars in Iraq and Afghanistan
and in his second term has repeatedly warned against the perils of
"perpetual war," he has shown himself no more able than his predecessor to take the country off what he criticizes as its "permanent
war footing." For all his power, in his repeated calls to end the war
the president increasingly appears to be a man fighting a stronger
force. He warns, he warns again. Little changes. Laocoön struggles
in the coils of the serpent.

What is that stronger force? Is it terrorism or the malign political currents still churning in its wake? Since the September 11 attacks only a handful of Americans have died at the hands of Islamic terrorists—twenty-four in 2014, fewer than were killed that year by lightning—and yet the war on terror has embedded itself deeply in our psyches and in our politics. The war on terror has taken on a life of its own, nourished by the politics of fear and nourishing in its turn powerful institutions of national security. United States' military spending, already greater than that of the next ten countries combined, nearly doubled. Its intelligence budget—so far as we know—more than doubled.

On the ground it has been a strange war, a mix of real and virtual, carried on partly in the glaring light by American warplanes and soldiers and partly in the darkness by special operators and unmanned aerial vehicles, or drones. Even as U.S. troops began to leave behind the hot wars in Iraq and Afghanistan, in Pakistan, Yemen, and Somalia, U.S. drones were killing thousands, some of them al Qaeda leaders but many more low-level militants in organizations that did not yet exist on September 11. This so-called third war—after Afghanistan and Iraq—has now given way to a fourth, the war on the Islamic State, which President Obama vowed in September 2014 "to degrade and ultimately destroy." In the cause of "taking out terrorists who threaten us, while supporting partners on the front lines"—a strategy, the president insisted, that "we have successfully pursued in Yemen and Somalia for years"—the United States sent thousands of troops back to Iraq and launched thousands of air strikes in Iraq and Syria. Months later, he had to hastily withdraw American security forces from Yemen as this particular "partner on the front lines" collapsed amid sectarian warfare.

After the attacks of September 11 the United States faced a global terrorist organization with thousands of trained fighters, a network of regional affiliate groups, and an innovative program of Internet-based propaganda and recruitment. After fourteen years of war the United States finds itself facing not one such organization but two, and the second the United States itself did much to create. The Islamic State, which governs a territory the size of the United Kingdom and a population greater than that of New Zealand, is a direct descendant of al Qaeda in Iraq, which itself was born of the Iraq War, a war of choice launched by President Bush that helped unleash a historic wave of destruction, instability, and sectarian fighting that has upended the traditional American-sustained order in the Middle East. President Obama's decision a decade later to bomb the Islamic State in order to "degrade and ultimately destroy" it has dramatically helped its recruiting, hastening a vast flow of foreign fighters into its ranks.

Also driving recruiting, as we are reminded each time we see an Islamic State prisoner kneeling in his orange jumpsuit, is the persistence of immensely damaging policies on detention and interrogation that hark back to the early days of the Bush administration. Despite President Obama's vow to close it, Guantánamo remains open with nearly a hundred detainees, and each new terrorist attempt within the United States brings with it loud calls for the suspect to be "given a one-way ticket to Guantanamo" and subjected there to what we have learned to call, politely, "enhanced interrogation techniques." Each new attack—and there have been several during the Obama years, from the young Nigerian who tried to blow up an airliner over Detroit to the Pakistani American who attempted to detonate a car bomb in Times Square to the couple who attacked a holiday party in San Bernardino—brings with it a revivifying of the politics of fear and a warning that the war on terror is nowhere near an ending. Even as President Obama calls for a replacement for his predecessor's original Authorization for Use of Military Force, he has seen to it that many of what he considers his most vital national security policies, from killing by remotely piloted drone aircraft to indefinite detention of prisoners, are legally grounded in it.

Many of these policies are tactics in search of a strategy, flailing at imminent threats today at the cost of creating more terrorists tomorrow. Even as "core" al Qaeda, the original organization that attacked the United States nearly a decade and a half ago, has been "decimated"—the word is President Obama's—it has sown successor organizations like dragon's teeth throughout the Middle East, North Africa, and South Asia. Many of these organizations have been greatly helped in their growth by American military interventions launched in the stated cause of making our country safer. The birth and growth of the Islamic State exemplifies a central theme of the war on terror: that across these fourteen and more years of war the United States through its own actions has done much to aid its enemies and has sometimes helped create them. Just as the invasion and occupation of Iraq sowed the seeds of the Islamic State, the ongoing drone wars in Yemen helped lead to the dramatic expansion of al Qaeda in the Arabian Peninsula and contributed to the collapse of the Yemeni state.

Though a vanishingly small number of Americans have died in terrorist attacks since September 11, the number of deaths from terrorism around the world has soared. According to U.S. government figures, nearly 33,000 people worldwide died from terrorism in 2014, an increase of 35 percent over the year before—and of *4,000 percent* since 2002. The number of jihadist groups and jihadists went on rising, in the case of fighters fielded by the Islamic State alone to perhaps 31,000. (Unofficial estimates are much higher.) In precisely those places where the United States has concentrated its violent attention—Iraq, Afghanistan, Pakistan, Yemen, Libya—the number of attacks, deaths, and terrorists rose most dramatically. In Iraq, American troops dramatically widened a Sunni-Shia rift that the Islamic State has exploited to destabilize the entire Middle East. In Yemen, the conflict has led to a bloody Saudi invasion that the United States is supporting. We have created in the war on terror a perpetual motion machine.

. . . . .

In the pages that follow I examine the persistence of the war that began so long ago and that has inscribed itself so prominently in our national life. My intent is to show how it is that terrorist attacks on a single day could have led a great power into the trap of endless war and how that war has degraded the country's values together with its security. Some of the underlying realities are unique to the United States, notably the country's history of adopting permanent "emergency state" procedures during the four-decade-long Cold War, which concentrated vast war-fighting powers in the president's hands and established under his sole command enduring secret bureaucracies such as NORAD, the Central Intelligence Agency, and the National Security Agency. Still, the dynamic of terror and counterterror, of terrorist bombings and kidnappings provoking torture, indefinite detention, and other harsh responses from the state, is all too familiar. Watching this dynamic take shape, I found myself discerning traces, faint but distinct, of a distant time and place.

More than three decades ago, when I was nearing the end of my last year in college, I met a fascinating man, a newspaper editor who had worked in Argentina during the "dirty war" that was then running its bloody course. He had gained a kind of quiet celebrity for daring to publish in his English-language paper the names of the disappeared—until the generals lost patience and his children were threatened, sending him and his family into exile. Under his tutelage I came to study the dirty wars of the Southern Cone and the dynamic of terror and counterterror that drove them forward: the bombings and kidnappings carried out by guerrilla groups, the disappearances and torture employed by the state. This last category included as a major component the practice of *el submarino*. In the paper I wrote at the time I translated that phrase as "the submarine"—in those days, I didn't know the expression "waterboarding," nor would I have guessed that the United States would one day employ this torture in interrogating prisoners and would do so under color of law.

The United States of the war on terror is not the Argentina of the dirty war. The United States did not disappear and torture and murder thousands of its own citizens. Yet during the war on terror the United States has disappeared people and it has tortured them, with the explicit and official approval of its leaders. Those leaders were not military officers who had seized power in a coup d'état but civilian politicians who had been elected by American voters. Whatever the striking differences between the American war on terror and the dirty wars of four decades ago, the bitter cycle of terror and counterterror kept in creaking inertial motion by the politics of fear seems hauntingly familiar. High-ranking members of the U.S. government have ordered terrorist suspects to be kidnapped, detained indefinitely, and tortured. Far from drawing official condemnation and punishment, these practices, together with widespread warrantless surveillance and assassination using remotely controlled drone aircraft, have come to define a new kind of quiet counterterror whose end is nowhere in sight. Torture itself, though no longer officially practiced, exists in a strange legal netherworld in which the current president and attorney general denounce it as "plainly illegal" but do nothing to punish or even repudiate their predecessors who now speak proudly of having ordered it. In the fall of 2012 we heard from advisers to the Republican candidate for president that, if elected, he would reinstate "enhanced interrogation techniques against high-value detainees that are safe, legal and effective." The leading Republican candidates for president in 2016 seem mostly to have embraced the same position, some of them vehemently. Even as indefinite detention, warrantless wiretapping, and assassination by drone have become normalized and legalized, torture, once an anathema, has become a policy choice.

During the Cold War the United States' de facto support for the repression unleashed by friendly regimes was kept officially sub rosa, an unmentionable necessity of the emergency state that had taken shape during the late 1940s to wage what was seen as a long twilight struggle against communist subversion. Torture was something *they* did and that we, if necessary, quietly supported but officially ignored; it was never brought out into the clear light of day to be defended as a regrettable but necessary tool of policy. Such public embrace came only with the war on terror. Only then were bright young officials in the Department of Justice set to work drafting legal memoranda to show that waterboarding, when examined with a sharp lawyer's eye, did not really violate the strictures of the United Nations' Convention Against Torture or the federal statutes that had until quite recently been used to prosecute it as a crime. Torture's official approval, and its acceptance by much of the American public, has thrust us into a new era, a legal twilight world from which we do not know how to escape. All evidence suggests that Americans remain deeply conflicted about torture, with substantial numbers—perhaps a majority, depending on how the question is posed—convinced it is sometimes necessary to protect the country.

Recognizing this political reality, understanding the fear behind it and how that fear is manipulated, is vital to gaining any understanding of the politics of torture and the other attributes of what has become our permanent emergency. It is one of the regrettable consequences of the war on terror that so many Americans are now convinced that the country cannot be adequately protected without breaking the law.

Amid this struggle, President Obama's declarations that "America must move off a permanent war footing" have come to sound less like the orders of a commander in chief than the pleas of one lonely conflicted man trying to persuade. Indefinite detention, warrantless wiretapping, assassination by drone: all seem to have become, despite the expressed ambivalence of a president who has made ready use of them, permanent parts of what the country does and thus what it is. Hundreds of thousands of people in Iraq and Afghanistan have died in the wars of September 11. Thousands more have been killed in U.S. drone attacks. Millions have had their email and telephone metadata collected without a warrant. Hundreds were disappeared into secret prisons. Scores remain in indefinite detention. No end is in sight. On the contrary, all elements seem in place to perpetuate a shadow war that few are willing to take the political risk of bringing to an end.

Meantime the permanent politics of fear makes the country uniquely vulnerable to the very terrorism it means to combat. A vast counterterror apparatus has arisen that serves to magnify the importance of each terrorist attempt, and politicians and the press do their part to multiply the fear. Only in the post–September 11 era would it have been conceivable for two young men using nothing more than two homemade pressure-cooker bombs to shut down the city of Boston or for an anonymous troublemaker with a "crudely written email threat" to close the entire Los Angeles school system. In our fear and anxiety we have become a highly tuned instrument, taut and tense, ever ready for terrorists to play upon. We have fallen into a self-defeating spiral of reaction and counterterror. Our policies, meant to extirpate our enemies, have strengthened and perpetuated them. To see this one need look no further than Iraq, where a repressive secular regime has been replaced in a third of the country by the self-proclaimed Islamic State; or Libya, where the U.S.-led overthrow of the Gaddafi regime has led to a lawless vacuum in which the Islamic State thrives; or Yemen, where under the constant "secret" bombardment of American drones al Qaeda in the Arabian Peninsula has grown from a few hundred militants to more than a thousand. Neither al Qaeda in the Arabian Peninsula nor the Islamic State existed on September 11, 2001. In the years since, even as we have sacrificed our values at the altar of our own fear, it is as if we have put our politics into their hands, and our policies at the service of their goals.

The public agonizing of our president, a man seemingly imprisoned in policies whose wisdom he has lately been given publicly to doubt, stands as a warning of how difficult it will be to escape this fear and its institutionalized consequences. Perhaps political up-heavals set in train by the war on terror will leave the country lit-tle choice: how to remain a status quo power where the status quo is collapsing? Or it may be that far-reaching changes in policy will come only after a true reckoning with the decisions that have thrust us into what has become a forever war. Perhaps somewhere over the horizon such a reckoning awaits. The Argentines, through three dec-ades of truth commissions, public inquiries, and criminal trials, are still struggling doggedly to work through and expiate what they did to themselves during those violent years of the late 1970s. That was a long time ago and the conflict was very different, but that their struggle still goes on might inspire in us a bit of faith that, however long it takes, this self-destructive cycle might be broken and its gen-esis examined and understood.

The pages that follow are intended as a modest contribution to-ward that effort, or at least toward understanding, a bit more fully, how we came to plunge into this spiral—this path that circles and circles while seeming to take us ever further from our destination. I seek to understand the dynamic of fear and reaction that took shape during the administration of George W. Bush and that has been modified and normalized under that of Barack Obama. At its center, at the heart of the forever war, I find the problem of tor-ture and the general forfeiture of moral and political legitimacy represented by the embrace of methods that are "not who we are." President Obama's repeated use of that phrase to describe policies embraced by the United States seems to reveal a kind of painful national schizophrenia. Guantánamo, insists the president, is not who we are. Yet Americans go on imprisoning without trial nearly a hundred detainees there. Torture, says the president, is not who we are. And yet he punishes no one for having tortured, contenting himself with the thought that "hopefully, we don't do it again in the future." Indefinite detention, torture, targeted assassination: all of these are not who we are. And yet they are what we do.

American exceptionalism, which held the country to be uniquely defined by its founding principles, has come to mean a country that routinely violates those principles while claiming its actions do not undermine the ideals it claims to embody. The contradiction here goes beyond simple hypocrisy to approach a kind of willed blindness. Perhaps that contradiction was always immanent in the American imperial vision and has emerged more clearly only as the American postwar order in the Middle East has begun its slow collapse. The attackers on September 11 were striking out at that order, at American support for the autocracies in Cairo and Riyadh, and their shocking success at undermining it could only have been possible with persistent, and unwitting, American help. I will describe that help in the pages that follow as I seek to understand how the self-proclaimed exceptional nation now finds itself trapped in a permanent state of exception, a spiral of self-defeating policies that carries us ever further from what had been our initial purpose: to reduce the number of terrorists seeking to do us harm. Determining how we might escape this spiral will mean exploring how we trapped ourselves in it in the first place, and finally questioning not only how America has "fought terrorism" but how it has exerted power as the "indispensable nation" it has long held itself to be.

PART ONE

BUSH: IMPOSING THE EXCEPTION
Constitutional Dictatorship, Torture, and Us

We are in a fight for our principles, and our first responsibility is to live by them.

—President George W. Bush, September 20, 2001

EXCEPTION

We are living in the state of exception. We don't know when it will end, as we don't know when the war on terror will end. But we all know when it began. The indelible images have long since been re-fitted into a present-day fable of innocence and apocalypse: The perfect blue of that September sky stained by acrid black smoke. The jetliner appearing, banking, then disappearing into the skin of the second tower, to emerge on the other side as a great eruption of red and yellow flame. The showers of debris, the falling bodies, and then that great blossoming flower of white dust, roiling and churn-ing upward, enveloping and consuming the mighty skyscraper as it trembles and collapses into the whirlwind.

These were unforgettable instants of metamorphosis: For the towers, transmuted before our disbelieving eyes from massive steel and concrete structures into great plumes of heaven-seeking dust. For thousands of families, slashed apart as husbands, fathers, moth-ers, sisters, brothers were ripped from them in an unbearably public moment of incomprehensible violence. And finally, for our country: For all of us as Americans, whose identity as citizens was subtly but perhaps irrevocably altered.

To Americans, those terrible moments stand as a brightly lit portal through which we were all compelled to step, together, into a different world. Since that day we have lived in a different country, and though we may have grown accustomed to these changes and think little about them now, certain words still appear often enough in the news—terrorism, Guantánamo, indefinite detention, drone warfare, extrajudicial killing, warrantless wiretapping, "enhanced interrogation"—to remind us that ours remains an altered America, a strange America. The contours of this strangeness are not unknown in our history: the country has lived through broadly similar periods, at least half a dozen or so, depending on how you count; but we have no proper name for them. State of siege? Martial law? State of emergency? None of these expressions, familiar as they may be to other peoples, fall naturally from American lips.

What are we to call this subtly altered America, this way we live now? Clinton Rossiter, the great American scholar of "crisis government," writing in the shadow of World War II, called such times "constitutional dictatorship." Others, more recently, have spoken of a "9/11 Constitution" or an "Emergency Constitution." Vivid terms all; and yet, perhaps too narrowly drawn, placing as they do the definitional weight entirely on law when this state of ours seems to have as much or more to do with politics, with how we live and who we are as a polity. This is in part why I prefer "state of exception," an umbrella term that gathers beneath it those emergency categories while emphasizing that this state has as its defining characteristic transcendence of the borders of the strictly legal: it occupies, in the words of the philosopher Giorgio Agamben, "a position at the limit between politics and law . . . an 'ambiguous, uncertain, borderline fringe, at the intersection of the legal and the political.'"

Call it, then, the state of exception: these years during which, in the name of security, some of our accustomed rights and freedoms are circumscribed or set aside. This exceptional time of ours has now extended more than fourteen years, the longest by far in American history, with little sense of an ending. Indeed, the very endlessness of our state of exception—a quality emphasized even as it was imposed—and the broad acceptance of that endlessness are among its distinguishing marks. "Our war on terror begins with al Qaeda," President Bush declared to the country nine days after the attacks, "but it does not end there. It will not end until every terrorist group of global reach has been found, stopped and defeated."

When we consider the state of exception that began that bright September morning and that continues today, we can point not only to its open-endedness and its increasing normalization, to its embedding as part of our politics, but also to the subtlety of its costs. The overwhelming majority of Americans have seen their daily lives change very little, certainly when set beside how their parents saw daily life altered during World War II. The particular burdens of our exception seem mostly to be borne by someone else: by someone *other*. Officially sanctioned torture, or "enhanced interrogation," however dramatic a departure it may be from our history, happens not to Americans but to others, as do extraordinary rendition, indefinite detention, and, in the main, targeted killing. It is possible for most of us to live our lives without taking note of these practices at all except as passing phrases in the news until, every once in a while, like a blind man who lives, all unknowingly, in a very large cage, one or another of us stumbles into the bars.

Whoever takes the time to examine that cage can see our country has been altered in fundamental ways. When President Barack Obama in his elegant address accepting the Nobel Peace Prize declares to the applause of the world that he has "prohibited torture," we should pause in our pride to notice that torture violates international and domestic law and that the notion that our president has the power to prohibit it follows insidiously from the pretense that his predecessor had the power to order it—that during the state of exception, not only because of what President George W. Bush decided to do but also because of what President Obama is every day deciding not to do, torture in America has metamorphosed. Before the war on terror, official torture was illegal and anathema; today it is a policy choice. Just as President Bush ordered torture and President Obama prohibited it, a future president might order it once more. In its implications for who we are this change is historic, and yet we live our lives, like the blind man behind the bars of his cage, not seeing it at all.

SKELETON

When it comes to the state of exception, our first task must be to see the bars of the cage. To do this, we must return to the weeks and months when the state of exception was imposed and watch it rise up in a series of historic, largely executive decisions as a scaffolding of interlocking orders, decision directives, memoranda, and laws.

The first of these came on September 14, 2001, when George W. Bush proclaimed a national state of emergency. That same day Congress declared war, after a fashion, by passing with only one nay vote the Authorization for Use of Military Force, or AUMF, a joint resolution that in sixty words empowered the president to "use all necessary and appropriate force against those nations, organizations, or persons he determines planned, authorized, committed, or aided the terrorist attacks that occurred on September 11, 2001, or harbored such organizations or persons, in order to prevent any future acts of international terrorism against the United States by such nations, organizations or persons." The resolution was extremely broad, though Congress did decline, notably, the administration's entirely open-ended request that it authorize force "to deter and pre-empt *any* future acts of terrorism or aggression against the United States." Still, the resolution included no sunset clause, no hint of an ending, and it is on the authority of these few words the president signed into law on September 18, 2001, that much of the war on terror continues to be fought.

This was the public war. The secret war had begun the day before, when President Bush signed a Memorandum of Notification, or Finding, empowering the CIA to proceed with "the capture and detention of Al Qaeda terrorists" and to take "lethal action against them" anywhere in the world. The language of this still secret fourteen-page declaration, a CIA lawyer who helped draft it tells us, "was simple and stark" and "filled the entire covert-action tool kit, including tools we had never before used." Out of this document sprang the CIA's network of secret prisons, or "black sites," its program of "enhanced interrogation techniques," and its assassinations by drone. A little more than two weeks later, on October 4, the president signed a secret directive that empowered the National Security Agency to search out and assemble, under what was code-named Stellar Wind but was later rechristened the Terrorist Surveillance Program, a vast collection of metadata, including data on the telephone calls of millions of Americans, which its analysts were allowed, without individual warrants, to search and mine for information.

In late October, Congress overwhelmingly passed and the president signed the USA PATRIOT Act, which awarded extraordinary powers to the FBI and other law enforcement agencies to conduct secret searches and surveillance without a court order and to detain noncitizens. A few weeks later, on November 13, President Bush issued his Presidential Military Order on the "Detention, Treatment and Trial of Certain Non-Citizens in the War Against Terrorism," which set up, under the president's sole authority, a system of military commissions to try at his own discretion suspected terrorists. The president reserved to himself as executive the power to determine who these terrorists were; to sentence them, even to life imprisonment or death, by vote of only two thirds of those empaneled as military judges, and to do so without any court review or appeal.

Prisoners were referred to not as "prisoners of war" but as "detainees" in this order and the administration soon began referring to them as "illegal enemy combatants" or "unlawful combatants." In an executive order of February 7, 2002, entitled "Humane Treatment of al Qaeda and Taliban Detainees," the president determined that "Taliban detainees are unlawful combatants and, therefore, do not qualify as prisoners of war" under the Geneva Conventions, and that the Conventions do not apply to the conflict with al Qaeda at all. All such detainees, the president ordered, were to be "treated humanely and, to the extent appropriate and consistent with military necessity, in a manner consistent with the principles of Geneva." To what extent was appropriate would only later become clear as, during the spring and summer of 2002, young Justice Department lawyers in the Office of Legal Counsel set about secretly drafting and delivering memoranda that came to be known as the "torture memos" determining that it was the position of the U.S. government that eleven of the twelve "enhanced interrogation techniques" the Central Intelligence Agency proposed for use on such "unlawful combatants," including stress positions, close confinement in boxes, sleep deprivation, and waterboarding, did not constitute torture under existing federal statutes and international treaties. Under this secret determination, waterboarding, which as recently as 1983 the federal government had prosecuted as torture, was now judged to be legal.

These are just a few of the declarations, presidential orders, findings, military orders, and memoranda, many public, some still secret, which form an intricate, all-embracing latticework that constitutes the state of exception's initial legal and administrative skeleton. Now let us examine the exception's flesh.

FLESH

Confronted with the attacks of September 11, any president would have taken emergency measures, imposed some state of exception, but only George W. Bush could have imposed precisely this one. And even after seven years of amending, reshaping, and fine-tuning, and, in a successor administration, a half dozen years of normalizing and legalizing, the impress of President Bush's original vision, however improvised and ad hoc it was in its initial expression, is still evident. What then can we identify as his state of exception's particular traits, its distinguishing characteristics? What sets it apart? What, as the Jesuits ask, is its *quiddity*: the essence of the thing?

To answer this, we need more than an accounting of laws and executive orders. We are after all at Agamben's "borderline fringe, at the intersection of the legal and the political." In this borderland, details are hazy, contested. Answers will—must—differ. Still, we can identify a number of policies and tendencies that, taking shape early on, embedded themselves in our practice and our laws and have formed a penumbra of exception around the subsequent functioning of our politics. Some remain strong, visible; others have faded to a ghostly remnant. All were vital to the original design. Here, in rough order of importance, are eight policies I believe critical to defining George W. Bush's state of exception:

First, *declaring the war on terror*. That is, self-consciously redefining the effort to protect the country from terrorists *as a war*, and purporting to separate this war, deliberately and cleanly, from the hybrid law enforcement and national security approach the U.S.

government had taken to protecting the country from terrorism before September 11, 2001.

Second, *defining this new war as unbounded in space and time.* That is, proclaiming, under what came to be known as the Bush Doctrine, that terrorists would be attacked wherever they might be found, that states harboring them would be considered enemies and liable to attack along with the terrorists, that a state's support for terrorism would put it on the other side of an "us versus them" ideological divide reminiscent of the Cold War, and that this new war would not conclude until all "terrorist groups of global reach" were destroyed—which could only be, if ever, in the indefinite future, thus making the war on terror, together with its accompanying state of exception, a war seemingly without end: a forever war.

Third, *redefining terrorists* not only as combatants, thus withholding from them the protections of the criminal law, but as "unlawful combatants" or "illegal enemy combatants," thus (in the administration's interpretation) depriving them of the protection of the laws of war, including the Geneva Conventions. Anyone designated a terrorist was thus transformed into a new kind of being understood *to enjoy the protection of no laws whatever.*

Fourth, *imposing in both law enforcement and national security the so-called preventive paradigm,* which shifted the intent of arrest, detention, and also military attack from punishment and response into the realm of preemptive and preventive action. Gathering proof, marshaling evidence, satisfying probable cause requirements, and other elements that had been central to adversarial judicial and administrative procedures were downgraded and the emphasis placed instead on acting aggressively and preemptively to *eliminate risk.*

Fifth, narrowly *grounding the legitimacy of much of the state of exception on the president's "inherent powers,"* pushing relentlessly to extend those powers, and using them to exclude from consideration or consultation the other two branches of government and the opposition party.

Sixth, *making use, in multifarious and creative ways, of the power of secrecy* in deciding what information is disseminated not only to the public but within the government itself, circumventing relevant bureaucracies, agencies, and experts, further narrowing the input of information and making it possible for tiny groups of officials to make the most momentous and consequential decisions, producing, in turn, a tendency toward . . .

. . . Seventh, *improvising solutions* to large and complicated problems, producing policies and methods that were often amateurish, because of lack of expertise and consultation, and difficult to sustain, because of the failure to build political support, not only among the public but within the government itself.

Eighth, *embedding the rhetoric of the war on terror in the political struggle* between the two parties and making increasingly blunt use of it as a political trump, especially during election campaigns.

All eight of these attributes, in their complex intertwining, haunt us still, in one form or another. Taken together, they produced a distinctive mode of acting, behaving, and reacting—call it the *style* of the exception—not only as the state of exception was imposed during George W. Bush's first term but as it matured during his second, and as it has evolved under the presidency of Barack Obama. Out of them came the trademark policies of the exception that we still hear echoing like ghostly footfalls behind the news: War on terror. Worldwide conflict. Forever war. National security letters. Warrantless wiretapping. Material support for terrorism. Extraordinary rendition. Unlawful combatants. Indefinite detention. Targeted assassination. Extrajudicial killing. Enhanced interrogation techniques. Torture.

It is the last of these, I would suggest, that forms what one might call the signal attribute of our state of exception, the policy that shadows and encapsulates, in its moral and legal transgressions, all the others. During the Civil War, Abraham Lincoln suspended the Great Writ of habeas corpus. As the country entered World War I,

Woodrow Wilson imprisoned or deported thousands who spoke out against it. After the attack on Pearl Harbor, Franklin Roosevelt interned 110,000 Japanese Americans. And after the attacks of September 11, George W. Bush tortured prisoners.

WHITE ROOM

I woke up, naked, strapped to a bed, in a very white room. The room measured approximately 4m x 4m. The room had three solid walls, with the fourth wall consisting of metal bars separating it from a larger room. I am not sure how long I remained in the bed. After some time, I think it was several days, but can't remember exactly, I was transferred to a chair where I was kept, shackled by [the] hands and feet for what I think was the next 2 to 3 weeks. During this time I developed blisters on the underside of my legs due to the constant sitting. . . .

I was given no solid food during the first two or three weeks, while sitting on the chair. . . . The cell and room were air-conditioned and were very cold. Very loud, shouting type music was constantly playing. It kept repeating about every fifteen minutes twenty-four hours a day. Sometimes the music stopped and was replaced by a loud hissing or crackling noise. . . .

During this first two to three week period I was questioned for about one to two hours each day. American interrogators would come to the room and speak to me through the bars of the cell. During the questioning the music was switched off, but was then put back on again afterwards. I could not sleep at all for the first two to three weeks. If I started to fall asleep one of the guards would come and spray water in my face.

A naked man is chained to a chair in a very cold white room, where he is bombarded, hour after hour, day after day, night after night, with sound and with light. There is no day, no night, nothing but paralysis, cold, brightness, sound. Oceans of time flow over him but he is denied sleep. Two weeks? Three? Later he would say three. In fact we are told in a later CIA inspector general report that it is after eleven successive days and nights without sleep that he begins to "break apart."

By now, sometime in the summer of 2002, as he sits woozy and drooling, chained naked to the chair, and though he doesn't know it, Zayn al-Abidin Muhammad Husayn is a famous man. His knowledge and status are debated in the world's press and argued over in the White House. When he was captured early on the morning of March 28, 2002, in a spectacular raid in Faisalabad, Pakistan, during which he was shot three times after he leapt from a rooftop, the man we now know as Abu Zubaydah, of Saudi birth and Palestinian nationality, had just turned thirty-one. His capture was an event of great moment, a trophy in the war on terror. "The other day," President Bush proclaimed at a Republican fundraiser in Greenwich, Connecticut, "we hauled in a guy named Abu Zubaydah.

"He's one of the top operatives plotting and planning death and destruction on the United States. He's not plotting and planning anymore. He's where he belongs."

Abu Zubaydah "was a close associate of" Osama bin Laden, Secretary of Defense Donald Rumsfeld told the world from his Pentagon lectern, "and if not the number two, very close to the number two person in the organization. I think that's well established."

It is an intriguing phrase, "well established": What does it take to make a fact a fact? What we actually know about Abu Zubaydah—and, even more, what we know he knows—will become a matter of intense debate. At this point in the spring of 2002 we know that in the course of his capture he suffered bullet wounds in the stomach, thigh, and groin, lost large amounts of blood, fell into a coma. On the other side of the world, in Baltimore, a celebrated trauma surgeon, awakened by an urgent call from the director of central intelligence, was rushed to a private jet and flown to Pakistan, where he managed to save the prisoner's life. Abu Zubaydah, bleeding, still unconscious, will be carried off to a famously "undisclosed location," and his whereabouts will remain a closely guarded secret, not least to him, even as he sits, several months later, chained immobile and woozy in his white room. Once again, we know a bit more than he does: the white room is at U-Tapao Royal Thai Navy Airfield, a military base in Thailand, one of the so-called black sites—secret prisons the CIA improvised hurriedly in the days after September 11, with the help of allies in Pakistan, Afghanistan, Thailand, Romania, Morocco, Poland, Lithuania, and perhaps other countries still not disclosed, to hold and interrogate prisoners, pursuant to President Bush's secret Memorandum of Notification of September 17, which gave this task to the CIA, an organization that officially had had nothing to do with detention or interrogation for two decades or more.

PUBLIC SECRECY

The critically wounded Abu Zubaydah had been "disappeared" into secrecy, but in fact all that was secret was his location. Thanks to the president himself and other senior officials, his capture had been instantly proclaimed a highly public victory in the war on terror. That he was in American hands and "where he belongs," being interrogated at an "undisclosed location," was boasted about, discussed, debated. We might call this strange confection of the known and unknown "public secrecy," a peculiar legerdemain by which the government withholds not so much information from the public—though some vital bits of information are withheld—but responsibility and liability from itself. Though the president of the United

States himself may boast of the capture of Abu Zubaydah, the government he heads refuses "officially" to acknowledge that it has possession of him and thereby rejects all claims that it has any legal obligation to account for him or to answer for his treatment. Such unacknowledged prisoners, with their strangely contemporary status as "secret celebrities," become, in effect, the new disappeared. These new disappeared—there will be well more than a hundred of them—are at once famous and absent. Without any legal status or even official acknowledgment that they are alive and in custody, such prisoners become the objects, as Giorgio Agamben put it, of "pure de facto rule, of a detention that is indefinite not only in the temporal sense but in its very nature."

Such disappearing, without official legal acknowledgment, stands in almost perfect opposition to the principle of habeas corpus, the Great Writ, an ancient core value of Western liberalism dating back to the twelfth century that limited government power. Securing a writ of habeas corpus—literally: "you should have the body"—requires authorities to acknowledge that an arrested person is indeed in custody by bringing that person before a judge. In adopting such disappearances as policy and in boasting about capturing people they refused to bring before a court or officially acknowledge holding, United States officials had moved to the other end of the spectrum, toward the antithesis of a government limited in its power over the individual person. Torture exists in the same dark realm: in its essence it is the state reaching through a person's skin and taking control of his nervous system by force in order to use it as a weapon against him. It is the ultimate destruction, by the state, of human autonomy. It seems no accident that the torments from which the American "alternative set of procedures" were drawn had been copied directly from techniques developed by the Soviets and the Chinese during the Cold War of the 1950s. Disappearing and torturing embody in action the totalitarian idea of a state unbounded in power.

WHAT WE KNOW

A few days after Abu Zubaydah woke from his coma he found at his bedside, in an unfamiliar location in an unknown country, a man he doesn't know, who asks him his name. Zubaydah shakes his head: he has heard the American accent. "And I asked him again in Arabic," remembered John Kiriakou of the CIA.

"And then he answered me in English. And he said he would not speak to me in God's language. And then I said, 'That's okay. We know who you are.'"

They did not quite know, as it happened. The "well established" facts that Secretary Rumsfeld had crowed about were not facts at all. Abu Zubaydah was not "a close associate" of Osama Bin Laden, nor "one of bin Laden's most trusted lieutenants," nor was he "number two," nor even "very close to the number two person in the organization." Nor, as the Department of Justice finally admitted in court documents in 2009, did he have any role in or advance knowledge of the 9/11 attacks, nor was he a member of al Qaeda or "formally" identified with it at all.

Still, to American officials desperate for information on al Qaeda six months after the attacks in New York and Washington, Abu Zubaydah seemed a rich prize indeed—as he seemed to recognize, according to Kiriakou's recounting of that initial bedside interview: "And then he asked me to smother him with a pillow. And I said, 'No, no. We have plans for you.'"

The plans even then were being fought over. Because those in charge of interrogations at the CIA's Counterterrorism Center didn't initially believe that the man captured was Abu Zubaydah, they had not sent their own people to the black site, and so two experienced interrogators from the FBI led the initial questioning. These interrogators began using traditional methods: nursing the wounded man back to health, changing his bandages, washing his wounds, building respect, rapport. One of these men, a Lebanese-born FBI

interrogator named Ali Soufan, would startle the prisoner by addressing him as Hani, an endearment his mother had used. Soufan
has argued strenuously, first as an unnamed source for journalists
and then in newspaper articles, congressional testimony, and a book
in his own name, that all the valuable information that was eventually gained from Zubaydah, including the identity of so-called dirty
bomber Jose Padilla and the code name of Khalid Sheikh Mohammed, alleged mastermind of the 9/11 attacks, was gained in those
initial discussions. Traditional interrogation, he and his colleagues
contend, was working.

Others in the government, however, particularly in the CIA, did
not believe it; they were convinced, as a Justice Department report
puts it, that Zubaydah "was not telling all he knew." How did they
come to this conclusion? It is a fascinating question. We are back
to the delicate calculation of knowledge and risk. For unlike the
famous Myth of the Ticking Bomb, in which officials know *almost*
everything, in the real world we are most often dealing with vast unknowns and it is these that we most fear: the deserts of ignorance,
unbounded by certain facts. Donald Rumsfeld famously distinguished between the "known unknowns"—what we know we don't
know, which can be frightening—and the "unknown unknowns"—
what we don't know we don't know, which can be terrifying. After
September 11, that terror of the unknown was expressed by policymakers in a simple calculus, well described by CIA inspector general
John Helgerson in his 2004 report on the interrogation program:
"lack of knowledge led analysts to speculate about what a detainee
'should know,' [versus] information the analyst could objectively
demonstrate the detainee did know."

Such lack of knowledge led those back at CIA headquarters to
make what they judged to be the "safer" but not always the most ac-
curate assumption, as the inspector general acknowledged: "[Head-
quarters'] assessments to the effect that detainees are withholding
information are not always supported by an objective evaluation of

available information and the evaluation of the interrogators but are too heavily based, instead, on presumptions of what the individual might or should know."

These assumptions, however unfounded they might be, however distant from any real evidence—and however distant those officials who made them might be from the source of that evidence—led interrogators in turn to take action, action on the bodies of detainees: "When a detainee did not respond to a question posed to him, the assumption at Headquarters was that the detainee was holding back and knew more; consequently, Headquarters recommended resumption of [enhanced interrogation techniques]."

In an atmosphere of fear and anxiety, it seemed the prudent course for officials to assume what the detainee "should know" and proceed accordingly. And make no mistake, the critical decisions laying the basis for the state of exception were taken in a state of intense anxiety and fear.

PANIC

"After September 11," as former White House counterterrorism adviser Richard Clarke put it simply, "we panicked." Terrorism, which had been downgraded as a threat by the incoming Bush administration, now became the single all-consuming obsession of a government suddenly "on a war footing."

We know from Clarke's vivid account of the atmosphere in the basement bunker of the White House on the day of the attacks, when a jetliner was hurtling toward Washington and, so it was thought, about to demolish at any moment the building above. And then the sustained terror of the days that followed: the mysterious and shocking anthrax attacks, the series of security alerts and threat warnings, ghostly emanations of the "second wave" strikes that all feared would come at any moment. The president and the first lady pulled out of bed because another attack was thought to be coming. The vice president warned that he had been fatally infected with botulism and had days or hours to live. If these reports weren't enough to keep those at the top of the government in a state of fevered anxiety, the president and other senior officials now began their day by poring over the "threat matrix," a document often dozens of pages long listing "every threat directed at the United States" that had been sucked up during the preceding twenty-four hours by the vast electronic and human information vacuum cleaner that was U.S. intelligence: warnings of catastrophic attacks with weapons of mass destruction, of conventional attacks, of planned attacks on allies—plots of all description and every level of credibility. "You simply could not sit where I did," Director of Central Intelligence George Tenet later wrote of the threat matrix, "and be other than scared to death about what it portended." One official compared reading the threat matrix every day (in an example of the ironic mirroring one finds everywhere in this story) to "being stuck in a room listening to loud Led Zeppelin music," which leads to "sensory overload" and "paranoia." He compared the task of defending the country against terrorism to playing goalie in a game in which the opposing players, the boundary lines, and the field are invisible yet you must stop every shot to escape instant defeat.

The sensory overload was in large part self-inflicted, a product of a panicked decision to pass on *everything* to policymakers. Having failed to provide specific information they had in their possession that might have led to action to stop the 9/11 attacks, intelligence officials now passed on any raw intelligence they thought might be relevant, and policymakers, who, writes Robert Gates, "had no idea after 9/11 whether further attacks were imminent," frantically immersed themselves in it. Gates, a former director of central intelligence who would become Bush's second secretary of defense and Obama's first, goes on: "Because the senior leadership was worried there might be warning signs in the vast collection apparatus of American intelligence, nearly all of the filters that sifted intelligence reporting based on reliability or confidence levels were removed, with the result that in the days and weeks after 9/11, the White House was flooded with countless reports of imminent attacks, among them the planned use of nuclear weapons by terrorists in New York and Washington. All that fed the fear and urgency."

These feelings, while understandable, sprang from specters and phantasms. "You're being flooded with some of the most dogshit, inaccurate threat reporting possible," recalled Roger Cressey, a White House counterterrorism official. "And the obligation was to put it out there. . . . So threat reporting that I would laugh out of my working group on threats was now making it directly . . . into the Oval Office because God forbid the FBI or the CIA didn't tell the president or the White House of a threat and it became true." Policymakers, unequipped to assess the quality of raw intelligence reporting, were suddenly overwhelmed. "We went from basically no information to floods," Condoleezza Rice, then national security adviser, told her biographer. "So now you were getting un-assessed intelligence. You know, just about anything anybody said might be a threat."

All that fear and urgency, writes Gates, "in turn, was fed by the paucity of information on, or understanding of, al Qaeda and other extremist groups. . . . Quickly filling those information gaps and protecting the country from another attack became the sole preoccupation of the president and his senior team. Any obstacle—legal, bureaucratic, financial, or international—to accomplishing those objectives had to be overcome."

This is the story of the decision making in the weeks and months immediately following the attacks: tiny groups of officials under enormous stress improvising policies with little or no input from those in government who could offer expertise, and caution. Thus the policy to try detainees before military commissions, later thrown out by the Supreme Court, was secretly improvised and imposed by a handful of officials led by Vice President Cheney and his counsel, David Addington, and put into effect during one of the president and vice president's weekly lunches. (Secretary of State Colin Powell learned of the policy while watching CNN.) And thus the decision to subject detainees to "enhanced interrogation techniques" was made secretly by a handful of people: those who prepared the way by composing the various presidential military orders and legal memoranda, and those who improvised the policy, all in secret, all pretty much on the fly, with the final decision to apply the techniques—having now been determined to be legal—taken by the president of the United States. Most of these officials were, the director of central intelligence confessed, "scared to death."

Such responses—the looming anxiety and fear, the panicked determination to *do something* to prevent the next attack, which everyone felt must be coming—are understandable, by which we mean that as human beings we can imagine ourselves reacting the same way. But if it is true that after 9/11 they panicked, the president and his highest officials did so in a way that magnified the effect of their personal fears and blind spots, including their instinctive ideological faith in American dominance in the world, and imposed them, in the most momentous and self-defeating policies of the state of exception, on the country they strove to protect.

WAR

All the poring over raw intelligence bespeaks not only an all-encompassing anxiety about information—the maddening absence of visible, identifiable threats like the movements of armies, the unremitting angst of making what could be life-and-death judgments based on the interpreting of inscrutable signs—but also deep-seated shame and guilt over what had been allowed to happen. There was, writes Robert

Gates, "a huge sense among senior members of the administration of having let the country down, of having allowed a devastating attack on America to take place on their watch." With it came a driving need to banish that shame and guilt, to start over, cleansed and immaculate. One must venture into this psycho-political realm, treacherous as it is, to begin to understand the Bush administration's particular crafting of the state of exception and its first principle: the insistence on a clear dividing line between the law enforcement paradigm of the past and the "global war on terror" that President Bush declared in the wake of the attacks. For an administration that had begun life with a historic contested election and a grave legitimacy problem, the bright line between past policy and the newly declared war on terror was in part meant to banish the attacks themselves to the realm of the irresponsible past, and to the responsibility of the other party.

That an attack was coming, of course, had been predicted: By Director of Central Intelligence George Tenet, who recalled that across the vast reaches of the country's intelligence universe throughout that fateful summer "the system was blinking red" and that he himself was running about with his "hair on fire" trying desperately to convey the urgency. By White House counterterrorism chief Richard Clarke, newly demoted from cabinet level, who desperately struggled to persuade Rice to schedule a Principals Meeting on al Qaeda and who, increasingly panicked, finally took to emailing the national security adviser warning of "hundreds of dead in the streets" and to shouting angrily in meetings that "something really spectacular is going to happen here and it's going to happen soon!" And it was predicted by U.S. intelligence officials, one of whom traveled to Texas in early August and personally read to President Bush these words:

BIN LADIN DETERMINED TO STRIKE IN US

Clandestine, foreign government, and media reports indicate Bin Ladin since 1997 has wanted to conduct terrorist attacks in the US.

Bin Ladin implied in US television interviews in 1997 and 1998 that his followers would follow the example of World Trade Center bomber Ramzi Yousef and "bring the fighting to America."

After US missile strikes on his base in Afghanistan in 1998, Bin Ladin told followers he wanted to retaliate in Washington. . . .

An Egyptian Islamic Jihad (EIJ) operative told an [redacted] service at the same time that Bin Ladin was planning to exploit the operative's access to the US to mount a terrorist strike. . . .

We have not been able to corroborate some of the more sensational threat reporting, such as that from a [redacted] service in 1998 saying that Bin Ladin wanted to hijack a US aircraft. . . .

Nevertheless, FBI information since that time indicates patterns of suspicious activity in this country consistent with preparations for hijackings or other types of attacks, including recent surveillance of federal buildings in New York.

What would have happened if the president, upon hearing these words, which were thought vital enough to be read directly to him during his Texas vacation—and which mention al Qaeda agents within the United States, their surveillance of federal buildings, their determination to hijack U.S. aircraft, along with other clear intimations of the attack that was to come fewer than five weeks later—what if, instead of dismissing his briefer with the words, "All right. You've covered your ass, now," the president had immediately called a National Security Council meeting, ordered increased surveillance at airports, directed the secretary of transportation to issue a threat warning to all civilian pilots, and generally put the various security agencies of the U.S. government on a heightened alert of the sort that the Clinton administration had ordered before the millennium celebrations?

Had senior Bush officials worked to focus the security agencies of the government on these threats during the summer of 2001, might they have prevented the attacks? We will never know. What we can say is that even without such pressure coming from the president and other senior officials, those within the security agencies came excruciatingly close. In July an FBI agent in Phoenix warned urgently in a memorandum to headquarters of "the possibility of a coordinated effort by Osama bin Laden to send students to the United States to attend civil aviation universities" and insisted on action to identify these students. He was ignored. Had there been pressure from the president, attorney general, or FBI director, would these students, among whom were the September 11 pilots, have been identified and tracked? On August 16 at a Minneapolis flight school FBI special agents arrested Zacarias Moussaoui, the fledgling pilot uninterested in learning how to land, but lawyers at the Department of Justice denied their desperate requests for a warrant to search his laptop. Had the attorney general been on alert, would the warrant have been granted and Moussaoui's laptop yielded up important details? Would Moussaoui have been connected to Mohammed al-Qahtani, the other supposed "twentieth hijacker" who had been turned away from the Orlando airport earlier in August? And, most tantalizing of all, would the FBI have been alerted much earlier to information about the two 9/11 "muscle hijackers" whom CIA officers had tracked from a planning meeting in Malaysia to their entry to the United States but had then failed, by accident or by design, to "hand off" to the bureau? What if, instead of ignoring these two men while they lived openly in San Diego for more than a year, FBI agents had been tracking them? Would they still have been able to board American Airlines Flight 77 and crash it into the Pentagon?

We will never know the answers to these questions. We do know that the senior officials brought in by President Bush, unlike their predecessors in the Clinton administration, did not consider al Qaeda and the threat it posed one of their highest security concerns. Despite the increasingly exasperated warnings of Clarke and Tenet, among others, Bush's national security officials preferred to focus their attention on what they saw as the challenge of a rising China and the growing threat of Saddam Hussein. (Faced with intelligence warnings of a coming attack, some senior officials in Donald Rumsfeld's Pentagon suspected that "bin Laden was merely pretending to be planning an attack to distract the administration from Saddam Hussein" and they exhorted the White House not to be "fooled.") But deep within the security bureaucracies, far below the level of Bush-appointed principals who denigrated the threat of terrorism as a Clinton-era obsession, what could happen was on everyone's mind, sometimes in eerily prophetic terms. The FBI supervisor in Minneapolis who met resistance to his urgent request to have Moussaoui's laptop examined responded angrily to Washington superiors that he was "trying to keep someone from taking a plane and crashing into the World Trade Center."

Even without the pressure that might have been applied from above, the intelligence and security agents on the working level came very close, and they knew it. Their bosses knew it too, which can only have increased their "huge sense"—in Gates's words—"of having let the country down." And the sudden frenzied activity of those same formerly uninterested Bush principals in the wake of the attacks should not blind us to what is a vital point: *none of the new laws and powers comprising the post-9/11 state of exception would have been necessary to stop the attacks*. Despite all the fevered post-9/11 talk of "taking the gloves off"—and the clear and plainly self-serving implication that if only those gloves had come off earlier, the attacks would have been stopped—in fact what allowed the attacks to succeed was not a paucity of available legal powers but negligence at the top together with spotty effectiveness in carrying out existing procedures and enforcing existing laws.

Just as the laying on of emergency powers after the fact embodies a subtle dynamic of self-exculpation—if only these laws had been in effect, if only these powers had been in the president's hands, the attacks never would have succeeded—so the declaration of the war on terror seemed to banish the successful attacks themselves to the supposed failings of the law enforcement model. The Bush people, after all, had inherited this model, under which terrorist attacks were treated as crimes, not acts of war, from the previous, Democratic administration. Now, after declaring the war on terror, they could ascribe the failure to stop the 9/11 attacks mostly to the previous administration, to *its* methods: as if the imposition of the state of exception, and the claim that the struggle to protect Americans from terrorists was in fact a "war on terror," marked a bright line between Republican and Democratic administrations.

This political dynamic is still with us; it was on dramatic display, for example, after the failed Christmas Day 2009 attack of the "Underwear Bomber," Umar Farouk Abdulmutallab, on an airliner over Detroit, when Republicans bitterly criticized the Obama administration for failing to send the suspect to Guantánamo for "enhanced interrogation" and instead "reading him his Miranda rights." Among those launching withering attacks on the new administration was former New York mayor Rudolph Giuliani, who in the wake of the Underwear Bomber's capture could be heard to claim that "we had no domestic attacks under Bush." Giuliani, who of course had led the city during the September 11 attacks, was joined in this odd rewriting of history by other prominent Republicans, including former Bush press secretary Dana Perino, who insisted that "we did not have a terrorist attack on our country during President Bush's term." Given that by an order of magnitude more Americans died from terrorist attacks during George W. Bush's administration than during all others combined, these might seem to be fantastic assertions, but they become comprehensible as revealing slips of the tongue if you consider that many truly believe that the Bush administration, as former Bush official Mary Matalin put it, "*inherited* the most tragic attack on our soil in our nation's history." Since those attacks occurred before the war on terror, in other words, they really could be said to have occurred on the Democrats' watch. For that, according to this reasoning, was *before,* when Democrats failed to treat terrorism as the warfare it truly was.

GLOVES COME OFF

Barely two weeks after the 2001 attacks, Cofer Black, then chief of the CIA's Counterterrorism Center, declared to the Senate Select Committee on Intelligence, "All you need to know: There was a 'before' 9/11 and an 'after' 9/11. After 9/11 the gloves came off." These resonant words carry within them the latent psycho-political argument of the state of exception. Simply put: that "the gloves came off" after the attacks meant that before the attacks the gloves were . . . on. And what exactly were these "gloves"? What many Republicans, including many senior Bush administration officials, believed were improper or at least unacceptable limitations on the president's power to conduct the country's foreign policy as he saw fit. The most important had been imposed three decades before: the Cooper-Church and Case-Church amendments, which limited the president's power to make war in Southeast Asia and led to the War Powers Resolution of 1973, requiring that the president secure congressional approval to maintain U.S. forces in hostilities; the Hughes-Ryan Act of 1974 (later replaced by the Intelligence Oversight Act of 1980), which restricted the president's power to conduct covert actions with "deniability," and the Foreign Intelligence Surveillance Act (FISA) of 1978, which required the executive to apply to a special court for a warrant to eavesdrop on an American.

It is no coincidence that the two most important architects of the state of exception, Vice President Dick Cheney and Secretary of Defense Donald Rumsfeld, had been serving as young senior officials of the Richard Nixon and Gerald Ford administrations when

Congress began imposing many of these laws on a wounded chief executive and his immediate successor during the last years of the Vietnam War. These years saw the modern nadir of presidential power, when the Watergate scandal brought the resignation of Nixon and the revelations by the Church and Pike committees of secret "dirty tricks" humiliated and humbled the CIA. If it is true, as Mark Twain purportedly said, that "History doesn't repeat itself but it does rhyme," then the imposition of the state of exception in the early 2000s, dramatically bolstering the president's power and authority, "rhymes" most resonantly with those post-Vietnam 1970s, when, as Vice President Cheney told reporters after the revelation of the administration's secret warrantless wiretap program in 2005, "Watergate and a lot of the things around Watergate and Vietnam both during the '70s served . . . to erode the authority . . . the president needs to be effective, especially in the national security area."

The gloves coming off meant not only freeing the president's hands at last but blaming the success of the attacks on the laws that had supposedly hindered him in his obligation to protect the country. Stripping off the gloves was a sign of commitment, of a determination to sweep away those inherited limitations that had let the terrorists succeed. Stripping off the gloves, along with the declaration of an unending war on terror and the redefinition of terrorists as unlawful combatants, was an affirmation that true responsibility belonged not to those on whose watch the attacks had occurred but to those who had put the gloves *on* the president in the first place and who had used and relied on the legal system, rather than the military, to "coddle" terrorists rather than fight them. That phrase, "coddling terrorists," clearly echoes time-honored Republican rhetoric denouncing Democrats' supposed softness on criminals. That it remains with us still suggests how deeply embedded this aspect of the state of exception has become in our domestic politics. Though no one would claim those policies were introduced in order to win elections, it is plain that they dovetail perfectly with the post–civil rights era, post-Vietnam political shadow play of Republican strength and Democratic weakness. Scarcely four months after the attacks, during a meeting of the Republican National Committee, senior Bush adviser Karl Rove set out the politics of the exception in explicit terms: "Americans trust the Republicans to do a better job of keeping our communities and our families safe. We can also go to the country on this issue [of terrorism] because they trust the Republican Party to do a better job of protecting and strengthening America's military might and thereby protecting America."

Rove offered this thought like one intoning ancient wisdom. And in a way he was: President Harry Truman would have well understood it. It was Truman who not only created the Department of Defense, the CIA, the National Security Council, and other institutions of the postwar emergency state but who in 1949 "lost China" (in the phrase his Republican adversaries coined to describe the Chinese Revolution) and thereby unwittingly helped to lay the groundwork for a half century of mostly Republican Party ascendancy in the area of national security, and its governing Cold War political question: In a world of unremitting danger, who can best keep us safe? In the case of both adversaries, the Soviet Union and al Qaeda, the threats were real, though al Qaeda's terrorism, unlike the Soviet nuclear arsenal, never posed an existential threat to the country. But what matters was the cleverness and determination brought to the task of extracting from the threat the political gold—fear, the most lucrative political emotion—and artfully maintaining and exploiting it for self-serving ends.

Out of these Cold War origins—the world of fellow travelers and security risks, of red-baiting politicians who depicted their opponents as soft on communism—came the lineaments of the politics of fear that we saw reemerge in the war on terror. Indeed, within ten days of the attacks President Bush was arguing quite explicitly that the two "wars" were continuous, insisting that the terrorists who had attacked New York and Washington were "heirs of all the murderous ideologies of the twentieth century." This passage, from the president's speech to Congress on September 20, which as much as any set forth the ideological foundation of the war on terror, is worth quoting in full:

> *We are not deceived by their pretenses to piety. We have seen their kind before. They are heirs of all the murderous ideologies of the twentieth century. By sacrificing human life to serve their radical visions, by abandoning every value except the will to power, they follow in the path of fascism, Nazism and totalitarianism. And they will follow that path all the way, to where it ends: in history's unmarked grave of discarded lies.*

Stirring words, and effective, for they domesticated the unthinkable in the categories of the accustomed. The terrorists become only the latest in a long line of "evildoers." Like the Nazis and the communists before them, they are Americans' evil twin: tyrants to our free men, totalitarians to our democrats. However disorienting the horror of the attacks, the war on terror could be narrated as a reprise of the Cold War, a return to its comforting categories of us and them.

As Truman christened the Cold War by explaining to Americans how "at the present moment in world history, nearly every nation must choose between alternative ways of life," so George W. Bush declared his global war on terror by insisting that "every nation, in every region, now has a decision to make. Either you are with us, or you are with the terrorists." Hating "our values" and "our freedoms," the evildoers were depicted as deeply irrational and committed to a nihilistic philosophy of obliteration. Nineteen men on September 11 had used box-cutters and airliners but thanks to much administration rhetoric reawakening the sleeping image of the mushroom cloud, in the American imagination every terrorist now came with a nuclear weapon in hand, or rather a "weapon of mass destruction." America must act, the president declared, "to answer these attacks and rid the world of evil."

The words are messianic, their roots deeply embedded in the exceptionalist tradition that saw the country even before its creation as a "shining city upon a hill." But in its breathtaking sweep and ambition to "rid the world of evil," the rhetoric bore scant relation to the practical realities of what the country, however powerful, could accomplish in its interactions with the Islamic world. And yet its grand ambitions were widely echoed, by pundits, foreign policy experts, political figures, and familiar media spokespeople. Dissenting voices were exceedingly rare. Those, scarcely more than a handful, who actively questioned the messianic tone, or sought to understand the attacks as anything more than an act of the purest evil, were drowned out beneath an avalanche of often savage criticism.

Such evangelical rhetoric not only fell easily on American ears, it provided a welcome boon to a vast national security bureaucracy created and shaped by the Cold War and, at its ending, left without clear purpose. "Washington policy and defense cultures still seek out cold-war models," as a Pentagon Defense Science Board study put it in 2004. "With the surprise announcement of a new struggle, the U.S. government reflexively inclined toward Cold War–style responses to the new threat, without a thought or a care as to whether these were the best responses to a very different strategic situation." Whether or not these were the "best responses," the September 11 attacks gave new life to the emergency state that had taken shape during World War II, that had expanded and gained permanence during the decades of the Cold War, and that had been actively seeking, in the wake of the fall of the Soviet Union in 1991, a new reason for being. Al Qaeda became that reason.

Al Qaeda was not the Nazis or the Soviets. Al Qaeda controlled no state, fielded no regular army. But it was treated from the start of the war on terror as an existential threat. The great security bureaucracies of the U.S. emergency state, having spent a decade without a Cold War adversary, began grinding fully back to life, fueled by the enormous expansion of funding and manpower that came with the war on terror: the defense budget nearly doubled, the intelligence budget more than doubled. At the same time, this powerful rhetorical idea anchored the war on terror in the familiar political constellation of the Cold War and restored to the Republicans their most potent foreign policy issue. The following fall, using powerful rhetoric that emphasized the gravity of the ongoing threat and insisted that only his party could adequately protect America from it, the president under whose leadership the country had suffered the most devastating terrorist attack in its history achieved what almost no first-term presidents had before: a decisive victory in his first midterm elections. In the shadow of the 9/11 attacks—and with the help of a terrorist-baiting campaign in which Democratic senator Max Cleland of Georgia, a war hero who had been severely wounded in Vietnam, in a notorious advertisement saw his face superimposed with that of Osama bin Laden—the Republicans won back control of the Senate. The national security trump that the Republicans had lost with the end of the Cold War was back in their hands. Waging war on terror had replaced being tough on communism as a defining cause in their political identity. Two years later, as President Bush struggled to win reelection during the increasingly unpopular war he had launched in Iraq, his vice president would take the rhetoric to a new level, warning voters that "if we make the wrong choice then the danger is that we'll get hit again and that we'll be hit in a way that will be devastating."

For all its usefulness as a political trump, Bush's declaration of a war on terror was in many ways the Original Sin of our state of exception, its founding category mistake, for it heralded a conflict that was not a war at all, at least not in the traditional sense of a state of belligerency between states. Instead, the war on terror was from the start a strange hybrid that was in large part worldwide counterterror operation, a combined police and intelligence struggle fought "on the dark side," as Vice President Cheney put it, onto which were grafted a conventional ground invasion and occupation, in Iraq, and a counterinsurgency campaign, in Afghanistan. These would themselves evolve, but it is important here to emphasize that an expansive war on terror was not foreordained. Many nations have confronted terrorists but none have gone so far as to grant them the prestige of declaring war on them. The British, to take just one example, have combated terror campaigns in Palestine, Ireland, Cyprus, and Malaysia. "But they never called them 'wars,'" writes Michael Howard. "They called them 'emergencies.'" Howard, an Oxford historian, goes on:

> *This terminology meant that the police and intelligence services were provided with exceptional powers and were reinforced where necessary by the armed forces, but they continued to operate within a peacetime framework of civilian authority. . . . The objectives were to isolate the terrorists from the rest of the community. . . . The terrorists were not dignified with the status of belligerents; they were criminals, to be regarded as such by the general public and treated as such by the authorities.*
>
> *To declare war on terrorists or, even more illiterately, on terrorism is at once to accord terrorists a status and dignity that they seek and do not deserve. It confers on them a kind of legitimacy. Do they qualify as belligerents? If so, should they not receive the protection of the laws of war?*

As we have seen, the Bush administration's answer to the question of whether terrorists in its war on terror were protected by the laws of war was a simple one: they were not. On the one hand, in Bush administration eyes terrorists were combatants, and thus would not fall under the protection of criminal law, but they were *unlawful* combatants, which meant, in the administration's reading, that they would not enjoy the protections of the Geneva Conventions either.

The Bush administration had strong political reasons for its fateful decision to declare war on terror. But the struggle's legal inscription as a war, without any broadly accepted definition about how such a conflict might be declared at an end, and the administration's determined grafting of law of war concepts onto a conflict that in some ways ill fits them, looms over us to this day. Indefinite detention without charge becomes, in the war model, legal capture and detention, leaving us with prisoners of war who are to be held until the end of a conflict that seems to have no end. Extrajudicial killing and assassination, not only of leaders of "core" al Qaeda but of foot soldiers, and of leaders and foot soldiers of "associated" groups that didn't exist when Congress voted the authorization for the use of force, becomes legal use of lethal force. Even the lowest-ranking militant can be targeted simply by virtue of his membership in an organization, whether or not he poses an imminent threat. Seen against the complicated reality of this conflict the terms seem makeshift, ill-fitted, not quite bridging a conceptual gap that, as the years go on and the prisoners sit in Guantánamo and the drones take their toll, has become increasingly difficult to ignore. Concepts that in traditional war had widely understood limits are suddenly rendered limitless, without border or duration. And an authorization to use force against al Qaeda and to defend the country against that group's future terrorism has been stretched into a boundless writ to target and assassinate militants from Yemen to Somalia to Libya and beyond, few of whom have been engaged in preparing imminent violence against the United States.

IMPROVISATION

So the leaders of the war on terror would not be "reading terrorists their Miranda rights." They would launch their new war with an unblemished record—since in their reconstruction the 9/11 attacks themselves had succeeded under the Democrats' law enforcement model—and with a willingness and commitment *to do whatever it takes.* In a war in which the United States would "work through, sort of, the dark side, if you will . . . spend[ing] time in the shadows," in Dick Cheney's resonant words to the nation five days after the attacks, this meant doing whatever it took to gain a bit of light: information. When it came to the interrogation of Abu Zubaydah, the victor in the struggle between the FBI's traditional law enforcement methods and the CIA's improvised "enhanced interrogation techniques" was preordained.

Though the judgment of how to interrogate the detainee would seem to be built on evidence, on the thinness of the information the detainee was providing, in fact it was based on conviction, as we've seen: on, as the CIA inspector general admitted, *lack* of knowledge. Zubaydah was *known* to be a high official in al Qaeda so he would know—wouldn't he?—of the second-wave attacks that were *known* to be coming. Therefore mustn't the very fact that he is giving up only modest information mean he is concealing what is most important? (And must not the fact that the United Nations inspectors can find no weapons of mass destruction in Iraq be *confirmation* that Saddam is hiding them?) It is a closed circle, self-sufficient, impervious to disobedient facts. Conviction of secret knowledge, set beside the paucity of what is revealed, proves deception.

By the late spring of 2002 officials at the CIA's Counterterrorism Center had accepted that the man at the black site in Thailand was indeed Abu Zubaydah. The argument about what he knew, about how best to make him tell it, escalated between CIA and FBI interrogators on the scene and between various factions back in Washington. Soon a CIA team arrived at the black site from headquarters at Langley, including a contractor whom Ali Soufan, the FBI interrogator who had begun the questioning, refers to as "Boris" in his account but who is actually James E. Mitchell, a retired psychologist who had been an instructor in the Air Force's survival program for downed pilots. "Washington feels," a CIA official tells Soufan, by his account, "that Abu Zubaydah knows much more than he's telling you, and Boris here has a method that will get that information quickly." That method, according to Boris, is to "make Abu Zubaydah see his interrogator as a god who controls his suffering." Zubaydah would have his clothes taken away, and if he still refused to cooperate harsher methods would be used. " 'Pretty quickly you'll see Abu Zubaydah buckle and become compliant,' Boris declared. 'For my technique to work,' he said, 'we need to send the message to Abu Zubaydah that until now he had the chance to cooperate, but he blew it. He has to understand that we know he was playing games and that game is over.' "

Soufan, appalled, asks Boris two simple questions:

> *"Have you ever questioned an Islamic terrorist before?"*
> *"No."*
> *"Have you ever conducted an interrogation?"*
> *"No," he said again, "but I know human nature." [I] was taken aback by his response. [I] couldn't believe that someone with no interrogation or terrorism experience had been sent by the CIA on this mission.*

If one knows Soufan's record as a professional interrogator of al Qaeda members, which is impeccable and unrivaled within the government, it is hard not to be shocked by his account. The exchange between Soufan and Boris embodied the bureaucratic struggle over interrogation methods that had escalated into a war of leaks in the press. "How Good Is Abu Zubaydah's Information?" asked a *Newsweek* Web Exclusive on April 27, 2002, less than a month after his capture. As *Newsweek* learned from "a senior U.S. official," presumably from the FBI, the prisoner was "providing detailed information for the 'fight against terrorism.' " Still, "U.S. intelligence sources"—presumably in the CIA—"wonder whether he's trying to mislead investigators or frighten the American public." This last was a reference to two "domestic terror warnings" that had been derived from

Zubaydah's "tips" about "possible attacks on banks or financial institutions in the Northeastern United States" and possible "attacks on U.S. supermarkets and shopping malls." That this highest of high-value detainees was being held in the strictest secrecy at an undetermined location on the other side of the world did not prevent his interrogators, or their bureaucratic overlords, from leaking information from him directly into the press in an effort to win the struggle over who would interrogate him and how.

One may note again here that CIA inspector general Helgerson supports one of Soufan's central points, which is that the entire assault on Zubaydah began with a misunderstanding born of ignorance of who precisely he was, how he was related to al Qaeda, and thus what he could be expected to know. CIA officers were convinced that, as President Bush announced when Zubaydah was captured, he was "chief of operations" of al Qaeda or anyway "the number two of three in the organization." As Soufan remarks, "To people who knew what they were talking about, the insistence that Abu Zubaydah was the number three or four in al-Qaeda was flatly ridiculous, as were the claims that he wasn't cooperating." Zubaydah was not even a member of al Qaeda, having served the group, as terrorism analyst Peter Bergen put it, as "a kind of travel agent." Not only did the FBI interrogators and others within the government know this but, as Soufan writes, a CIA officer at the black site "dutifully wrote it up and sent it in cables to Langley," which made it "very surprising to see him publicly described by Bush administration officials as being a senior al-Qaeda member, and even the terrorist group's number three or four in command." But once the president, the secretary of defense, and other senior officials had identified Abu Zubaydah as "a senior al-Qaeda member," it was very hard to "walk it back." ("I said he was important," Bush would later tell Tenet at one of their daily meetings. "You're not going to let me lose face on this, are you?" "No Sir, Mr. President," Tenet replied.)

So CIA officers, led by two contractors—Mitchell (Boris) and his colleague, Bruce Jessen—who had been Air Force instructors in the Survival Evasion Resistance Escape (SERE) program designed in the 1950s to prepare downed pilots for hostile interrogation by Soviet and Chinese enemies, set about preparing an interrogation plan for Abu Zubaydah. The plan, which included twelve "enhanced interrogation techniques," or EITs, was passed to CIA headquarters and discussed in the White House. As Condoleezza Rice tells us in her memoir, "The intelligence agencies and those who were interrogating him were certain that he knew far more than he let on, perhaps even crucial information about impending plots. It was under these circumstances that the Central Intelligence Agency sought authorization to use particular procedures they referred to as 'enhanced interrogation techniques.' The President asked two questions: Would the proposed interrogation program be legal? Is it necessary?"

The second question, of course, had already been addressed—by "Boris" and the CIA. And so, in effect, had the first; by the president's own decision, taken months before, to declare detainees in the war on terror outside the protections of the Geneva Conventions, including, according to the Bush lawyers' arguments, Common Article 3, which was meant to set standards for the treatment of *all* persons taken prisoner or detained. This decision, among other things, removed the bar from subjecting detainees to "cruel, inhuman and degrading treatment"—or that, anyway, was the interpretation of administration lawyers, who argued in effect that the president's decision on Geneva had made it possible, "legally," to apply cruel, inhuman, and degrading treatment to prisoners. "The Geneva decision," as Alberto Mora, the general counsel of the Navy at this time, later put it, "had the primary purpose of making room for cruelty." Undersecretary of Defense Douglas Feith put it more succinctly: "That's the point."

So the groundwork had already been laid. At the Department of Justice, Deputy Assistant Attorney General John Yoo and a young colleague were working furiously on a memorandum that judged specifically whether the CIA's twelve proposed techniques—including slamming the detainee's head against a wall and suffocating him with water—violated the statutes of the U.S. criminal code and the U.S. government's international agreements forbidding torture. Because cruel treatment was no longer barred, or so he and other administration attorneys argued, the task became one of how to define torture itself. The answer: very narrowly, by placing the bar very high. Using an obscure medical insurance statute, Yoo defined torture as treatment causing pain "equivalent to that accompanying major organ failure or death." The definition is bizarre and almost meaningless— some deaths seem not to be painful, for example—but it seemed to serve Yoo and his colleague as a way to limit the legal application of the word torture to techniques that would cause only the most severe and unendurable pain. The memos went through several drafts. "Bring the Bad Things Memo," Yoo emailed his young colleague before one high-level White House meeting. "I like the opinion's new title," she replied brightly. More than a dozen years later, these exchanges make strange reading: one senses in them, amid the intensity of that first heady spring after 9/11, all the breathless excitement of ambitious young professionals breaking new legal ground.

Late in the late summer of 2002, Zubaydah was moved from the ministrations of Ali Soufan and his FBI colleagues, stripped naked, and taken to the very cold, very bright white room. When Soufan discovered the prisoner there, he angrily protested. Soon after, he and his colleagues were withdrawn by the Justice Department; henceforth the FBI's interrogators, the most experienced and able in the federal government, would no longer take part in the CIA-led interrogations.

In their wake, CIA officers and their colleagues began applying what President Bush would later prefer to call an "alternative set of procedures." Abu Zubaydah had entered the realm of improvisation, of an interrogation program developed largely by two private contractors who knew nothing about al Qaeda, who had the distinction of never having carried out a single real interrogation, and who were intent on "reducing" this detainee, according to the CIA's description of the program's intent, "to a baseline, dependent state . . . to demonstrate that he has no control over basic human needs . . . [to] create . . . a mindset in which he learns to perceive and value his personal welfare, comfort, and immediate needs more than the information he is protecting."

NO EXIT

As the Justice Department lawyers worked on their memos that summer, the CIA, according to Rice, "was soon pressing for an answer. The Agency was absolutely convinced that Zubaydah knew something crucial and that time was running out." Those officials who could point most convincingly to the desert of knowledge, who could dwell on and profit from the fear of the vast threatening unknown, were victorious, and indeed nothing more dramatically embodies the style of the exception: Assume the worst. Act preemptively, aggressively. Don't hesitate. If there is a risk, the possible consequences are so grave that you must not let uncertainty about evidence slow you down. The apotheosis of this style of thought and action is Vice President Cheney's "one-percent doctrine": "If there was even a one percent chance of terrorists getting a weapon of mass destruction . . . the United States must now act as if it was a certainty."

That such a fevered and eccentric attitude toward risk—that only *lack* of action poses dangers to the country—followed from the failure to act before September 11 perhaps should not surprise us. Soon the administration itself would prove that *taking* aggressive action— in Iraq, most obviously—could also threaten the country's security but not before this attitude—act aggressively, preemptively; ask questions later, if ever—came to be embodied in the vast worldwide detention regime the Bush administration's state of exception very quickly spawned: five thousand locked up in U.S. detention centers; tens of thousands imprisoned in Bagram and Abu Ghraib and other sites in Afghanistan and Iraq; nearly eight hundred held incommunicado in Guantánamo Bay; hundreds disappeared and held secretly in the various black sites around the world. As embodied in this global detention regime, which at its height held more than eighty thousand prisoners, Cheney's one-percent doctrine had a peculiar and contradictory effect. Call it "the one-way funnel": men were swept into the system, often handed over by people tempted by enormous U.S. bounties—in Afghanistan the military offered for supposed al Qaeda members as much as $20,000, an enormous sum—and once there, stayed there, clogging and debilitating it. Not only was there no adversarial system in place to judge their guilt or evaluate the threat they posed, which, had it existed, would at least have forced the gathering of information, but those in charge strongly resisted releasing anyone. According to one interrogator, officers in Afghanistan charged with deciding what prisoners should be shipped to Guantánamo felt "great fear . . . that they were going to somehow manage to release somebody who would later turn out to be the 20th hijacker. So there was real concern and a real erring on the conservative side." This "erring on the conservative side"—this attitude of "better safe than sorry"—pervaded the system. On the ground, there was no real incentive to release anyone from detention and a very great disincentive. No wonder that, as Lawrence Wilkerson, Secretary of State Colin Powell's chief of staff, discovered in the summer of 2002, "of the initial 742 detainees that had arrived at Guantánamo, the majority of them had never seen a U.S. soldier in the process of their initial detention and their captivity *had not been subjected to any meaningful review.* . . . Often absolutely no evidence relating to the detainee was turned over, so there was no real method of knowing why the prisoner had been detained in the first place."

Wholesale arrests based on paltry or nonexistent information weren't confined to Afghanistan. Parallels can be found throughout the detention regime of the state of exception. For example, in Iraq's Abu Ghraib prison, where, according to an officer on the Detainee Assessment Board, "85 to 90 percent of the detainees were of no intelligence value." What is more, the officer went on, the "failure . . . to sort out the valuable detainees from the innocents who should have been released soon after capture, [led,] ultimately, *to less actionable intelligence.*"

Which is to say that the sweeping arrests and indefinite detention—the refusal to make discriminations of risk, which would have entailed a willingness to get it wrong, in favor of sweeping judgments based on pervasive fear—crippled the intelligence-gathering system itself. The various prisons, secret and public, were flooded with detainees who knew nothing, but who could not be set free because, as in Abu Ghraib, the detaining officers objected or because, as in Guantánamo, as Wilkerson says, "it was politically impossible to release them." Had hundreds been released—as eventually happened, though it took years—"the detention efforts at Guantánamo would be revealed as the incredibly confused operation that they were." We see here again the limits and distortions of the particular war paradigm the Bush administration invented: men became prisoners, or rather "detainees," not because of the uniforms they wore or the fact that they were found on the battlefield but because they were turned over, almost always for cash bounties, by people who claimed they were the enemy, often on little or no evidence. What evidence did exist was, in any case, rarely recorded. Once in the system, there was often no way to get them out: they had become "prisoners of war," or rather "unlawful combatants," who could seemingly be held "for the duration of the conflict," though no accepted determination had been reached about when that conflict might end or what might even constitute such an ending.

The injustice of the system was increasingly recognized around the world. It was a blessing in particular to al Qaeda's cause in Islamic countries in what was, after all, a political war. But quite apart from its propaganda value to the enemy, of which we are reminded whenever the Islamic State displays one of its hostages in an orange jumpsuit, the detention regime failed even on its own terms: the system meant to gather the resource judged most vital to success in fighting the war on terror—information—was debilitating itself.

CREATIVE INSTABILITY

From the beginning of the war on terror, tactics developed in the name of preventing attacks imagined as imminent, from torture to indefinite detention to drone warfare, have often undermined or debilitated broader efforts to weaken and eliminate terrorist groups. Strategic choices themselves have sometimes been contradictory or self-defeating, with the invasion of Iraq again the preeminent example. But time and again tactical choices have helped enemies thrive. To understand this, we must return to a question that is too seldom asked: What exactly were the leaders and the foot soldiers of al Qaeda trying to achieve on that bright September morning in 2001?

They intended to kill Americans and they succeeded in killing nearly three thousand. But "killing Americans" no more describes al Qaeda's ultimate goal than "killing jihadists" would describe America's war aims. On September 11, al Qaeda's true weapon of choice was neither box cutters nor airliners but that powerful American invention, the television set. One goal of the attacks, brilliantly achieved, was to create an indelible image that would spread fear—but also, critically, hope. Hope to young Muslim men that the United States, the great superpower standing behind the oppressive, idolatrous puppet states of Egypt and Saudi Arabia and Pakistan, was vulnerable, that it could be attacked and defeated. For the strategic goal of al Qaeda was and remains to reestablish the

Caliphate, a Muslim superpower stretching from the Strait of Gibraltar to the Strait of Malacca. To do that the jihadists must sweep away the entire post–World War I, post-imperial order of the Middle East and with it those they view as illegitimate, American-backed autocrats, the apostate leaders ruling, and repressing, Muslims. Up to the mid-1990s al Qaeda and its precursor groups had done battle directly with these "near enemies"—the Sadat and Mubarak regimes of Egypt, the House of Saud—but with little success. They then decided to try a different strategy, turning to attack the "far enemy," without whose support, so the theory went, these local apostate regimes would eventually crumble.

So al Qaeda began to attack the United States, first its embassies, in Nairobi and Daar es Salaam in 1998; then its warships, in Aden, Yemen, in 2000; and finally, in September 2001, its military headquarters in Washington and its commercial center in New York. The purpose was in part the purpose of all terrorism, as defined by the late Israeli prime minister and (as leader of the Irgun terrorist group) dynamiter of the King David Hotel, Menachim Begin: to dirty the face of power. The dirtied face of American power—the iconic, unforgettable image of the burning collapsing towers—was meant to serve as a giant recruitment poster for the jihadist cause. Every time that image reappears on television screens around the world it says to potential jihadists: We can win. We can defeat them. *Join us.* It is an image not only of terror but, grotesque as this may seem, of idealistic struggle. For Osama bin Laden was engaged, first and foremost, in building a movement. His ultimate goals, and those of his successors, are not military but political.

The second major goal of the jihadists in attacking New York and Washington in such spectacular fashion, and earlier in attacking American embassies and warships, was to provoke the United States to react by taking dramatic, brutal, and, the hope was, *telegenic* action against Muslims. Much evidence suggests bin Laden assumed the United States would immediately invade and occupy

Afghanistan, allowing itself to be drawn into, as Michael Scott Doran has put it, "somebody else's civil war," and leading to an endless, grinding conflict. This quagmire was to have inspired bin Laden's Arab legionnaires from throughout the Islamic world to heed the call to join with the Taliban holy warriors and defeat the sole remaining superpower in that mountainous "graveyard of empires," destroying the United States in a grand reenactment of the destruction of the Soviet Union a dozen years before.

In the event, of course, the Bush administration, after initially contenting itself largely with aerial bombardment of Afghanistan, did bin Laden one better, invading and occupying Iraq, an Arab country much more central to the average Muslim's concerns. That quixotic effort produced exactly what bin Laden had hoped for in Afghanistan, a bloody quagmire. And in creating it and attempting to slog through it, the United States quickly came to embody the caricature that the jihadists had depicted: a blundering, blasphemous, muscle-bound, violent superpower intent on humiliating, repressing, and murdering Muslims. By the spring of 2003 the day-to-day repression carried out by the United States' main Middle East client states had been embodied for all to see in a violent occupation of a major Arab country by the "far enemy" itself. Muslims were fighting and dying heroically at the hands of American soldiers on televisions across the Islamic world. Thus the strategy of *la politique du pire*—"the politics of the worst" or "the strategy of provocation"—whereby you provoke your enemy to strip off his peaceable mask and make manifest the true underlying dynamics of repression.

By attacking the United States and provoking American attacks on Muslims, then, bin Laden aimed to "awaken the inattentive" Muslims to the true depredations of the United States, depredations usually shrouded in the secondhand repression of American client regimes. Once awakened—so the theory went—those Muslims would launch or escalate various local rebellions that would eventually coalesce into a worldwide fundamentalist revolution that would overthrow the "apostate regimes" and reestablish the Caliphate across the Islamic world. The series of attacks that reached its climax in September 2001 was to be the spark that set off a conflagration to consume the present Muslim world, divided and humbled after World War I by the imperialist powers, and make way for the rebirth of Muslim unity, Muslim piety, and Muslim power.

It is an age-old strategy of insurgents and guerrillas and terrorists: if you are weak, if you have no army of your own, borrow your enemy's. Provoke your adversary to do your political work for you. Use your enemy's strength to make up for your own weakness. And al Qaeda's leaders know that they *are* weak. "However far our capabilities reach," Ayman al-Zawahiri, then bin Laden's deputy and now his successor, wrote, "they will never be equal to one thousandth of the capabilities of the kingdom of Satan that is waging war on us." Recognizing their own meager manpower and resources, the jihadists sought to take advantage of the unlimited power of the United States. And in launching the war on terror, eventually occupying two Muslim countries and producing in Guantánamo and Abu Ghraib celebrated images of repression and torture, the United States proved all too happy to oblige.

Against this background, former secretary of state Henry Kissinger's explanation for why he supported the Iraq War becomes almost poignant. The United States had to invade Iraq, Kissinger said, "because Afghanistan wasn't enough. Because we needed to humiliate them as they wanted to humiliate us." In Kissinger's conception, the image of American tanks rumbling down the main streets of an occupied Arab capital would supplant the scene of the collapsing World Trade towers and restore the prestige and credibility that the superpower had lost on September 11, thereby cleansing the dirtied face of power. This reasoning, by which the United States was obliged to respond to the attacks by reasserting itself as the invincible, dominant superpower, played directly into al Qaeda's political strategy.

Some officials of the Bush administration understood the Iraq expedition to be an answer to the political and ideological challenge presented by bin Laden. The war and the transformation of the Middle East that it promised, according to Condoleezza Rice, then Bush's national security adviser, "is the only guarantee that it will no longer produce ideologies of hatred that lead men to fly airplanes into buildings in New York and Washington." In the view of many influential thinkers in the administration at the time, as I wrote five months before American troops invaded, overwhelming victory in Iraq was to offer a democratic vision that would have rivaled and indeed triumphed over the fundamentalist revolution promised by bin Laden:

> *It envisions a post–Saddam Hussein Iraq—secular, middle-class, urbanized, rich with oil—that will replace the autocracy of Saudi Arabia as the key American ally in the Persian Gulf, allowing the withdrawal of United States troops from the kingdom. The presence of a victorious American Army in Iraq would then serve as a powerful boost to moderate elements in neighboring Iran, hastening that critical country's evolution away from the mullahs and toward a more moderate course. Such an evolution in Tehran would lead to a withdrawal of Iranian support for Hezbollah and other radical groups, thereby isolating Syria and reducing pressure on Israel. This undercutting of radicals on Israel's northern borders and within the West Bank and Gaza would spell the definitive end of Yasir Arafat and lead eventually to a favorable solution of the Arab-Israeli problem.*

Perhaps, had the Americans managed to install a stable democratic Shia regime in Baghdad and withdraw almost all their troops within three months, as Secretary of Defense Rumsfeld and others envisioned, the "creative chaos" or "creative instability" that the Bush officials and their think tank sympathizers hoped to provoke would have done its work and a "Democratic Tsunami" would have swept from Tehran to Damascus to Ramallah, bringing in its wake popular, democratic, America-supporting regimes. But this fantasy was built on another: that of an instant, clean, democratic transformation in Iraq and a population grateful to have it.

The Iraq expedition produced instead an inept U.S. occupation, a brutal insurgency, a sectarian civil war, and daily television footage of Muslims fighting and dying at the hands of American soldiers. And in the spring of 2004, a year after President Bush proclaimed victory ("mission accomplished") from the deck of the USS *Abraham Lincoln,* the occupation gave the world the most lasting images so far of the entire war on terror: hooded, naked Muslim men in the squalor of Abu Ghraib prison chained to the bars of cells, forced to masturbate, to climb naked on top of one another under the eyes of beefy American soldiers. Consider the image of Leashed Man: an Arab male stretched out nude and helpless on the dirty floor of Abu Ghraib, his face convulsed in pain and humiliation as a young American woman in military fatigues stands smiling triumphantly over him, the leash tethering his neck grasped in her hand. Had bin Laden gone to Madison Avenue and offered to pay millions for a propaganda poster that would embody his message, could he have found anything more effective? These images, on television and on the Internet, on the front pages of newspapers and the covers of magazines, on murals painted across city walls, swept through the Islamic world. Could bin Laden have hoped for a more dramatic victory in the strategy of provocation?

ALTERNATIVE PROCEDURES

Bureaucracy, by creating regular pathways of procedure and practice, makes the unusual routine. By the time officials of the Central

Intelligence Agency had codified their "combined use of interrogation techniques" in late 2004, "high-value detainees" (HVDs)
would have to immediately and "willingly provide information on
actionable threats and location information on High-Value Targets
at large—not lower level information—for interrogators to continue
with the neutral approach." That is, a high-value detainee's failure
to offer such immediate and complete cooperation upon capture,
as judged by the interrogator, would result in his immediate sub-
jection to the "conditioning phase" of the enhanced interrogation
program, which involved, in the CIA's description:

a. Nudity. The HVD's clothes are taken and he remains
   nude until the interrogators provide clothes to him.
b. Sleep Deprivation. The HVD is placed in the vertical
   shackling position to begin sleep deprivation. Other
   shackling procedures may be used during interrogations.
   The detainee is diapered for sanitary purposes, although
   the diaper is not used at all times.
c. Dietary manipulation. The HVD is fed Ensure Plus or
   other food at regular intervals. The HVD receives a target
   of 1500 calories a day per OMS [CIA Office of Medical
   Services] guidelines.

Throughout these documents the language is neutral and bureaucratic: "The procedures he is subjected to are precise, quiet, and
almost clinical and no one is mistreating him."

Even in the CIA documents, though, which strive to describe the
program so "clinically," every once in a while a bit of reality peeps
through: one interrogator, chastised for blowing cigar smoke in a
detainee's face, claims he is obliged to smoke the cigar "to cover up
the stench." Think of those diapers, which are used for humiliation
as well as for "sanitary purposes." Or consider Khalid Sheikh Mohammed's description of the "vertical shackling position," which,

by the time he was captured, in Rawalpindi, Pakistan, in March 2003, nearly a year after Abu Zubaydah, CIA interrogators had begun using in preference to "long-term sitting" to "begin sleep deprivation":

> *I was kept for one month in the cell in a standing position with my hands cuffed and shackled above my head and my feet cuffed and shackled to a point in the floor. Of course during this month I fell asleep on some occasions while still being held in this position. This resulted in all my weight being applied to the handcuffs around my wrist resulting in open and bleeding wounds. Both my feet became very swollen after one month of almost continual standing.*

The Red Cross interviewer, who took down Khalid Sheikh Mo-hammed's account in late 2006, notes that "scars consistent with this allegation were visible on both wrists as well as on both ankles."

Like all of the CIA's "enhanced interrogation techniques," forced, extended standing has a long tradition. The Soviets, who called it simply *stoika*, "standing," relied on it heavily as the most important "softening" tool in their interrogations. Pondering the effectiveness of this method, Lawrence F. Hinkle and Harold G. Wolff, in a classic 1956 paper, "Communist Interrogation and In-doctrination of 'Enemies of the State,'" observe that "after 18 to 24 hours of continuous standing, there is an accumulation of fluid in the tissues of the legs. . . . The ankles and feet of the prisoner swell to twice their normal circumference. The edema may rise up the legs as high as the middle of the thighs. The skin becomes tense and intensely painful. Large blisters develop, which break and exude watery serum."

Set against this stark description the bureaucratic terms of the CIA's description—"quiet, precise, almost clinical," "OMS guide-lines"—are particularly striking, not least the presence of doctors to make sure "no one is mistreating him." One detainee, Wallid bin

Attash, who had lost a leg fighting in Afghanistan and who spent days and weeks with his hands chained to the ceiling, described periodic visits he received from a doctor, whose task was to measure the swelling in his remaining leg using a tape measure.

Many trained observers have pointed out the similarities of the CIA's "alternative set of procedures" to "the basic KGB technique . . . sleep deprivation, stress positions, cold." The association is no accident: the CIA contractors improvised their methods based on techniques they had used as instructors in the SERE program, which in turn had been designed during the early Cold War "to simulate conditions" pilots might face if imprisoned by the Soviets or the Chinese—"enemies," that is, "that did not abide by the Geneva Conventions."

We see here perhaps the prime example of the improvisation inherent in the state of exception. First, the critical security bureaucracies in the U.S. government, the CIA, and the military derived their "enhanced interrogation techniques" from a Cold War–era pilot training program that intentionally reproduced techniques the Soviets and Chinese had used in their *illegal exploitation . . .* of prisoners over the last 50 years," as one former SERE instructor later told the Senate Armed Services Committee. Then they placed before government attorneys the Through-the-Looking Glass task of proving that those same interrogation techniques were perfectly permissible under the tenets of international law that they had been expressly designed to violate. A central line of reasoning running through the torture memos drafted by the Department of Justice lawyers is the peculiar notion that because the pilot trainees, who were volunteers and who could, of course, halt the procedures at any time, did not suffer long-term psychological harm, then detainees involuntarily and repeatedly subjected to these techniques for real—who might reasonably fear that during waterboarding, for example, they might actually drown—would not suffer long-term harm either.

EXTRAORDINARY BUREAUCRATIC FEAT

So an interrogation program deemed absolutely essential to protect the country during a national emergency was reverse engineered from a training program for pilots from the 1950s by contract instructors who knew nothing about al Qaeda and had never carried out an actual interrogation. Then the highest of America's "high value detainees," who supposedly knew about deadly attacks soon to come, were placed in the hands of those contractors, who applied to them techniques that had been "reverse engineered" from Soviet and Chinese tortures of half a century before. The story is too bizarre and strange to be credible in any novel.

And yet it happened. How can we begin to account for it? The United States, after all, had had considerable experience in interrogating prisoners, not least during World War II, a time of no small national emergency, during which the military managed to produce in short order an interrogation program that was legal, subtle, and by all accounts immensely effective. But there is no evidence that anyone in the Bush administration looked at this history or indeed had any interest in finding out what solutions to these problems the government had devised in the past. To understand the decisions about interrogation we have to look to attitudes about history and about government held by the most senior and powerful figures in the Bush administration, notably the vice president, the secretary of defense, and the president himself. As Ron Suskind notes in *The One Percent Doctrine*, "Sober due diligence, with an eye for the way previous administrations have thought through a standard array of challenges facing the United States, creates . . . a kind of check on executive power and prerogative." Such a check was precisely what the president, in the wake of September 11, did *not* want. As President Bush evolved, writes Suskind, from

the early, pre-9/11 president, who had little grasp of foreign affairs and made few major decisions in that realm . . . to the post-9/11 president, who met America's foreign challenges with decisiveness born of a brand of preternatural, faith-based, self-generated certainty.... His view of right and wrong, and of righteous actions—such as attacking evil or spreading 'God's gift' of democracy—were undercut by the kind of traditional, shades-of-gray analysis that has been a staple of most presidents' diets.... The hard, complex analysis ... would often be a thin offering, passed through the filters of Cheney or Rice, or not presented at all.

During the post-9/11 Bush administration the "interagency"—the process by which government departments and agencies study, develop, debate, and approve ideas and policies, by which policies rise gradually through the assistant secretary, deputy secretary, and then principal level—went on, with the bureaucracy whirring along as it always had. But when it came to many of the most vital policies of the state of exception, the recommendations produced were ignored or circumvented. When we search for a record of the policy discussion that preceded the momentous decision to approve and use "enhanced interrogation techniques," for example, we find very little there, beyond Rice's approval of the Abu Zubaydah interrogation plan. As Philip Zelikow, executive director of the 9/11 Commission and later Secretary Rice's counselor at the Department of State, remarked, in this and other grave policy choices in the state of exception, the tendency seemed to have been to call in the lawyers to tell policymakers the limits of "what we can do." There is little or no record of anyone ever discussing "what we should do." If officials argued this question, no record of it has yet been made public. We don't even know who came up with the idea that, in Zelikow's words, "the CIA—an agency that had no significant institutional capability to question enemy captives—[would improvise] an unprecedented, elaborate, systematic program of medically monitored physical torment to break prisoners and make them talk."

How was it then that this "extraordinary bureaucratic feat," by which this "program was conjured out of thin air"—the words are Zelikow's—actually came about? No study seems to have been undertaken of various interrogation methods, no effort to consult allies— the English, the French, the Israelis—who had grappled intimately with these issues themselves. No record has been made public of any effort to examine, let alone adapt, the remarkably effective and noncoercive interrogation program developed during World War II. Faced with the momentous decision to torment America's prisoners, writes Zelikow, "none of the moral or policy issues connected with these choices, including the merits of using SERE-type methods, appear to have been analyzed in a serious way." Instead, secret meetings with a handful of people and then a "presidential-level decision."

We have seen this movie before. During the fall of 2001 the policy of trying detainees before military commissions was developed the same way, by David Addington, then Vice President Cheney's counsel, and a handful of others, and then presented by Cheney for the president's signature during one of their private lunches. And like Colin Powell, Condoleezza Rice, who as national security adviser was supposedly running the interagency process, found out about the decision on CNN. A tiny cabal of officials, led by Cheney and including Addington, Tenet, counterterrorism official Cofer Black, and Deputy Assistant Attorney General John Yoo, and a few others, essentially constructed, themselves, the critical national security policies of the U.S. government during the weeks and months after September 11. The National Security Council system, set up in the National Security Act of 1947 as the means by which critical decisions would be made, by which information and analysis would be drawn upward from the essential security bureaucracies and decisions imposed downward, was effectively bypassed. Senior officials were kept in the dark, sidelined, ignored. It was a mechanism for creating a series of faits accomplis, and it worked.

Of course, that depends on what we mean by "worked." The military commissions system proved to be a disaster, a political and diplomatic embarrassment that was unworkable in practice and that the Supreme Court finally threw out. Out of nearly eight hundred "unlawful combatants" that had been brought to Guantánamo during President Bush's time in office, his military commissions managed to convict a total of three. Hundreds were simply released. But the cabal had succeeded in creating the commissions under the president's sole authority, circumventing those in the government who would have raised objections that would likely have blocked or certainly modified the program, and making it the law of the land for four years.

We know how the "alternative set of procedures" came to be approved. In the wake of Abu Zubaydah's capture in March 2002, the CIA director and the vice president argued that the program was necessary. Rice tells us in her memoirs how Director of Central Intelligence Tenet described the alternative set of procedures to the president:

> George said . . . the program was necessary, explaining why the CIA thought Zubaydah was the key to understanding impending plots. He described in general terms what techniques he'd recommend, including waterboarding, and the safeguards that would be employed, including the presence of medical personnel, to ensure that the interrogations were conducted safely. The DCI emphasized that the techniques were safe and effective and had been used in the military training of thousands of U.S. soldiers.

Justice Department officials, based on the decisions that had been taken months before withholding from detainees Geneva Convention protections (and thus sidestepping, at least to their satisfaction, the ban on "cruel, inhuman and degrading treatment"), and armed with John Yoo's memoranda affirming that the techniques did not rise to the level of torture, had pronounced the program legal. "In other words," as Zelikow puts it, "the President was told that an al Qaeda leader with knowledge of possible plots was in our hands, that this was the only way to find out what he knew, and that the proposed program was legal." Given these points—severe threat, necessity, legality—the decision of the president—at least this president—was foreordained. He approved.

BLACK BOX

As it happens, almost everything the president was told, beginning with who Abu Zubaydah was and what he could be expected to know, was wrong. These misconceptions and errors would soon come to be inscribed, as it were, on Zubaydah's body. That improvisation and experimentation, inherent in the style of the state of exception, can be seen in the evolution of the "enhanced interrogation techniques" Abu Zubaydah himself came to recognize. He recounts the second, or "correction," phase of his interrogation in the cold white room:

> *Two black wooden boxes were brought into the room outside my cell. One was tall, slightly higher than me and narrow. Measuring perhaps in area [3½ by 2½ feet by 6½ feet high]. The other was shorter, perhaps only [3½ feet] in height. I was taken out of my cell and one of the interrogators wrapped a towel around my neck, they then used it to swing me around and smash me repeatedly against the hard walls of the room. I was also repeatedly slapped in the face. . . .*
>
> *I was then put into the tall black box for what I think was about one and a half to two hours. The box was totally black on the inside as well as the outside. . . . They put a cloth or cover over the outside of the box to cut out the light and restrict my air supply. It was difficult to breathe. When I was let out of the box I saw that one of the walls of the room had been covered with plywood sheeting. From now on it was against this wall that I was then smashed with the towel around my neck.*

In a 2004 memorandum to Assistant Attorney General Daniel Levin an unnamed CIA officer noted that this "walling"

> *is one of the most effective interrogation techniques because it wears down the [high-value detainee] physically, heightens uncertainty in the detainee about what the interrogator may do to him and creates a sense of dread when the HVD knows he is about to be walled again. . . . An HVD may be walled one time (one impact with the wall) to make a point or twenty to thirty times consecutively when the interrogator requires a more significant response to a question.*

What about the mysterious appearance of the plywood, evidently introduced to prevent the kind of bodily injury that would make further "exploitation" of the detainee difficult or impossible? Where precisely did that change in procedure come from? As CIA officer John Kiriakou reminds us,

> *Each one of these steps . . . had to have the approval of the Deputy Director for Operations. So before you laid a hand on [a detainee], you had to send in the cable saying, "He's uncooperative. Request permission to do X." And that permission would come. . . . The cable traffic back and forth was extremely specific.*

This hour-by-hour approval of specific techniques issuing out of CIA headquarters was the near end of an interlocking system of notification and briefings that ensured that knowledge of the enhanced interrogation program was spread among top officials of the government. CIA officials who approved the program and the use of specific techniques made an assiduous effort to brief "NSC policy staff and senior Administration officials," according to the CIA inspector general's report. "The Agency specifically wanted to ensure that these officials and the [Congressional Oversight] Committees continued to be aware of and approve CIA's actions."

The Church and Pike committee investigations of the CIA in the 1970s exposing agency assassinations, coups, and other misdeeds brought in their wake scandals and indictments. CIA leaders and officers of the national security state were determined that this time, no matter how national attitudes on interrogation and torture might change, they could never again be accused of rogue behavior. Instead of the former policy of putting nothing on paper, which had allowed a convenient deniability for the president and other high officials when misdeeds were exposed, this time CIA officers would insist on briefings, meetings, records, memoranda, documents: explicit approval. This time, they made certain that high officials wouldn't be able to claim they didn't know. In so doing, they ensured that responsibility was spread very high and very wide indeed. "Why are we talking about this in the White House?" Attorney General John Ashcroft is said to have asked during one Principals Meeting conducted to choreograph and approve what "enhanced interrogation techniques" should be applied, and in what combination, to a hooded prisoner on the other side of the globe. "History will not judge this kindly."

DRIFTING DOWNWARD

Of the eleven "enhanced interrogation techniques" deemed legal in August 2002 by the Department of Justice (a proposed twelfth, burial alive, the government lawyers rejected), ten techniques, according to John Yoo, "did not even come close to the [legal] standard [of torture]" but "waterboarding did." "I had actually thought that we prohibited waterboarding," Yoo confessed to Department of Justice investigators. "I didn't recollect that we had actually said that you could do it." He went on: "The waterboarding as it's described in that [August 2002] memo, is very different than the waterboarding that was described in the press. And so when I read the description in the press of what waterboarding is, I was like, oh, well, obviously that would be prohibited by the statute."

Indeed the International Committee of the Red Cross, legally charged under the Geneva Conventions with investigating and judging the treatment of prisoners, declared without qualification in its extensive report on American treatment of high-value detainees that waterboarding and other "enhanced interrogation techniques" as practiced at the black sites "amounted to torture and/or cruel, inhuman, or degrading treatment" and that "the ill-treatment to which [the detainees] were subject while held in the CIA program, either singly or in combination, constituted torture." But Yoo's observation underlines the difference between what is prescribed in the legal and policy documents—in which Yoo memorably dismissed waterboarding as "simply a controlled acute episode"—and what happens when these techniques are actually applied by human beings to human beings at the black sites.

Here is Abu Zubaydah's account:

> After the beating I was then placed in the small box. . . . As it was not high enough even to sit upright, I had to crouch down. . . . The stress on my legs held in this position meant my wounds both in the leg and stomach became very painful. . . .The wound on my leg began to open and started to bleed. . . .
>
> I was then dragged from the small box, unable to walk properly and put on what looked like a hospital bed, and strapped down very tightly with belts. A black cloth was then placed over my face and the interrogators used a mineral water bottle to pour water on the cloth so that I could not breathe. After a few minutes the cloth was removed and the bed was rotated into an upright position. The pressure of the straps on my wounds was very painful. I vomited. The bed was then again lowered to horizontal position and the same torture carried out again with the black cloth over my face and water poured

on from a bottle. On this occasion my head was in a more backward, downwards position and the water was poured on for a longer time. I struggled against the straps, trying to breathe, but it was hopeless. I thought I was going to die. I lost control of my urine. Since then I still lose control of my urine when under stress.

I was then placed again in the tall box. While I was inside the box loud music was played again and somebody kept banging repeatedly on the box from the outside. I tried to sit down on the floor, but because of the small space the bucket with urine tipped over and spilt over me. . . . I was then taken out and again a towel was wrapped around my neck and I was smashed into the wall with the plywood covering and repeatedly slapped in the face by the same two interrogators as before.

I was then made to sit on the floor with a black hood over my head until the next session of torture began.

This then is the famous waterboarding, a time-honored technique deployed by the priestly interrogators of the Spanish Inquisition, by American soldiers during the Philippine rebellion of the early twentieth century, by French paratroopers during the Algerian War of the late 1950s and early 1960s, by the Argentines during their dirty war of the 1970s, and by the Khmer Rouge and the Salvadorans during their wars of the 1970s and 1980s. Techniques varied: the French would strip the prisoner, beat him, strap him to a bench, and tilt his head backward into a bucket of dirty or soapy water, or of urine. The Argentines devised a hinge joining bench and water basin that would allow the interrogators to strap the prisoner down, lift the bench, and tilt his head backward into the water. In developing their modern version, the CIA interrogators seem to have relied most heavily on the technique used by the venerable Spanish inquisitors in which, according to one contemporary description, "a wet cloth is laid over the prisoner's mouth and nostrils, and a small stream of water constantly descending upon it, he sucks ye cloth into his throat . . . and puts ye unhappy wretch into the *agonies of death*." Whatever the variation in technique, the principle of waterboarding remains the same: drowning the prisoner, provoking the uncontrollable panic this causes, and interrupting the drowning just in time to save his life.

That American interrogators were waterboarding prisoners first appeared in the press in May 2004, in a report in *The New York Times*. As early as December 2002, *The Washington Post* had run a lengthy report on its front page on "stress and duress" techniques, and the *Times* had followed with its own report several months later. In the spring of 2004, in the wake of Abu Ghraib, the trickle of leaks about torture became a flood. The two narratives, the story of what was "secretly" done and the story of what we know was done, crossed very early. Despite the secrecy of the black sites, we've now had more than a decade to debate waterboarding and its effectiveness, and we have seen discussion about these "secret" techniques evolve, from Kiriakou's assertion in 2005 that Abu Zubaydah "broke" almost immediately when waterboarded for the first time to the revelation, three years later, that in fact Zubaydah had been waterboarded no fewer than eighty-three times, to the description, in the voluminous but still largely classified Senate Select Committee on Intelligence's torture report, that these waterboardings produced from Abu Zubaydah "hysterical pleas" and "immediate fluid intake and involuntary leg, chest and arm spasms," until he became "completely unresponsive, with bubbles rising through his open full mouth." After the eighty-second waterboarding, officials back at headquarters insisted he must be waterboarded again—in the face of strong objections from interrogators on the scene who argued that the first eighty-two applications of the waterboard had left the detainee "compliant"—because he still hadn't given up information about the attacks that these officials were convinced he knew were coming. Finally, even they were forced to conclude that Abu Zubaydah didn't know. So when CIA officers judged that the use of "enhanced interrogation techniques" had been a "success," they meant not that they had forced him to give up more information but that they had made him suffer enough to prove to their satisfaction that he didn't know what they had been convinced he did. Torture was successful because it let them alleviate their own anxiety. And their anxiety was in no small part based on their ignorance about who Abu Zubaydah actually was and what he could be expected to know.

This dynamic arises in the Senate report again and again. CIA officials are convinced that detainees know about pending attacks, and when they don't reveal them, officials push for more days of "forced standing" and sleep deprivation, more walling and water dousing and close confinement, more waterboarding. What the weeks and weeks of torture finally prove is that detainees don't know. Terrorist organizations are cellular structures, with information supplied only to those who need to know it. Unless American forces chance to capture a person about to conduct one, they are going to have a very hard time finding people who know about coming attacks. Because of this reality, the narratives of torture after 9/11 for all their numbing brutality tell a simple, ugly story: we translated our ignorance into their pain.

Already in 2004 the CIA inspector general had concluded in his report that in waterboarding Zubaydah the interrogators used more water and performed the procedure much more frequently than prescribed in the legal documents. The Senate Select Committee on Intelligence concluded that the techniques as applied had been much more brutal than had been reported to the Department of Justice, the Congress, or the White House: Detainees were kept chained to the walls of bare concrete cells in constant darkness, bombarded with unceasing white noise. One detainee left chained to a wall in a dark, unheated dungeon half naked was found frozen to death. Two detainees whose feet were broken were tortured by "forced standing," their hands shackled to the ceiling for days at a time. One detainee, after "56 hours of standing sleep deprivation," was "barely able to enunciate" and "visibly shaken by his hallucinations of dogs mauling and killing his sons and family." Five detainees were force-fed rectally "without documented medical necessity."

The Senate investigators also concluded that the CIA had repeatedly and systematically misled its overseers in the White House and in Congress about the effectiveness of torture. And if, as the committee found, the "CIA repeatedly provided inaccurate information to the Department of Justice, impeding a proper legal analysis of the CIA's Detention and Interrogation Program," then the golden shield the Department provided in its torture memos was based on false information. What was done in those sunless rooms, in other words, might well have been illegal even according to the extremely lenient analysis of John Yoo and his colleagues. The waterboarding performed on detainees so differed from what had been described to Justice Department lawyers that the acts likely constituted torture, even under Yoo's exceedingly narrow definition.

Whether or not the agency intentionally misled the lawyers, the actual application of the techniques certainly reflected a general "drifting downward" into greater cruelty that we see throughout the various plotlines of this story. In testimony before the Senate Judiciary Committee, the FBI's Ali Soufan, who carried out the initial interrogation of Zubaydah, explained the dynamic behind this inevitable devolution. An interrogator using harsh techniques, Soufan explained, "tries to subjugate the detainee into submission through humiliation and cruelty. The approach," he went on,

> applies a force continuum, each time using harsher and harsher techniques until the detainee submits. The idea behind the technique is to force the detainee to see the interrogator as the master who controls his pain. . . . The detainee is stripped naked and told: "Tell us what you know." If the detainee doesn't immediately respond by giving information . . . then the next step on the force continuum is

introduced, for example sleep deprivation, and the process will con-
tinue until the detainee's will is broken and he automatically gives
up all information he is presumed to know.

There are many problems with this technique. A major problem
is that it is ineffective. Al Qaeda terrorists are trained to resist torture.
As shocking as these techniques are to us, the al Qaeda training pre-
pares them for much worse—the torture they would expect to receive
if caught by dictatorships, for example. This is why the contractors
had to keep getting authorization to use harsher and harsher meth-
ods, until they reached waterboarding and then there was nothing
they could do but use that technique again and again. Abu Zubaydah
had to be waterboarded 83 times and Khalid Shaikh Mohammed
183 times. In a democracy there is a glass ceiling of harsh techniques
the interrogator cannot breach, and a detainee can eventually call
the interrogator's bluff.

At the time Zubaydah was strapped to that hospital gurney, in
fact, any such "rules" limiting his treatment were in effect administrative, not legal. In arguing that waterboarding was nothing more
than "a controlled acute episode" and thus did not constitute torture, John Yoo had appended a final and rather striking section to
his August 1, 2002, memorandum, in which he argued that, even if
this and other "alternative procedures" *were* in fact torture—he of
course had claimed otherwise—then the president, as commander
in chief, could still, legally, order them applied to detainees. Re-
gardless of what treaties or statutes might say, in other words, the
president of the United States could legally order torture. This most
notorious passage of legal argument was apparently added to the
memo after the Justice Department refused to give CIA officials, as
they demanded, a "letter of declination," a full *ex ante* pardon for
any actions CIA officers might take in interrogating detainees. The
final passage of Yoo's memorandum seems to have been intended
as a substitute for such a letter, in order to offer a final, bulletproof

"golden shield" to the CIA, so that, come what may—even if this ex-
treme reasoning was eventually disowned and discarded, as in fact
it was—all involved could claim to have acted "in good faith, on the
advice of their attorney."

Yoo, in composing this part of his memorandum—the idea for
it seems originally to have come from David Addington, Vice President Cheney's counsel—was not arguing anything he did not himself believe, as demonstrated in his other writings and, most vividly,
in this 2005 exchange during a debate with Professor Doug Cassel
of the Notre Dame Law School:

> CASSEL: If the President deems that he's got to torture
>   somebody, including by crushing the testicles of the per-
>   son's child, there is no law that can stop him?
> YOO: No treaty.
> CASSEL: Also no law by Congress. That is what you wrote in
>   the August 2002 memo.
> YOO: I think it depends on why the President thinks he
>   needs to do that.

Yoo is quite right, of course, that his memorandum, which was
the official policy of the United States government for several years,
does in effect claim that if the president of the United States ordered any atrocity and did so pursuant to his commander in chief
authority, such an order would be legal. Presumably he could order
the child burned alive or dipped in acid or boiled in oil, and that
would be legal as well. He is the president and the commander in
chief.

We all know of governments in which the leader may command
that atrocities be committed and can do so in full confidence that
his actions are legal because he is the head of state or commander in
chief. Certainly Jefferson and Madison and the other framers knew
of such governments—they had all read Voltaire on torture and

tolerance and limited power, understood that forbidding torture stood as an ultimate test case of limited government—and it was not the kind of government that they thought they were creating. Such a government is one of men and not of laws, based on the principle, famously enunciated by Richard Nixon, that "when the president does it, that means that it's not illegal." After September 11, that principle, which is the clear implication of Mr. Yoo's memorandum, became the de facto policy of our government, and in important ways remains inscribed within our laws. Fourteen years after the coming of the state of exception, and six years after a new president was elected in part to end it, we remain imprisoned within it.

SCANDAL FORETOLD

Though his moment of secret fame is long past, Abu Zubaydah is still with us. Before they began torturing him at the black site in the summer of 2002, his interrogators cabled CIA officials that "in light of the planned psychological pressure techniques to be implemented," they needed "reasonable assurances that [Abu Zubaydah] will remain in isolation and incommunicado for the remainder of his life." But after three and a half years in black sites in Thailand, Poland, and other undisclosed locations, he was moved in September 2006 to Guantánamo—an event hailed by President Bush in a historic White House speech revealing and defending his "alternative set of procedures"—and he remains there today, in his thirteenth year of imprisonment without trial.

Thinking of Abu Zubaydah, his undetermined future, and the questions his mistreatment raises, it is impossible not to think as well of his American partners in these black site scenes enacted more than a decade ago. Some remain in the CIA and elsewhere in the security bureaucracy. Others have moved on, to private law firms, to university faculties, to corporate security jobs, even, in the case of Jay Bybee, John Yoo's boss and the signatory of Yoo's most notorious torture memorandum, to the federal bench. But Abu Zubaydah, Khalid Sheikh Mohammed, and the others are still with us: their story has not ended and so neither can that of their American interrogators.

The CIA and Justice Department documents, now public, are full of the drama of the interrogators and CIA officials demanding that they be granted if not advance immunity for what they were about to do then at least a golden shield that would protect them from any future attempt to prosecute. And they were provided with such a shield, first, in the torture memos produced by John Yoo and his successors at the Justice Department and later in the Military Commissions Act of 2006, which explicitly shielded Bush administration officials from prosecution under the War Crimes Act. In April 2009, in what would turn out to be one of its last acts of aggressive transparency when it came to the state of exception, the new Obama administration released to the public the full texts of the torture memos, as tarnished tokens, perhaps, of an era that had been left behind, or so it was then thought. But as one looks today at those documents, and through them at these ghostly figures—not only at the lawyers who deemed these techniques legal but at the policymakers sitting in their offices who ordered them and the interrogators who practiced them on men chained naked in cold sunless rooms—one has the haunting sense that they are all looking forward at us, that they were all anticipating the day we might be standing here judging what they did. If we know anything, it is that they knew this moment would come. They were determined to prepare for it, and in a sense they succeeded brilliantly. The legal memos, however grotesque in their reasoning and however widely denounced, have in effect held sway. In this sense, the state of exception, enduring as it is, had inscribed within it the chronicle of a scandal foretold.

RUMSFELD'S QUESTION

During the dark days of October 2003, after he had finally been forced to admit that the great Iraq "Mission Accomplished" had indeed become a grinding insurgent war, with ardent young Muslim volunteers flooding into Iraq to fight the American occupiers as they had once flooded into Afghanistan to fight the Soviets, embattled Secretary of Defense Donald Rumsfeld let fall on the Pentagon one of his famous "snowflakes," a memorandum asking broad questions that he directed his top generals and strategists to ponder. Dated October 16, 2003, and entitled "Global War on Terrorism," the memo, after pointing out that "we lack metrics to know whether we are winning or losing the global war on terror," posed with characteristic precision the key question: "Are we capturing, killing or deterring and dissuading more terrorists every day than the *madrassas* and the radical clerics are recruiting, training and deploying against us?"

Read today, Rumsfeld's question has a certain poignancy, for we know that the secretary of defense was posing it just after having invaded Iraq, thereby broadening the war on terror far beyond the initial battlefield and giving an enormous boon to all "the *madrassas* and radical clerics . . . recruiting, training and deploying" against the United States. It was slowly dawning on him, perhaps, that instead of moving smartly forward toward his destination he found himself trapped in a spiral that circled ever further away from it. Not only had he and his colleagues, by invading Iraq before "finishing" Afghanistan, embroiled the United States in a two-front war, they had gone far beyond even the vastly ambitious goals President Bush proclaimed to the American people nine days after the 9/11 attacks. "Our war on terror begins with Al Qaeda but it does not end there," the president declared. "It will not end until every terrorist group of global reach has been found, stopped and defeated." Now finding, stopping, and defeating every terrorist group of global reach was no longer enough. Iraq and Afghanistan must somehow be pacified and made over into workable democracies. Responding to an attack by an insurgent group that seeks to expose the United States as the ultimate oppressor of Muslims, the United States had not only sent paramilitary and special operators around the world to conduct secret operations, including capturing, secretly imprisoning, and torturing terrorist suspects, it had invaded and occupied two Muslim countries and pledged to remake the region. In doing so, instead of narrowing the list of enemies, as insurgency expert Jeffrey Record writes, "the administration has postulated a multiplicity of enemies, including rogue states, weapons of mass destruction (WMD) proliferators, terrorist organization, and terrorism itself." He goes on: "It has also . . . conflated them as a general, undifferentiated threat. In so doing, the administration has arguably subordinated strategic clarity to the moral clarity it seeks in foreign policy and may have set the United States on a path of open-ended and unnecessary conflict with states and non-state entities that pose no direct or imminent threat to the United States."

By the time it invaded Iraq in March 2003, the United States in its global war on terror was following not the strategy of disaggregation suggested by many experts, whereby it would concentrate on destroying al Qaeda itself, and attacking its links to associated terrorist and insurgent organizations, thereby isolating al Qaeda and narrowing and concentrating the war. By invading Iraq, the United States had adopted a de facto strategy of aggregation, which meant, wrote military strategist David Kilcullen in 2004, "lumping together all terrorism, all rogue or failed states, and all strategic competitors who might potentially oppose U.S. objectives in the war" and which "tends naturally to the logical outcome of a war against all terrorists or—far worse—all Muslims simultaneously. This creates enormous potential for overstretch, exhaustion of popular will, and ultimate failure."

It also creates the distinct likelihood that in the process the Americans, with their high-profile military occupations and the insurgent reactions that those occupations spawned, would be doing the jidhadists' political work for them. Ayman al-Zawahiri, then bin Laden's deputy, recognized this early, noting in 2004 that the Iraq insurgency had "turned America's plan upside down. The defeat of America in Iraq and Afghanistan has become just a matter of time, with God's help. The Americans in both countries are between two fires. If they carry on, they will bleed to death—and if they pull out, they lose everything."

For Secretary Rumsfeld, perhaps, this reality had begun to dawn. He put his query about whether the United States was creating more terrorists than it was "capturing, killing or deterring and dissuading" to the Pentagon's Defense Science Board. In 2004, the board delivered a report in which the authors identified "negative attitudes [toward the United States] and the conditions that create them" in the Middle East and South Asia as "the underlying sources of threats to America's national security." The authors were quite specific:

- American direct intervention in the Muslim World has paradoxically elevated the stature of and support for radical Islamists, while diminishing support for the United States to single-digits in some Arab societies.
- Muslims do not "hate our freedom," but rather, they hate our policies. The overwhelming majority voice their objections to what they see as one-sided support in favor of Israel and against Palestinian rights, and the longstanding, even increasing support for what Muslims collectively see as tyrannies, most notably Egypt, Saudi Arabia, Jordan, Pakistan, and the Gulf states.
- Thus when American public diplomacy talks about bringing democracy to Islamic societies, this is seen as no more than self-serving hypocrisy. . . .
- Furthermore, *in the eyes of Muslims,* American occupation of Afghanistan and Iraq has not led to democracy there, but only more chaos and suffering.

The result, the authors conclude, is that "the dramatic narrative since 9/11 has essentially borne out the entire radical Islamist bill of particulars." The United States is the threat and jihadist groups "portray themselves as the true defenders of an Ummah (the entire Muslim community) invaded and under attack—to broad public support."

The answer to Rumsfeld's question: Not only was the United States not killing, capturing, deterring, or dissuading terrorists as fast as the madrassas and the radical clerics could produce them, but it had chosen, by expanding its global war on terror to places it need never have gone, to give its enemies an enormous helping hand. Even as the drones began flying and al Qaeda had begun to suffer damage in the tribal areas of Pakistan, another great force was rising in the deserts of western Iraq, a Sunni movement that would combine the Islamist resistance forces that had risen up against the American occupiers, the foreign mujahideen that had flooded into the country to fight the infidels, and the Baathist military and intelligence specialists that the Americans had thrown out on the street when they dissolved Saddam's army and security forces. The American invasion had given bloody birth to al Qaeda in Iraq, the future Islamic State, a second great multinational terrorist enemy in the looming forever war.

PART TWO

OBAMA: NORMALIZING THE EXCEPTION
Terror, Fear, and the War Without End

Turns out I'm really good at killing people. Didn't know that was gonna be a strong suit of mine.
—President Barack Obama, September 30, 2011

This war, like all wars, must end.
—President Barack Obama, May 23, 2013

ENDURING EXCEPTION

Our forever war began with a transformative image of unending resonance and power: the violent metamorphosis of those great New
York towers, taller than the builders of the Tower of Babel could
have dreamed, into heaven-reaching plumes of white dust. As they
were transformed, so were we, stepping through the portal into the
state of exception. Permanent war, both conventional and covert; extraordinary rendition, indefinite detention, enhanced interrogation,
warrantless surveillance: these and other emergency procedures
quickly became the accepted currency of the national security state.

More than fourteen years later that state of exception endures
and bears now within it a prodigious contradiction: it is an exceptional state that shows all signs of becoming normalized. The one
element that since the early Roman dictatorships all states of exception have shared—that they are temporary, that they *end*—seems
lacking in ours. In this, our state of exception seems to contradict
the basic purpose that has always motivated "constitutional dictatorship." Clinton Rossiter, the scholar who coined that term, declared that the intent of the exception was *"to end the crisis and restore
normal times."* Normal times he defined simply as "the complete restoration of the *status quo ante bellum*."

In the United States normal times have not been restored. Our state of exception, created to fight a war on terror that by its own definition would not end, endures. This does not mean that it has not evolved and changed, even as our political leaders have. Most notably, President Obama "prohibited" torture, an act that, in itself, gives a sense of the twilit new normal we now inhabit. Though moving from practicing torture to prohibiting it, as President Obama did by publicly signing an executive order to that effect, is most significant, it is emphatically not a return to the *status quo ante bellum*. Though strictly forbidden by domestic statute and international law, which forbids it at all times and explicitly in times of emergency, torture now lies within the president's power to prohibit—or to order. In refraining from officially torturing before the state of exception, our government was following the law; in refraining from torturing now, the government is in effect following the directive of the current chief executive, an executive who, even as he calls waterboarding "plainly illegal," refrains from prosecuting or sanctioning in any way his predecessors who speak proudly of having ordered it.

Managing such subtle evolutions has been President Obama's distinctive contribution. He grasped certain central weapons of the exception and, instead of returning them to the arsenal of emergency measures, legalized, regularized, normalized them. And yet this had not been his stated intent. During his first presidential campaign his words on the issue were plain, and eloquent; for example, this ringing statement in August 2007:

> Too often since 9/11, the extremists have defined us, not the other way around. . . .
>
> As President, I will close Guantánamo, reject the Military Commissions Act, and adhere to the Geneva Conventions. Our Constitution and our Uniform Code of Military Justice provide a framework for dealing with the terrorists.
>
> This Administration also puts forward a false choice between the

liberties we cherish and the security we demand. I will provide our intelligence and law enforcement agencies with the tools they need to track and take out the terrorists without undermining our Constitution and our freedom.

That means no more illegal wire-tapping of American citizens. . . . No more ignoring the law when it is inconvenient. That is not who we are. And it is not what is necessary to defeat the terrorists. The FISA court works. The separation of powers works. Our Constitution works. We will again set an example for the world that the law is not subject to the whims of stubborn rulers, and that justice is not arbitrary.

This is not who we are: words that candidate and then president would utter again and again, pointing to the gap between American aspirations and the reality of the war on terror. Seventeen months later, after his improbable rise to the White House, the tone and the evident determination had not changed. On his second full day in office, President Obama sat before the television cameras and signed executive orders prohibiting torture by limiting permissible interrogation techniques to those explicitly contained in the Army Field Manual, creating a special task force to recommend how the U.S. government should interrogate high-value detainees, directing that the status of all detainees at Guantánamo be reviewed, and ordering that the offshore prison itself be closed within one year.

It seemed a powerful first step on the road to ending the state of exception. Yet today it is hard not to see this moment, two days into the new administration, as the high point, a moment of bold aspiration pointing toward a future that was never achieved. Rather than ending the state of exception, the Obama administration normalized it. Unlike George W. Bush, who often grounded his secret actions on his own authority as president, Obama and his team have worked hard to inscribe his predecessor's improvisations into law and to make them permanent. And even as President Obama has taken to warning that the country must not remain "on a perpetual war-time footing," he seems trapped in a prison of his making, perpetuating the very policies he demands must end.

We live with Guantánamo, an offshore prison and "legal black hole" that, a half dozen years after Obama vowed to close it, still holds nearly a hundred detainees, most of whom have been imprisoned there without trial for more than a decade, and more than forty of whom now officially comprise, thanks to yet another Obama executive order, a new type of legal being: prisoners who can neither be tried nor released. Justice Department lawyers have determined that not enough evidence exists to try these detainees, and yet to set them free is judged to pose too great a danger to the country. We accept from our president instead explicit rules, based not on his own authority but on the Congress's Authorization for Use of Military Force, to govern and manage their indefinite detention.

We live with daily targeted killing as a central tool of U.S. foreign policy, carried out by unmanned aerial vehicles, or drones, on al Qaeda's "associated forces"—many of which didn't exist on September 11—under the authority of executive orders the most important of which remain secret. We live with warrantless surveillance of American citizens. And for the mass murderers whose attacks plunged us into the state of exception, we live with trials conducted not in the sunlight of our civilian courts but in a strange new half darkness, a twilight military world that has been conjured as a kind of darker twin subsisting alongside the law.

TRIAL OF THE CENTURY

As I write, five defendants who stand accused of plotting the attacks of September 11, whom President Obama had first boldly vowed to try in federal court in New York, are being judged before a military commission at Guantánamo. Military commissions had been the object of great contention during the Bush administration: devised in secret by a handful of administration appointees in 2001, the commissions had staggered along under various legal challenges until June 2006, when the Supreme Court in its *Hamdan v. Rumsfeld* decision declared them unconstitutional without an act of Congress. The following fall Congress finally ratified them in its Military Commissions Act. During the campaign Obama vowed to abolish the commissions and during his first days in office he suspended them. Four months later, after instituting certain reforms—limiting the use of hearsay evidence, banning evidence gathered by means of cruel treatment, making it easier for defendants to choose their own lawyers—the president reactivated the commissions. After the great outcry from New York politicians and the Republican opposition at the prospect of civilian federal trials for the 9/11 plotters, the commissions became the only alternative.

In spring 2012 the accused masterminds of the attacks of September 11 stood trial before a military commission at Guantánamo. Though one might have thought, with defendants facing charges of murdering nearly three thousand Americans, that this would truly be the Trial of the Century, few Americans even know the trial is taking place. The offshore courtroom differs markedly from any they might recognize. Those among the handful of journalists able to gain permission to fly into Guantánamo find themselves ushered into a room separated from the actual courtroom by thick soundproof glass. Through the glass they see people, many in uniform, enacting the roles of lawyers, judges, defendants, but though their lips move it is only after a forty-second delay that the journalists can hear the actual words they say, which are piped in through a special speaker system. This peculiar delay, like so much else in this peculiar place, is dictated by "security concerns." When "something sensitive" is uttered behind the glass, notes reporter Carroll Bogert,

the infamous "hockey light" on the judge's bench lights up and the com-
ment is bleeped out. . . . The degree of classification of banal matters
is bewildering. A former camp commander issued a memo on exactly
what material the defense lawyers were allowed to bring in to their cli-
ents. One thing that was not allowed to be brought in? The memo itself.

The defendants include Khalid Sheikh Mohammed, the confessed mastermind of the September 11 attacks, who after he was
captured to great fanfare in Pakistan in March 2003 immediately
disappeared into the CIA's network of secret prisons, spending time,
reportedly, at black sites in Afghanistan, Poland, Romania, possibly Lithuania, and Guantánamo, an odyssey during which he was
subjected to prolonged sleep deprivation, beatings, forced nudity,
"walling," cold water immersions, and waterboarding. Though that
information comes from CIA documents that have long been public, in this court any mention of his or other defendants' treatment
while in custody is strictly forbidden. And yet torture, as Bogert
writes, "is Guantánamo's Original Sin. It is both invisible and om-
nipresent." Which puts the government in a difficult position:

> *The U.S. government wants coverage of the 9/11 attacks, but not*
> *the waterboarding, sleep deprivation, prolonged standing, and other*
> *forms of torture that the CIA applied to the defendants. It's tricky,*
> *prosecuting the 9/11 case while trying to keep torture out of the pub-*
> *lic eye.*

As one of the psychiatrists present told the reporter, "Torture
is the thread running through all of this. You can't tell the story
[of 9/11] without it." And indeed proceedings had to be halted
while the mental condition of one defendant—who kept shouting,
"This is my life. This is torture. *TOR! TURE!*"—was evaluated. In the
event, reporters never learned what else the defendant said. Partway
through his statement the audio feed was cut off.

During the last few decades American prosecutors have convicted hundreds in federal court on terrorism charges. But what is happening in that strange bifurcated courtroom in Guantánamo bears little resemblance to those trials. This peculiar procedure, a futile attempt to render in the shadows a kind of disfigured justice to those charged with killing thousands of Americans and upending the history of the country, is one more legacy of the misshapen response to the attacks, a sign that torture is not a remnant of a past we want to forget but of a present we still struggle to ignore.

EDITING THE EXCEPTION

When President Obama and his senior officials took office, they confronted a state of exception already in place, including two ongoing hot wars in Iraq and Afghanistan; a counterterrorism war being fought "on the dark side" around the world by CIA paramilitaries and by the special operators of the military's Joint Special Operations Command; a network of secret black site prisons stretching around the globe, from Morocco to Poland to Thailand, and a CIA that under explicit presidential and Justice Department approval had set up those prisons and had designed and run a program of "enhanced interrogations" there; a military prison at Guantánamo Bay that held 242 detainees; a military commissions system that had finally been passed into law by Congress—and much of this operating under the general legal authority of a sixty-word Authorization for Use of Military Force that Congress had passed three days after the September 11 attacks, more than seven years before.

Whatever his desire, it would not be within the new president's power to begin anew, to start afresh. First and foremost Obama's policies reflect the fact "that the Bush policies," in the words of Bush's former assistant attorney general Jack Goldsmith, "were woven into the fabric of the national security architecture in ways that were hard if not impossible to unravel." The new president would have to work with what he had, altering what he could: editing, if you will, Bush's state of exception.

He began boldly, suspending the military commissions, prohibiting torture, closing the black sites, and vowing to close Guantánamo within a year. More broadly, he moved to bring to a close, as expeditiously as possible, the "dumb war" his predecessor had launched in Iraq and to expand and win the "good war" that had dragged on and on in Afghanistan. Soon, and especially after Umar Farouk Abdulmutallab's foiled attempt to blow up an airliner over Detroit on Christmas Day 2009, President Obama would vastly accelerate the rate of drone attacks on targets in Pakistan and Yemen, "secretly" killing, during the remainder of his first term, thousands of people by drones alone.

By the time President Obama took office, what I have called the "skeleton of the exception," the latticework of laws, executive orders, and other legal instruments defining the emergency state, had evolved considerably since the early years of Bush's presidency. During the second Bush administration, under the force of court decisions and congressional votes, the changes had accelerated. "One reason the Obama practices are so close to the late Bush practices," as Goldsmith observes, "is that the late Bush practices were much different than the early ones." Goldsmith, who ran the Office of Legal Counsel at the Department of Justice after John Yoo had left, notes that during the last years of the Bush administration, "Congress and the courts have engaged on terrorism issues, pushing back on some, approving others, and acquiescing in yet others."

Congress not only passed into law Bush's military commissions, it largely did the same for his surveillance program two years later. The Supreme Court in 2006 ruled that Common Article 3 of the Geneva Conventions does in fact apply to al Qaeda prisoners and fashioned a form of federal judicial review, albeit a strikingly ineffective one, for their detention. Obama's acceptance of the war on terror paradigm and his moves to regularize the exception, issuing executive orders on indefinite detention, among other things, and basing much of the exception more explicitly on Congress's Authorization for Use of Military Force, calmed some of the struggles between the executive, Congress, and the courts and brought to the exception a kind of "institutional settlement"—in the words of Professor Robert M. Chesney—based on "the emergence of a cross-party and cross-branch consensus."

And what about the "flesh of the exception"? If we were to try to define the style of the Obama state of exception, plotting his changes to and innovations on that state bequeathed him by his predecessor, its most striking elements might comprise the following:

First, *bringing to an end the explicit "war" part of the war on terror*: that is, working—with varying degrees of success—to end the American role in the shooting wars in Iraq and Afghanistan and bring the troops home.

Second, at once *narrowing and broadening the use of violence*: focusing on al Qaeda and other terrorist groups, and on the Taliban, not on states that may or may not support them, while broadening the secret targets to include associated terrorist groups, a category very broadly conceived, from al Shabaab in Somalia to the Islamic State.

Third, *developing a "light footprint" strategy with heavy covert use of remotely piloted vehicles (drones) and special operators* to kill presumed terrorists and militants secretly from "over the horizon."

Fourth, *crafting a hybrid criminal justice–military approach to apprehending, interrogating, trying, and incarcerating terrorists* that to some extent harks back to the pre-9/11 era and moves away from Bush's war and preventive paradigms.

Fifth, *working to legitimize and normalize those elements of the state of exception that had been grounded only in his predecessor's inherent powers as "unitary executive,"* collaborating with Congress to embody them in law or in executive orders.

Sixth, *making expansive use of the power of secrecy, including the state secrets privilege,* not only to cloak selectively many of the main offensive elements of the light footprint approach, including the drone program, but also to protect the state of exception from legal challenge and to threaten and prosecute aggressively leakers and reporters who convey unsanctioned information to the public.

Seventh, *creating a playbook and doctrine for the light footprint approach that delineates and regularizes its procedures,* such as target selection and its legal underpinnings, and that will make it possible for the program to continue, perhaps indefinitely, under future administrations.

Eighth, *while working to diminish the political profile of the war on terror,* still making use of selected successes, such as killing Osama bin Laden, as political trumps.

For better and very much for worse, on coming to power in January 2009, President Obama went to war with the exception we had, to paraphrase Donald Rumsfeld, and in the years since he has worked hard to regularize, normalize, legalize these policies, even as he began to speak out against the country's "perpetual wartime footing." This has comprised his distinctive contribution to the state of exception: honing its rough edges, legalizing and regularizing its procedures, furthering its evolution into permanency—and, after his reelection, increasingly expressing publicly his apprehensions about the quiet permanent war he had done so much to create.

WAR PARADOX

If we look for the vital element of the state of exception's persistence, we come face-to-face with what I identified as the most important of its original distinctive attributes: declaring the war on terror *as a war,* and a war unbounded in space and time. Only nine days after the attacks President Bush had declared that the war on terror "will not end until every terrorist group of global reach has been found, stopped and defeated." Six days earlier Congress had not only voted to authorize the president to "use all necessary and appropriate force against those nations, organizations, or persons he determines planned, authorized, committed, or aided the terrorist attacks that occurred on September 11, 2001" but also "to prevent any future acts of international terrorism against the United States by such nations, organizations or persons." The authorization is not unlimited but it is extremely broad and potentially unending, and the Obama administration, in including in its secret list of adversaries al Qaeda's "associated forces"—a phrase that does not appear in the original resolution—has broadened it further, seemingly making it possible to wage war on an apparently endless chain of successor organizations, all of whose members, from leaders to the lowest-ranking militants, whether engaged in preparation for imminent attack against the United States or not, become legally targetable. The legal and political consequences of this open-ended war on terror still imprison us, from the president on down, in a network of poisonous paradoxes, of which those indefinite detainees at Guantánamo, imprisoned for the duration of a conflict that seems to have no ending, are living embodiments.

The problem with a "war on terror" is not only that, as many have pointed out, it is nonsensical to declare war on a tactic. The problem is that the word "war" is misapplied. War is traditionally defined as "a state of belligerency between sovereigns" and this condition of belligerency is in turn defined by its limitations: by what it does *not* include. Who are belligerents and who are not? Where does the battlefield extend and where does it not? When does the conflict end? How is the state of peace to be distinguished from the state of war? Once these concepts are blurred and corrupted, as they are by the ill-defined notion of a war on terror, the road to endless war, and an endless grant of power to the sovereign, lies open before us. Such a

"selective adaptation of doctrines dealing with war," as Bruce Ackerman put it more than a decade ago, "predictably leads to sweeping in-
cursions on fundamental liberties." Ackerman, a professor at Yale Law
School, had in mind specifically the Bush administration's military
commissions to try al Qaeda members, which were modeled after the
military tribunals President Franklin Roosevelt established by executive proclamation in 1942 to try eight Nazi saboteurs, two of whom
were American citizens. "It is one thing," Ackerman wrote, "for President Roosevelt to designate a captured American citizen serving in the
German army as an 'enemy combatant' and try him without standard
scrutiny by the civilian courts; it is quite another for President Bush to
do the same thing for suspected members of al Qaeda."

The problem is one of clear borders and limits; for example, the
distinction between ordinary people and members of the German
army. "Only a very small percentage of the human race is composed
of recognized members of the German military," Ackerman wrote,
"but anybody can be suspected of complicity with al Qaeda. . . .

> All of us are, in principle, subject to executive detention once we treat
> the "war on terrorism" as if it were the legal equivalent of the war
> against Germany.

And just as the reach of a war on terror is in principle unlimited,
so too is its duration:

> War between sovereign states also comes to an end; some decisive act
> of capitulation, armistice, or treaty takes place for all the world to
> see. But this will not happen in the war against terrorism. . . . Even
> if [al Qaeda] disintegrates, it will likely morph into other terrorist
> groups. . . . So if we choose to call this a war, it will be endless.

Such "morphing" has long since begun, al Qaeda having sown its
affiliates like dragon's teeth across the Middle East and North Africa.

Though President Obama tells us as a matter of course that al Qaeda has been "decimated," U.S. drone and other airborne and special operator attacks have long since focused on al Qaeda in the Arabian Peninsula as well as al Shabaab and the Islamic State, groups that did not exist in September 2001. Though President Obama has repeatedly declared his determination to take the country "off a permanent war footing," he has found that the war on terror retains its own powerful political and institutional momentum. Though he prefers not to utter the phrase "war on terror," Obama found himself embracing the war paradigm as early as March 2009 in a filing in federal court arguing that the government has the power to detain prisoners indefinitely in Guantánamo under the law of armed conflict, and grounding his authority on the 2001 Authorization for Use of Military Force.

While the Justice Department brief sought to define limits—only those already in custody at Guantánamo, for example, could be subject to open-ended detention without trial—Pentagon officials have done quite the opposite, arguing that under the 2001 resolution the president retains the power to send in U.S. military forces anywhere, from Yemen to the Congo. In voting to authorize President Bush's use of military force three days after the September 11 attacks, members of Congress might have envisioned U.S. forces fighting in Pakistan's tribal areas. But in Yemen? Congo? And more than a dozen years later?

The open-endedness, the impossibility of finding an ending when facing the inertial momentum of the institutionalized war on terror, was a potential inherent in the original ill-defined declaration of war. For once "we accept a conflict with no apparent spatial or temporal boundaries," as former Obama defense official Rosa Brooks observed, "we give to our executive branch a virtually open-ended ability to use lethal force, anywhere, any time." Ackerman foresaw this more than a decade ago, noting that defining the response to terrorist attacks as a war "not only subject[s] *everybody* to the risk of detention by the Commander in Chief, but . . . subject[s] everybody to the risk of *endless* detention." The war on terror has survived bin Laden and seems likely to survive Obama's presidency, as will, almost certainly, the indefinite detention of those in Guantánamo.

POLITICS OF FEAR

If it was a new Democratic president, despite his bold rhetoric, who found himself creating of the state of exception a "new normal," he was pushed strongly toward this by a revitalizing of the politics of fear in the wake of his inauguration. That surge in the rhetoric of fear was owed not to a terrorist attack—the first major attempt would not come until Christmas Day eleven months later—but largely to the determined efforts of one man. With breathtaking speed in early 2009, Dick Cheney seized his place as the new administration's bête noire on national security issues. Within days of leaving office, the former vice president stepped forward as a highly visible and relentless advocate of "enhanced interrogation techniques" and a dark prophet of the disaster he claimed must inevitably befall the United States once their use was renounced.

Ten days after Obama's inauguration, scarcely a week after the new president had prohibited torture, Cheney launched a public attack, telling a television interviewer:

> When we get people who are more concerned about reading the rights to an Al Qaeda terrorist than they are with protecting the United States against people who are absolutely committed to do anything they can to kill Americans, then I worry. . . . These are evil people. And we're not going to win this fight by turning the other cheek.
>
> If it hadn't been for what we did—with respect to the . . . enhanced interrogation techniques for high-value detainees . . . then we would have been attacked again. Those policies we put in place,

*in my opinion, were absolutely crucial to getting us through the last
seven-plus years without a major-casualty attack on the U.S.*

A few weeks later Cheney went further, citing his worry about a

*9/11-type event where the terrorists are armed with something much
more dangerous than an airline ticket and a box cutter—a nuclear
weapon or a biological agent of some kind. That's the one that would
involve the deaths of perhaps hundreds of thousands of people, and
the one you have to spend a hell of a lot of time guarding against.*

*I think there's a high probability of such an attempt. Whether
or not they can pull it off depends [on] whether or not we keep in
place policies that have allowed us to defeat all further attempts, since
9/11, to launch mass-casualty attacks against the United States.*

Those policies included, the former vice president made clear, not
only enhanced interrogation but the use of that notorious offshore
prison that the new president had vowed to shutter:

*If you release the hard-core Al Qaeda terrorists that are held at
Guantánamo, I think they go back into the business of trying to kill
more Americans and mount further mass-casualty attacks. If you
turn them loose and they go kill more Americans, who's responsible
for that?*

Who indeed? Cheney's dark admonitions were both exculpatory,
pointing back to and justifying what the Bush administration had
done, and menacing, warning about attacks that he claimed were
coming and laying down a clear predicate for who would be blamed
in their wake. His words, lavishly covered both in the mainstream
press and on the cable news programs, had a powerful political effect. How could they not? As all politicians, and all terrorists, know,
fear is the most powerful political emotion. In the wake of Cheney's

relentless public campaign, which, despite his personal unpopularity, had wide resonance at a time when the Republican Party lacked recognized leaders, support among lawmakers for the plan to close Guantánamo steadily declined. Within three months, the new president's promise to liberate the country from a symbol of torture and repression that was "not who we are" had become a plan to "put terrorists in our neighborhoods."

The story of the struggle over closing Guantánamo included significant mishandling by Obama officials, who never managed to put forward a specific plan of action. But the broader political plotline of the story had long since been established, emerging from the politics of fear as it had developed after September 11 and owing much, in turn, to earlier embodiments, notably, the "soft on communism" battles of the Cold War and the "soft on crime" debates of the 1960s and 1970s. Even as Cheney was showing Obama's opponents what they could gain politically by attacking a plan to close Guantánamo, he was showing the president's allies what they could lose. "The debate became suffused with fear," concluded *The Washington Post*, "fear that closing Guantánamo would be electoral suicide. Some Democratic lawmakers pleaded with the White House not to press too hard." That the administration made little effort to lobby on the Guantánamo issue worsened the political predicament, as one anonymous "senior Democratic aide" explained: "Vulnerable senators weren't going out on a limb and risk being Willie Hortonized* on Gitmo when the White House, with the most to lose, wasn't even twisting arms. They weren't breathing down our necks pushing the vote or demanding unified action."

---

* Willie Horton was a convicted African-American murderer whose crimes while "on furlough" from a Massachusetts state prison the George H. W. Bush campaign used during the 1988 election to stigmatize Democratic nominee Governor Michael Dukakis as "soft on crime."

The tactical dynamic here—pleading with administration officials "not to press too hard," then blaming them for not "twisting arms"—is pure Washington. But the underlying element is fear. Under Cheney's attacks, Democrats saw the political risk growing—by June 2009 polls showed more than half the public disapproved of closing Guantánamo—without any compensating rewards. Even if no one had suggested releasing "terrorists in our neighborhoods," what exactly did a senator gain by voting to close Gitmo and taking the risk of being "Willie Hortonized" when election time rolled around, especially when the administration, and its most potent spokesman, seemed to be making so little effort to speak out and change the broader politics of the issue?

President Obama clearly understood this political dynamic. During the signature speech he devoted to national security and terrorism, at the National Archives on May 21, 2009, he had been frank on the politics of fear:

> Now as our efforts to close Guantánamo move forward, I know that the politics in Congress will be difficult. These are issues that are fodder for 30-second commercials. You can almost picture the direct mail pieces that emerge from any vote on this issue—designed to frighten the population. I get it. But if we continue to make decisions within a climate of fear, we will make more mistakes. And if we refuse to deal with these issues today, then I guarantee you that they will be an albatross around our efforts to combat terrorism in the future.

However prophetic, the words were too little, too late. Minutes after the president spoke, Cheney, across town at the American Enterprise Institute, launched an unrestrained attack on the Obama administration, asserting that "to bring the worst of the worst terrorists inside the United States would be cause for great danger and regret in the years to come." As for the "enhanced interrogation techniques" that the new president had prohibited, they "were legal, essential, justified, successful and the right thing to do," and, what's more, "they prevented the violent death of thousands, if not hundreds of thousands, of innocent people." That there was no evidence for that last claim did not prevent Cheney from repeating it, while bemoaning the fact that the facts to back him up "remain classified."

When Cheney took up proposals for a "so-called 'Truth Commission'"—recently put before the Senate by Patrick Leahy of Vermont—and demands "that those who recommended and approved the interrogations be prosecuted," the former vice president's tone turned grim, even threatening: "I would advise the administration to think very carefully about the course ahead. All the zeal that has been directed at interrogations is utterly misplaced. And staying on that path will only lead our government further away from its duty to protect the American people."

"*Further* away": Already under the Democrats the American people had become less protected—almost by definition, for, as Karl Rove had argued, Americans "trust the Republicans to do a better job of keeping our communities and our families safe." Cheney's speech was a ruthless attack on Obama's entire approach to human rights and national security, starting with the premise that Guantánamo and Abu Ghraib have been propaganda boons for al Qaeda, which the former vice president mocked as Obama's "recruitment-tool theory" of torture and terrorism:

> On this theory, by the tough questioning of killers, we have supposedly fallen short of our own values. This recruitment-tool theory has become something of a mantra lately, including from the President himself. And after a familiar fashion, it excuses the violent and blames America for the evil that others do. It's another version of that same old refrain from the Left, "We brought it on ourselves."

"After a familiar fashion": Cheney's attack incorporates Obama's national security policies into the traditional Republican critique of

Democrats: that they are weak, indecisive, guilt-ridden, self-hating liberals given to putting the public at risk by "coddling criminals" and now by coddling "hardened terrorists." As such they are incapable of protecting the country. In the wake of a future successful attack Cheney and company could be expected to shed all restraint in blaming the administration and its policies for the death and destruction. Indeed they were blaming it already, months into the new president's term.

Against these savage accusations, Obama and his administration offered nuance and ambivalence. In April, to a burst of criticism from Republicans, the Justice Department had released the torture memos that had been written by John Yoo and his successors in the Department of Justice. In a statement the president bemoaned this "dark and painful chapter in our history" while insisting that "this was a time for reflection, not retribution." The following month, the administration publicly reversed an earlier pledge and declined to release additional photographs of American soldiers abusing detainees at Abu Ghraib. And in May, during that same National Archives speech, President Obama announced that at Guantánamo there were "a number of people who cannot be prosecuted for past crimes, in some cases because evidence may be tainted, but who nonetheless pose a threat to the security of the United States." When it came to such detainees, the president was clear: he would not end indefinite detention but instead place it within "a legitimate legal framework . . . that involves judicial and congressional oversight." In this war without end nearly fifty detainees would be held in captivity indefinitely, without charge or trial.

And they would be staying right where they were. In June, in placing the first of a series of legislative roadblocks that were to stymie Obama's plan to close Guantánamo, the Senate voted to restrict any transfer of Guantánamo detainees to U.S. prisons. The tally was 90 to 6.

THE END OF ACCOUNTABILITY

Perhaps the decision that expresses most purely the tormented ambivalence of the Obama administration, torn between a boldly stated desire for justice and a growing reluctance to confront the political costs of supplying it, is the decision not to investigate or prosecute those who tortured. Or rather, the decision to investigate but *possibly* prosecute only those who might have gone beyond the Bush administration's immensely forgiving limits on what could be done to detainees during interrogations. Even as president-elect, Barack Obama had emphasized his "belief," when it came to interrogation and torture, that "we need to look forward as opposed to looking backward": "At the CIA, you've got extraordinarily talented people who are working very hard to keep Americans safe. I don't want them to suddenly feel like they've got to spend all their time looking over their shoulders."

A dilemma, then: having made solemn vows to "set an example for the world that the law is not subject to the whims of stubborn rulers," the new president now confronted well-documented acts committed during the previous administration that contravene U.S. and international law and that much of the world considered torture. At the same time he confronted opinions from Justice Department lawyers finding those acts to be legal, a paper trail showing that the highest officials, including his predecessor, had approved them, and laws passed by Congress explicitly protecting from prosecution those who ordered them. Finally, he confronted a Central Intelligence Agency whose officers had taken on the job of "enhanced interrogation" only after having received written assurances they were acting within the law and who insisted, even as those interrogations were being carried out, that senior administration officials and key members of the Congress be briefed about them in detail. This same CIA remained the lead agency charged with tracking terrorists, stopping plots, directing drones: leading the war on terror.

Given Obama's shift toward a more focused counterterror policy, the CIA's role was becoming only more vital. And the CIA had now become *his* CIA.

Given these realities, all evidence suggests that President Obama had little interest in investigating past acts of torture. His initiatives on torture and interrogation, including the release of the torture memos in April 2009, had attracted withering criticism. By summer it had become clear that Guantánamo would remain open long after the one-year deadline the president had set and perhaps indefinitely. Not only had White House officials made it plain that the president would not support the Truth Commission to look into Bush-era crimes that Senator Leahy proposed, but the increase in the pace of drone attacks in Pakistan—the number killed nearly doubled in 2009—showed how aggressive Obama would be in using the CIA to fight what had become his war on terror. Ending conventional ground and air wars, ramping up the secret war: he had set out this strategy during the campaign, vowing to "ensure that the military becomes more stealthy, agile and lethal in its ability to capture or kill terrorists." In Pakistan, the CIA, not the military, was responsible for revving up the drone attacks. Obama needed his CIA officers looking ahead as they fought his new "stealthy, agile and lethal" war.

In the end the task of investigating whether prosecution was merited fell to the Department of Justice. In August 2009, Attorney General Eric Holder, who had read the CIA inspector general's 2004 report, asked John H. Durham, an experienced and well-respected federal prosecutor from Hartford, Connecticut, to examine whether the acts of CIA interrogators at the black sites merited prosecution. Durham was well acquainted with the issue: at the request of the outgoing Bush administration he had been investigating the CIA's destruction, in 2005, of ninety-two videotapes recording the interrogations of Abu Zubaydah and another detainee. At the same time, the attorney general made clear that "the Department would not prosecute anyone who acted in good faith and within the scope of the legal guidance given by the Office of Legal Counsel regarding the interrogation of detainees."

Obama administration officials, in other words, had decided that they would take as their guide for what was legally "questionable" precisely the guidelines that had been handed down by John Yoo and other Bush Department of Justice lawyers in the memos that had permitted the torture in the first place. As a practical consequence Durham was not permitted to prosecute, for example, a former interrogator for waterboarding—that procedure Yoo and his successors had deemed legal—but he could (in theory) prosecute him for waterboarding too frequently or waterboarding with more than the prescribed amount of water. Durham could not prosecute an interrogator for keeping a naked prisoner shackled by his wrists to the ceiling for two weeks but he could prosecute him for racking his semiautomatic pistol next to the detainee's hooded head and threatening to execute him, or for threatening him with a power drill, or for vowing to rape his wife and murder his family. At the black sites interrogators had committed all these acts, as the CIA inspector general had described. Still, had Durham decided to bring such prosecutions, while leaving uncharged those who had ordered waterboarding and those who had applied it within the bounds of Yoo's memo, it would have been very hard to claim that this was justice. In the event, after examining more than a hundred cases, Durham advised further investigation in only two, both involving detainees who had died from abuse while in custody. In the end, he and the Department of Justice declined to bring any prosecutions against interrogators or those who directed them.

Even as Durham investigated whether anyone who had tortured could be charged, President Obama spoke out against violations of the laws of war. "Where force is necessary," he declared during his Nobel Peace Prize Lecture in Oslo in December 2009, "we have a moral and strategic interest in binding ourselves to certain rules of conduct." He went on:

And even as we confront a vicious adversary that abides by no rules, I believe that the United States of America must remain a standard bearer in the conduct of war. That is what makes us different from those whom we fight. That is a source of our strength. That is why I prohibited torture. That is why I ordered the prison at Guantánamo Bay closed. And that is why I have reaffirmed America's commitment to abide by the Geneva Conventions. We lose ourselves when we compromise the very ideals that we fight to defend. And we honor those ideals by upholding them not just when it is easy, but when it is hard.

In Oslo this eloquent statement of American idealism and multilateralism drew applause, not least for its sharp contrast with the radically unilateralist philosophy of Obama's predecessor. Bush's go-it-alone, great-power-rules thinking had been perfectly encapsulated in the National Defense Strategy of 2005: "Our strength as a nation-state will continue to be challenged by those who employ the strategy of the weak using international *fora*, judicial processes and terrorism." In this bleak vision, international laws and the multilateral institutions that embody them are placed alongside terrorism as "weapons" that "the weak" will use to limit the world's preeminent power. International life, in this view, is a zero-sum game, in which the strongest state simply has no inherent interest in adhering to international law, for by the nature of things the strongest is better off when the only limits it recognizes are those placed on it by its own power. It was this nightmare of an unbounded United States that President Truman and his advisers sought to banish from the international imagination after World War II by embedding American power in the North Atlantic Treaty Organization, the United Nations, and other multilateral institutions.

In his rhetoric and his sympathies, Obama seems far from that grim view, and doubtless it was that distance and the hope it inspired that led the Nobel Committee to award him the Peace Prize so soon after he had taken office. But if President Obama's rhetoric suggests a radical break in philosophy from Bush, his practice has not. His very statement that he "has prohibited torture," as noted earlier, suggests how far we have come from beneath the shadow of international law. In declaring that he has the power to prohibit a practice that is illegal under international treaty and domestic statute, Obama in effect reaffirms the president's putative power to order it. No wonder that during both the 2012 and 2016 presidential campaigns Republican candidates have let it be known—indeed, have sometimes boasted—that if elected they were likely to reinstate "enhanced interrogation techniques." President Bush, after all, beyond seeing the practice "prohibited" by his successor, suffered no legal consequences for ordering torture.

What action would President Obama have had to take to return torture definitively beyond the legal pale, beyond the power of any president to order or to prohibit? Consider these words, from later in his Nobel lecture:

> *America cannot insist that others follow the rules of the road if we refuse to follow them ourselves. For when we don't, our action can appear arbitrary, and undercut the legitimacy of future intervention—no matter how justified. . . .*
>
> *First, in dealing with those nations that break rules and laws, I believe that we must develop alternatives to violence that are tough enough to change behavior—for if we want a lasting peace, then the words of the international community must mean something. Those regimes that break the rules must be held accountable.*

Accountable: Is it possible to reenter the realm of justice and legality without accountability? No one, beyond a handful of low-ranking soldiers from Abu Ghraib, has been held accountable for torture. No elected leader, no high official, no senior military officer. And yet the crimes are well documented. We have thousands of pages of reports from the various departments, including the CIA,

the Department of Defense, and the Department of Justice, and mi-
nutely detailed investigations from committees in Congress. Our
highest officials, including the former president and vice president,
have been frank in their memoirs and public statements.

Torture was undertaken on orders from the president and other
high officials. Techniques that were discussed so carefully at the
upper levels of the CIA and the White House were discussed, specifically and in detail, in the Department of Justice. Lawyers there
approved them. Those documents, some public since the aftermath
of the Abu Ghraib revelations in 2004, some made public by the
Obama administration, make astonishing reading. They show us
not only the so-called golden shield but the process by which lawyers in the Justice Department and in the White House forged it,
how officials at the highest levels of the administration approved it,
and how they looked on while that daily grinding work was carried
on in interrogation chambers on the other side of the world under
the "legality" of its protection.

Small wonder that Obama, when confronted with the problem of accountability, has exhorted us to "look forward as opposed
to looking backward." Yet it is a sad but immutable fact that the
refusal to look backward leaves us trapped in the world without
accountability that his predecessor made. In making it possible,
indeed likely, that the crimes will be repeated, the refusal to look
backward traps us in the past. The only way to move ahead into a
future unshackled by past lawbreaking is to look forthrightly at the
past and to demand clarity and at least some true accountability for
what happened there.

Demanding that accountability is made immeasurably harder
by the fact that those who did the torturing and those who ordered
it did so only after they, as it were, "looked forward"—after they had
looked ahead to the time when, after the emergency had passed,
their fellow citizens would begin questioning what they did. They
had seen such questioning before, during the Church and Pike

committee hearings of the 1970s, and they were determined that this time, when the music stopped in Washington, they would not be the ones left searching vainly for a chair. And so when they demanded the golden shield the intent was clear. "The requests for advice" from the Justice Department, as Ralph S. DiMaio of the CIA's National Clandestine Service told a federal court bluntly in April 2008, "were solicited in order to prepare the CIA to defend against future criminal, civil, and administrative proceedings that the CIA considered to be virtually inevitable." And they prepared not only by demanding the Justice Department memoranda but by ensuring that responsibility for ordering Bush's "alternative set of procedures," and knowledge that they had been ordered, was spread broadly among all the senior national security officers of the government.

At the same time, they in effect constructed both a legal and a public defense for the revelations and condemnations they knew would come: that torture "saved thousands of lives." In the wake of the release of the Senate Select Committee on Intelligence torture report it is no accident that we heard these claims countless times. It is one of the fascinating revelations of the report itself that CIA lawyers and administration officials crafted the claims that "enhanced interrogation techniques" were essential to saving the lives of thousands of people before the program even existed. Even before any high-value detainees had been captured, CIA lawyers seemed bent on constructing a "necessity defense," claiming that torture—the lawyers used that word—was necessary to stop imminent attacks. Thus necessity could be invoked to protect from prosecution "U.S. officials who tortured to obtain information that saved many lives." This idea predated the program's inception and it has survived the program's demise as its main defense, uttered again and again by officials from former President Bush and former Vice President Cheney on down. This included three former CIA directors who in the wake of the report's release rallied publicly to torture's defense by insisting that they had been living "the classic 'ticking time bomb scenario' every single day" and that the torture program, yes, "saved thousands of lives." Yet the Senate report meticulously demonstrates that these claims that torture was critical to obtaining essential, lifesaving intelligence are simply not true. If in torturing we transformed our ignorance into their pain, we did not succeed in transforming their pain into our safety.

We did succeed in placing torture permanently in the realm of legal limbo. Senator Dianne Feinstein, who as chair of the Select Committee on Intelligence presided over the writing of the Senate report, joined with John McCain, the only senator to have suffered torture, to produce an amendment that codifies into law President Obama's executive order of January 2009, when on his second day in office the new president "prohibited" torture and explicitly limited lawful interrogation to those techniques contained in the Army Field Manual. That manual is not perfect—it contains an appendix that would seem in some cases to permit forced isolation, stress positions, and other questionable techniques—but the McCain-Feinstein amendment, in transforming what could be an ephemeral executive order into explicit law, would seem to be a step forward. And yet when the Senate passed it 78–21 in June 2015, the response was distinctly muted, for the fact that torture is already illegal, both by federal statute and international treaty—that it was illegal when the president ordered it—tempers one's faith in the power of yet another law. The fact that the amendment is needed at all reminds us that in the state of exception a determined executive with accommodating lawyers, a timid legislature, and deferential courts can run roughshod over the law, however plainly it is written. Until there is some accountability, can anyone doubt that a future president—perhaps one of the Republican candidates who are calling for torture even as I write—could reinstitute torture if he or she were set on doing so?

While Yoo's handiwork and that of his Bush administration

successors may be gone now—President Obama ordered the memoranda withdrawn in that televised ceremony on his second day—the authority of their conclusions has in effect held sway, and imprisoned us in a painful unremitting moral limbo. When Eric Holder let it be known what could and could not be investigated, he was in effect reaffirming the *ex ante* pardon Yoo had granted, concluding that accountability had been foreclosed by the decisions of the Bush administration. And it has been foreclosed too by members of the United States Congress, who had voted, in the fall of 2006, to pass the Military Commissions Act, which, by amending the War Crimes Act to narrow the definition of cruel and inhuman treatment and to eliminate retroactively violations of several provisions of Common Article 3 of the Geneva Conventions as crimes under U.S. law, explicitly shielded members of the Bush administration from prosecution.

Waterboarding, prosecuted within the United States as recently as 1984—and reaffirmed as illegal by Obama's first attorney general in his confirmation hearings—now amounts, in these exhaustively documented cases, to no more than the "controlled acute episode" of Yoo's description. The former vice president speaks defiantly in his memoirs of his approval of these techniques, asserting, in direct contradiction of the findings of the International Committee of the Red Cross, that "they complied with the law, including international treaty obligations such as the United Nations Convention Against Torture." While Obama is on record asserting that waterboarding is illegal, Bush proudly recounts in his own memoir how, when asked for approval to waterboard Khalid Sheikh Mohammed, he replied without hesitation, "Damn right!" The words bear a perverse eloquence: the decision was indeed a damning one, inscribing in the country's history a wrong that has so far proved impossible to set right.

SOMETHING JUST SHORT OF WAR

Sometime late in the first Bush administration or early in the second the first phase of the secret war came to an end. One might see as a symbolic turning point the CIA inspector general's report on interrogation in 2004, which in its harsh criticisms of how the "enhanced interrogation techniques" had been applied and its intimations of possible legal consequences sounded within it a death knell for a secret war based on kidnapping and torture. A month after the report was completed, on June 18, 2004, the CIA used a Hellfire missile launched from a Predator drone to kill Nek Muhammad Wazir, a prominent tribal leader in South Waziristan who earlier that year had fought regular Pakistani army forces to a standstill. So far as we know Nek Muhammad posed no threat to Americans. Killing him was the CIA's end of a bargain concluded with Pakistan's Directorate for Inter-Services Intelligence (ISI): in exchange the CIA was allowed to fly its drones in certain defined "flight boxes" in the Tribal Areas and, subject to ISI approval, "take out" certain al Qaeda and Taliban figures. Few in the West noticed—all eyes were turned to the ongoing disaster in Iraq—but the drone war had begun.

It would start slowly but by 2008, when President Bush issued secret orders that allowed the CIA to strike without the approval of its Pakistani counterpart, the United States was launching a drone strike in the tribal areas on average every ten days, killing that year perhaps 350 people. Under President Obama, the numbers increased dramatically and by 2010 the CIA was striking Pakistan with Hellfire missiles on average every three days and killing that year alone perhaps a thousand people.

As the troops began to come home from Iraq this new phase of the forever war gradually revealed itself: Obama's "light footprint," a seemingly permanent covert war fought with Special Operations Forces and unmanned aerial vehicles in South Asia, the Arabian Peninsula, and, increasingly, the Horn of Africa. Every day, twenty-four hours a day, American airmen serving their shifts at bases outside Las Vegas, Nevada, in upstate New York, in northern Virginia, and elsewhere in the United States and abroad "pilot" these lethal flying robots, staring at computer screens through which they track from above the movements of men on the other side of the globe. What is it like to be in the cockpits of the combat planes in this new war? "It was an ordinary-looking room located in an office building in northern Virginia," a former CIA lawyer, John A. Rizzo, recalled to a *Newsweek* reporter, "filled with computer monitors, keyboards, and maps. Someone sat at a desk with his hand on a joystick." The lawyer and several others from the CIA "hovered nearby."

> *Together they watched images on a screen that showed a man and his family traveling down a road thousands of miles away. The vehicle slowed down, and the man climbed out.*
>
> *A moment later, an explosion filled the screen, and the man was dead. "It was very businesslike," says Rizzo. An aerial drone had killed the man, a high-level terrorism suspect, after he had gotten out of the vehicle, while members of his family were spared. "The agency was very punctilious about this," Rizzo says. "They tried to minimize collateral damage, especially women and children."*

Who was this man, killed without warning in front of his family, thousands of miles away? We are not told. Perhaps he had stepped out of his car in Pakistan, where in the decade since that first attack in 2004 the CIA has launched perhaps four hundred drone strikes, killing between three and four thousand people. Despite the agency's punctiliousness, perhaps as many as one in four of these were civilians.

Or perhaps the man had stepped out of his car in Yemen, where as early as 2002, and especially since 2009, the U.S. military and the CIA have launched perhaps 120 attacks, killing as many as eleven hundred people, of whom a hundred or so have been civilians. It is quite possible that the deskbound warriors in that ordinary-looking room in northern Virginia did not know the man's name. While the men they shadow in Pakistan and Yemen and, more recently, Somalia are sometimes known militant suspects—the targets of what are known as "personality strikes"—often they are unidentified "military-aged" men, targeted only because they are behaving in ways deemed to fit known terrorist "profiles." These "signature strikes," according to one account, made President Obama uncomfortable. "He would squirm," an unnamed Obama adviser said. "He didn't like the idea of kill 'em and sort it out later."

Whether the target is a known "personality" or a man behaving according to a certain terrorist "signature," the desk-borne pilots of the Central Intelligence Agency and the Joint Special Operations Command spend their days observing them, and in many cases pulling the trigger that launches a missile that streaks down and kills them and whoever is unlucky enough to be near them at that fateful moment. How many have been killed altogether? The short answer is, no one knows. This is a covert war, a war cloaked not in darkness but in the twilight I call "public secrecy": even as most drone strikes are publicly reported in the target country as well as in the United States, the U.S. government routinely denies official knowledge of or responsibility for them. We thus have only estimates of the number killed compiled by various nongovernmental organizations. Those pilots working quietly in ordinary-looking rooms in office buildings or in air-conditioned trailers on U.S. military bases have killed as many as five thousand people, according to credible sources, and the most conservative estimates suggest that at least one in ten of these have been noncombatants. At least six—and this the U.S. government has confirmed—have been American citizens.

This secret war that is no secret is President Obama's "focused" version of George W. Bush's global war on terror. Though the number of drone strikes increased dramatically during Bush's final year, Obama embraced drones as Bush never did, in part as a stopgap measure when a planned counterinsurgency campaign in Afghanistan proved too open-ended and expensive. During the Bush administration an American drone struck in Pakistan once every forty-three days; during the first two years of the Obama administration one struck every four days. The gunsights shift from here to there—northern Pakistan, various provinces in Yemen, the occasional strike in Somalia. The numbers have diminished since 2010 and 2011 but the secret drone war shows no sign of coming to an end. It is Obama's signature policy, his "light footprint" embodied, his answer to how, after putting an end to the full-bore occupations of Iraq and Afghanistan, the United States can continue quietly prosecuting the war on terror.

Together with the intensified use of drones came an increased reliance on raids by the elite troops of the Joint Special Operations Command, or JSOC, whose numbers have more than doubled since the start of the war on terror, to nearly seventy thousand. On any given day U.S. Special Operations Forces are deployed in seventy or so countries around the world, though their primary focus is on conducting black ops raids and kill/capture missions in Pakistan, Afghanistan, and Yemen and various other nations in the Middle East and Central Asia. Both of these quiet weapons, in the words of *New York Times* reporter David Sanger, "dramatically expanded the president's ability to wage nonstop, low-level conflict, something just short of war, every day of the year."

No doubt some of those killed in drone attacks posed an imminent threat to American citizens, though the definition of what exactly that means, of what criteria must be satisfied for the U.S. government to order someone's death, remain classified. But there is much evidence to suggest that many, at least by any reasonable definition of "threat," do not. At the height of Obama's drone war in Pakistan, the targeting shifted from al Qaeda to the Taliban and from leaders to foot soldiers. Of the 482 people U.S. intelligence estimates drones killed in the twelve months ending in September 2011, 265 were "assessed" to be "Afghani, Pakistani and unknown extremists," not senior al Qaeda leaders. Nearly half of the strikes over that period—forty-three out of ninety-five—struck members of groups other than al Qaeda, including some that would not seem to be covered by the Authorization for Use of Military Force. Though President Obama in his comments on drones has insisted that they are used to attack people who pose "a threat that is serious and not speculative" in situations where "we can't capture the individual before they move forward on some sort of operational plot against the United States," intelligence documents show something different. During his administration the focus of drone warfare moved from "personality strikes" to "signature strikes" that were launched, as we've seen, based on "patterns of merely suspicious activity by a group of [unidentified] men"—to the point that as many as 94 percent of those killed in the strikes were "mere foot soldiers," low-level sometime militants about whom, in the words of terrorism expert Peter Bergen, "it's hard to make the case that [they] threaten the United States in some way." The United States directed its drone pilots to kill militants trying to establish shariah law, militants fighting the Pakistani security services, militants sympathetic to the Taliban. Some of the strikes seem to have been "side payment strikes" that killed Pakistani Taliban as a favor to the Pakistani government. As the drone campaign passed its peak in Pakistan in 2011, the Obama administration began to ramp up attacks in Yemen, where the following year the military and CIA between them launched forty-seven strikes, many of them signature strikes. Far from limiting drone targets to leaders "before they move forward on some sort of operational plot against the United States," as the president claimed, evidence suggests his administration used drones to attack hundreds of people who are not plotting against the United States, few of whom appear to be leaders. As one militant told a reporter, "It seems they really want to kill everyone, not just the leaders."

Though the drone strikes remain "secret"—U.S. officials refer to them freely off the record—President Obama has spoken about them publicly on several occasions, in interviews and in formal speeches. In "taking 'direct action,' we must uphold standards that reflect our values," the president declared at West Point in May 2014, and this means "taking strikes only when we face a continuing, imminent threat, and only where there is near certainty of no civilian casualties, for our actions should meet a simple test: We must not create more enemies than we take off the battlefield."

With these words one confronts a tangle of paradoxes. What, for example, is a "continuing, imminent threat"? Given their plain meaning, "continuing" and "imminent" would seem to contradict each other. And so they would, had government lawyers not redefined them: "imminence," according to a leaked Department of Justice 2011 white paper, "does not require the United States to have clear evidence that a specific attack on U.S. persons and interests will take place in the immediate future." This document and others have made it clear that for the purpose of targeting militants with drone strikes Obama administration officials have redefined the word "imminent" to be mean roughly the opposite of what the dictionary says. Among national security lawyers, we have been told more recently, the current term of art is "elongated imminence," which means that "a president doesn't have to deem the country under immediate threat of attack before acting on his or her own." There is imminence and there is imminence.

As for the president's demand for "a near certainty of no civilian casualties," it appears that "near certainty" has also been redefined. Though perhaps a thousand civilians have died in strikes, it does seem to be true that the percentage of civilians killed and wounded in each strike is decreasing. It seems to be true as well that attacking these militants with other methods—launching cruise missiles, dropping bombs or missiles from fixed-wing aircraft, raiding with special operators—might kill even more civilians. Still, for that very reason these other methods would not be used at anything close to the rate at which drone strikes have been. Without drones, in other words, greater numbers of civilians would not be dead; without drones many of those thousand civilians would likely still be alive. It seems a bitter paradox that many of these civilians have died in part because of the relatively low numbers of civilian casualties that drone strikes make possible.

Whatever the numbers, how do we judge Obama's program of drone strikes against his "simple test"—that "we must not create more enemies than we take off the battlefield"? This test—like Rumsfeld's question about whether we are "capturing, killing or deterring" more terrorists than are being recruited to replace them—may seem simple, but how does one go about applying it?

Evidence that the drone strikes create enemies is easy to find. "What radicals had previously failed to achieve in my village," a young Yemeni activist told the Senate Judiciary Committee in April 2013, "one drone strike accomplished in an instant. There is now an intense anger and growing hatred of America." It is not in dispute that these killings of thousands of Muslims, conducted by remote control by a distant superpower, have caused enormous resentment and hatred of the United States in Pakistan and throughout the Islamic world, and have led at least two would-be Muslim American terrorists—Najibullah Zazi, the intended New York City subway bomber, and Faisal Shadzad, the Times Square bomber—to attempt attacks of their own. Deeply unpopular, drone strikes perpetuate many of the political sentiments at the root of the war on terror.

But how much anger is there, how many enemies have been created, and how do we weigh the anger and the enemies against the enemies the drone campaign has killed and the lethal plots that they might have otherwise brought to fruition? President Obama claimed in May 2013 that the drone attacks have meant that "the core of al Qaida in Afghanistan and Pakistan is on the path to defeat" for their "remaining operatives spend more time thinking about their own safety than plotting against us." And yet during that time the membership of al Qaeda in the Arabian Peninsula, the group that engineered two of the most serious recent plots against the United States—the Underwear Bomber in December 2009 and the UPS plot the following October—has multiplied. From a few hundred militants when the drone campaign began the group now numbers perhaps three or four times that. This growth echoes broader trends, as the authors of the Stimson Center's *Task Force on US Drone Policy* explain:

> *While tactical strikes may have helped keep the homeland free of major terrorist attacks, existing evidence indicates that both Sunni and Shia Islamic extremist groups have grown in scope, lethality and influence in the broader area of operations in the Middle East, Africa and South Asia. Prior to 9/11 such extremist groups operated in a generally confined geographic area near the Afghanistan/Pakistan border area. Today, such groups operate from Nigeria to Mali, to Libya, to the Sinai, to Syria, to Iraq, to Pakistan, Afghanistan and beyond, and there is no indication that a US strategy to destroy al-Qaida has curbed the rise of Sunni Islamic extremism, deterred the establishment of Shia Islamic extremist groups or advanced long-term US security interests.*
>
> *The use of targeted UAV [unmanned aerial vehicle] strikes to gain tactical advantage has led to some successes in various geographic areas of operations, but evidence about the scope, number and lethality of terrorist attacks worldwide suggest that al-Qaida elements still have a broad reach and, potentially, a decades-long lifespan. These weapons will be part of that struggle, but they will not defeat the broader strategic threat. In fact, evidence suggests that the broader strategic struggle against terrorist entities is not succeeding.*

Behind this grim appraisal lies a clash between tactics and strategy that dates back to the beginning of the war on terror. Tactics developed to prevent attacks, from torture to drone warfare, worsen the underlying resentment and anger that nourish the jihadist movement while confirming the story it tells. Think of it as the difference between a strategy of counterterrorism—one designed to destroy terrorist groups by killing terrorists—or a strategy of counterinsurgency, which treats the broader jihadist movement as a worldwide insurgency that must be combated through various military and political methods. As military specialist David Kilcullen wrote in 2004, "methods that treat the enemy primarily as a target set—seeking to destroy key nodes and hoping this will unhinge the insurgency—cannot work. Instead," he goes on,

> *we must focus on taking the insurgency off the boil by denying it energy, thus reducing the coherence and stability of Islamist movements and allowing nonmilitary measures (governance, development, the constitutional middle way . . .) to have an effect.*
>
> *This means that a decapitation strategy aimed at eliminating key Islamist leaders will not work here. Decapitation has rarely succeeded in counterinsurgency, with good reason—efforts to kill or capture insurgent leaders inject energy into the system by generating grievances and causing disparate groups to coalesce. . . . Moreover, although leaders are key nodes, their destruction would do little damage to the linked but separate groups in the global jihad. Rather, their martyrdom would inject energy into the system and allow a new class of leaders to emerge.*

These words, written more than a decade ago by a key adviser to the U.S. government in its war on terror, proved prophetic. If it is true, as the 2004 Defense Science Board report had it, that "the dramatic narrative since 9/11 has essentially borne out the entire radical Islamist bill of particulars," then it is within this dramatic narrative that the story of the drone war must be told. A tactical response to the threat of imminent attack, by enraging the targeted public, leads toward strategic defeat, or at best strategic stalemate: an unending dependency on violent methods of tactical intervention to stave off attacks, even as the broader insurgency grows and flourishes. "The increasing use of lethal UAVs," note the authors of the *Task Force on US Drone Policy* report, "may create a slippery slope leading to continual or wider wars." The Israelis refer to such periodic and persistent interventions as "mowing the grass," a task that, once undertaken, must be undertaken again and again and again. "The problem with the drone is it's like your lawn mower," former CIA analyst Bruce Riedel put it, expanding the metaphor. "You've got to mow the lawn all the time. The minute you stop mowing the grass is going to grow back." Even as one pushes the mower, one plants the seed for the grass to grow back thicker than before.

Drones appear seductively low-cost and low-risk: no pilots are shot down and captured, relatively few civilians are killed, the American public cares little and thus the political cost seems negligible. And yet they are a stopgap measure, at best disrupting attacks at the cost of nourishing and expanding the movement itself. Relying on them implies an inherent movement toward expansion: applied narrowly at first to address specific threats, they grow addictive, becoming the go-to short-term method for dealing with groups that pose much more diffuse political problems to policymakers. The more drones are used, the more they are needed. Killing enemies and creating more, killing and creating more, they are deadly perpetual motion machines, prime symbolic instruments of permanent war.

THE TRIUMPH OF FEAR

Beyond human rights organizations and a few college campuses, one finds surprisingly little debate about the drone war. During Obama's campaign for reelection in 2012, drones were scarcely mentioned. Asked about drone killings during the second presidential debate, former governor Mitt Romney said little more than that he "support[ed] that entirely," clearly implying that if he became president he'd order more such attacks. Of course, very little about the state of exception found its way into the campaign. One might have thought a great democracy in choosing its leader could have found time at least to consider its ongoing and seemingly endless war: to debate, for example, whether the drone strikes might be creating at least as many terrorists as they are killing or to ask whether Americans truly believe that their president should have, in Rosa Brooks's words, "the unreviewable power to kill any person, anywhere on earth, at any time, based on information that is secret and has been collected and evaluated according to secret criteria by anonymous individuals in a secret procedure"—or even to inquire of their leaders, actual or prospective, how many thousands will need to be killed in this manner before the war on terror could finally be declared at an end, if in fact it ever can be.

Obama's reelection powerfully demonstrated the bipartisan ascendency of the politics of fear. In 2004, George W. Bush had defeated John Kerry, a highly decorated Vietnam War veteran, thanks in part to unanswered Republican warnings that, in Vice President Cheney's words, "if we make the wrong choice then the danger is that we'll get hit again and we'll be hit in a way that will be devastating." If in the 2012 campaign the word "drones" was hardly uttered—and if, when it finally was, the Republican challenger found himself vigorously supporting their use—it is not least because when it came to Cheneyesque intimations of weakness, Obama had taken a position so strongly in favor of quiet and unremitting military violence that he left his Republican rival, struggle though he might to shoulder his way past him, no place to stand. If during the campaign the politics of fear had lost its magic for the Republican right this was not least because its methods had been co-opted by the Democrat in the White House, who had proved relentless in hunting down terrorists, and those who may look like terrorists, and killing them by the thousands. No one could criticize President Obama for prosecuting CIA officers for torture, for he had conducted no such prosecutions. No one could attack him for abandoning Bush's indefinite detention policy because he had regularized and legalized it. And no one could denounce him for closing Guantánamo because Guantánamo had not been closed.

Indeed Republicans, who had reportedly planned in a Romney administration to reinstate "enhanced interrogation techniques against high-value detainees that are safe, legal and effective," made the plausible claim that Obama, after officially halting torture, had in practice avoided the knotty questions of interrogation, "enhanced" or otherwise, by managing during his light footprint version of the war on terror to avoid taking prisoners. Drones, they argued, had replaced the interrogation room. But our leaders and those seeking to replace them need have no debate on drones because on this as on other pressing matters raised by the permanent war on terror there was no longer an opposition. Both parties had enlisted themselves full-force in the struggle to be tough, and tougher. If Obama had made himself largely invulnerable to the politics of fear it is because he had shielded himself from it by his cool and ruthless methods and left little political space for discussion. Across fourteen years of the war on terror, and two presidents, the politics of fear had not been forestalled, or banished, or defeated. The politics of fear had been embodied in the country's permanent policies, largely without comment or objection by its citizens. The politics of fear had won.

SHELTER IN PLACE

On a cool overcast day in April 2013 the city of Boston, birthplace of American independence, was shut down. Massachusetts's governor had ordered Boston's 700,000 residents to stay off the streets—or, in the new term of art, to "shelter in place." Boston's subways were shuttered, its buses garaged, its train stations closed. Rumbling through the eerily deserted streets as the light rose over the great metropolis came black-body-armored SWAT teams in armored cars, the vanguard of thousands of paramilitary forces of the FBI, the Bureau of Alcohol, Tobacco, Firearms and Explosives, the Department of Homeland Security, the National Guard, and the Massachusetts State Police. These armored cars roared through residential neighborhoods. Helicopters swooped and clattered overhead. Tanks blocked off streets. Snipers in camouflage gear crouched on rooftops. Paramilitary fighters pounded on doors, pulled people out of their houses, and searched them at gunpoint. Though their nominal purpose was finding the two young men who had planted pressure cooker bombs at the Boston Marathon four days before, killing three people, this was also, according to CBS News, "the first major field test of the interagency task forces created in the wake of the September 2001 attacks." Congressman Ron Paul spoke more vividly, describing the show of force as "a military-style occupation of an American city" that looked like a "military coup in a far-off banana republic."

Watching these tanks rumbling down deserted Boston streets, I was beset by a nagging memory. Not until Dzhokhar Tsarnaev, the nineteen-year-old University of Massachusetts marine biology major who with his older brother, Tamerlan, had set the pressure cooker bombs, was finally captured did scattered images finally coalesce in my mind into a battered streetscape I recognized as occupied Baghdad. It was October 2003, the first day of the Ramadan Offensive. Five suicide bombers had blown themselves up and, reaching the scene of one bombing moments afterward, I found torn bodies strewn around a great fire burning, the remains of the exploded vehicle glowing red-hot at its center. An hour or so later, still covered in oily soot and grime, I remarked to a top American intelligence officer that such suicide attacks must be nearly impossible to prevent. "No, we could stop these things entirely," the general replied sharply, "*if* we were willing to do what was necessary! We could stop car bombers if we stopped all driving. But that would be inconsistent with another, overriding imperative—letting Iraqis live a reasonably normal life. . . . We could stop them but to do it, we would have to *shut the place down.*" What prevented the military stopping them was that, in Baghdad in 2003, "politically at least, we can't take those steps."

Now, I thought in some wonder, in Boston, Massachusetts, a decade later we *can* take those steps, in the cause of finding a nineteen-year-old college student who had used a homemade pressure cooker bomb to kill three people. Or rather, politically, it seems, we can't afford not to take them. And it was this, Congressman Paul had said, that "should frighten us as much or more than the attack itself." A dozen years after the attacks of September 11, 2001, we have made, in panic in the months immediately after the attacks and in mostly uncaring acquiescence in the years since, a different country. It is a disfigured land, a land at peace in which it has become politically imperative to take those steps which were unthinkable in a Baghdad beset by brutal civil war. It has evolved slowly but inexorably, as the fear has institutionalized itself in our police forces, our intelligence bureaucracies, and most of all in our politics. And even as the temper of emergency has become the intermittent backdrop of our politics, bloating our security budgets and ever ready, when the right buttons are pushed, to flare into crisis, it has meant that in the guise of shielding itself from attack our country is ever prey to it. The ingrained obsession with security makes it possible for a couple of young men with pressure cookers to attack a great city and *shut the place down.* It has disfigured us not least by rendering us defensive, reactive. It puts *our* politics in *their* hands.

Drones striking on the other side of the world, detainees subsisting quietly at Guantánamo: unseen and unheard, these attributes of the state of exception touch us little in our daily lives. Yet the closing of the city of Boston by two young men on an overcast April day suggests a question about our politics of fear. If the goal of terrorists is to spread terror, how is it that, years after the attacks of September 11, we seem to be doing so much to help them?

A SELF-DEFEATING SPIRAL

Like fever lines tracing jagged paths above our politics, fear and political posturing spike and ebb with the day's news. The time of the terrorist "spectacular" of 9/11 scale seems long past—the "planes plot," the last Grand Guignol bloodbath, was foiled by British and American intelligence nearly a decade ago. But smaller attempts come regularly, sponsored by regional franchises—the Underwear Bomber and UPS plot, courtesy of al Qaeda in the Arabia Peninsula; the Times Square bomber, courtesy of the Pakistani Taliban— or undertaken by lone wolves like the Boston bombers or the San Bernardino attackers. As each plot is uncovered it brings with it a predictable rhetorical attempt to reignite the politics of fear.

Throughout the country's history, from "waving the bloody shirt" in the wake of the Civil War to charging that adversaries were "soft on communism" during the Cold War, some politicians have worked hard to frighten the people. But working to gin up fear about terrorism is special. What terrorists ultimately aim to produce, after all, is not death or mayhem or destruction—these are only the means to an end—but terror. To say that the politics of fear has become embedded in our politics is to say that, in a permanent war on terror, the rich political benefits of that most lucrative emotion are being shared, between the terrorists themselves and some politicians who portray themselves as leading the fight against them. Our institutionalized overreaction to terrorism is a boon to the terrorists, for it multiplies the power of their actions. It is what granted two young men with pressure cookers the power to shut down the city of Boston.

More than a dozen years after the attacks of September 11 the politics of fear has joined hands in a self-defeating spiral with *la politique du pire*. As we saw, this time-honored French phrase—meaning, roughly, "the politics of the worst"—describes the insurgent strategy of staging attacks intended to provoke the adversary into taking reckless actions that "strip off his mask" and make manifest the underlying dynamics of repression. Al Qaeda stages acts of terrorism intended to provoke the United States into taking actions that reveal itself as an oppressor of Muslims. The strategy of *la politique du pire*—sometimes called "the strategy of provocation" and drawn originally from revolutionaries of the nineteenth century—depends on a dialectical escalation, on provoking a response and then provoking another. The first terrorist attack provokes counterattack and repression, which in turn produces recruits for the revolutionary cause, who undertake more terrorist attacks, provoking harsher repression, and so on. By so doing, al Qaeda's theoreticians believed they could turn the United States and its Arab puppet states "into recruiting sergeants for their cause," in the words of historian Michael Ignatieff:

> *Success depends less on the initial attack than on instigating an escalatory spiral, controlled not by the forces of order but by the terrorists themselves. If terrorists can successfully draw democracies into this spiral and control its upward acceleration, they will begin to dictate the terms of the encounter. Success becomes a matter of inflicting losses, enduring harms, and gambling that the enemy has less endurance than they do.* Since a state will always be too strong for a cell of individuals to defeat in open battle, it must defeat itself. *If terrorists can provoke the state into atrocity, this will begin to erode the willingness of a democratic public to continue the fight.*

That initiating such an "escalatory spiral" puts the power in the terrorists' hands—that it makes our politics prey to their actions—is a vital point and it is where *la politique du pire* links so dramatically with the politics of fear. Terrorists produce death and destruction not as their primary goal but as a means to an end. That end is fear. Fear incites reaction, and overreaction. Fear produces policies that are self-defeating. Fear puts our politics in their hands.

A similar dynamic of reaction played out in Iraq after the U.S. invasion removed Saddam Hussein in 2003. Saddam had led a minority Sunni government. The great underlying political problem the Americans faced in Iraq was how to transfer power to the Shia, the long suppressed majority, while persuading the displaced Sunnis to accept without violence their loss of power. Little evidence exists that the Americans even understood the problem, let alone had a solution. But Abu Musab al-Zarqawi, the Jordanian-born Sunni leader of what became al Qaeda in Iraq, certainly understood it: scarcely had the occupation begun before he launched a vicious campaign of suicide bombings against the Iraqi Shia. "If we succeed in dragging [the Shia] into the arena of sectarian war," Zarqawi wrote in a letter to al Qaeda leaders in 2004, "it will become possible to awaken the inattentive Sunnis as they feel imminent danger and annihilating death." In launching hundreds of suicide attacks on the Iraqi Shia, Zarqawi was trying to provoke the Shia to launch counterattacks on the Iraqi Sunni, in the hope that this would lead the Sunni, his potential allies, to rise up, defend themselves, and retake power.

Zarqawi's violence against the Shia was meant to be a remedy for the political unpopularity of his own cause among Sunnis, his own allies, a way to force his enemies to do the political work for him. The suicide bombing campaign, as David Kilcullen writes, "was driven by a brutal political logic":

> In provoking the Shi'a, Zarqawi hoped to back the Sunni community into a corner, so that his group would be all that stood between

Sunnis and the Shi'a death squads, giving people no choice but to sup-
port AQI [al Qaeda in Iraq], whatever they thought of its ideology.
This cynical strategy . . . meant that Shi'a killing Sunni was actually
good for AQI, and so they'd go out of their way to provoke the most
horrific violence against their own people.

And indeed after hundreds of vicious suicide attacks on Shia neighborhoods and mosques, Zarqawi finally succeeded, after his militants blew up the Golden Mosque in Samarra in February 2006, in provoking widespread counterattacks by Shia death squads on Sunnis, which brought on Sunni counterattacks and a bloody dynamic, in 2006 and 2007, of near all-out civil war in which several thousand a month were dying at the hands of suicide bombers and death squads. During the years since, after a brief respite during the "surge" of American forces of 2006–2008, Iraq's underlying dynamic of sectarian conflict has persisted and worsened, helping produce the Islamic State, the stepchild of al Qaeda in Iraq and the jihadists' greatest victory yet in their strategy of provocation.

BULL'S-EYE

At the end of 2011 the last American soldiers rumbled across the Kuwaiti border in quiet ignominy, leaving behind the failed occupation of Iraq. Now the great bulk of American troops have departed Afghanistan, leaving behind contingents of military trainers and special operators and drone maintenance men. In both countries the wars the United States began go on. In both the forces the United States vowed to destroy remain strong. Several thousand Americans have now returned to Iraq and more will likely soon join them. They train Iraqis to fight a reincarnation of familiar enemies, an alliance of Islamists and Baathists that took shape during the early years of the American occupation a decade ago and has now grown and matured into a "new Caliphate" stretching in its power from the suburbs of Aleppo to the outskirts of Baghdad and in its growing influence from the Strait of Gibraltar to the Strait of Malacca, and beyond.

On the day after September 11, 2001, what dedicated jihadist would have dreamed a mere decade and a half would bring such success? Given the reality of those years, what exactly has the forever war been about? Ridding the world of evil? It has been fourteen years and more since President Bush offered that answer to Americans staggered by the attacks of September 11 and if it wasn't clear then, it has long since become so that the United States will never succeed in ridding the world of "evildoers." But perhaps American leaders might have followed, in the wake of the attacks, a strategy that would have avoided creating more. Perhaps they might have tried to avoid actions that dramatically increased their numbers.

Imagine for a moment a target. In its yellow bull's-eye imagine grouped together those Muslims most committed to violent jihad: the leaders of jihadist groups and the men and women willing to blow themselves up to support them. In the surrounding first, red circle of the target are committed supporters who actively aid the cause. In the next circle are those who contribute money to the jihadists, in the next those who argue for its goals and aspirations, in the next those who are politically sympathetic but who take no action, and near the outer edge are Muslims who watch and follow the struggle but who remain uncommitted.

For Osama bin Laden and his successors, the political task was to take actions that would encourage Muslims to move toward the bull's-eye: that would lead apolitical Muslims to move into the circle of those sympathetic to the cause, that would lead those sympathetic into the circle of those who contribute money and support, and so on. Al Qaeda's remaining leaders, those of its "associated forces," and those of the Islamic State all have in common that they want to do what they can to "awaken the sleeping Sunnis" and thereby cause a general migration toward the center, toward committed and violent activism, not only by encouraging radicalization directly in their propaganda but by provoking the United States to take actions that will do that political work for them.

For the United States the strategic goal in this war from the beginning was, or should have been, to slow and ultimately reverse that movement toward the center by following policies that discourage the radicalization of Muslims. When he asked in 2003 whether we are "capturing, killing or deterring and dissuading more terrorists every day than the *madrassas* and the radical clerics are recruiting, training and deploying against us," Secretary of Defense Rumsfeld appeared to be grasping his way to this reality, at the very moment that the United States had embroiled itself in a politically catastrophic counterinsurgency in Iraq. His formulation, precise as it may appear, was telling, for the verbs subvert one another. Killing and capturing can seriously undermine deterring and dissuading. Capturing and detaining in Guantánamo and Abu Ghraib promote radicalization and recruitment, not deterrence and dissuasion. Throughout the Bush years we saw these contradictions vividly, for even as the rhetorical emphasis evolved during the second term the bleeding sore of the Iraq War and the lingering images from Guantánamo and Abu Ghraib made it impossible to gain ground in the "battle of the story." Until 2009, the America of the Bush administration remained an America that invaded Muslim countries and imprisoned and tortured Muslims.

Even as a presidential candidate Barack Obama made clear that he grasped in all its subtlety bin Laden's strategy of provocation. "Bin Ladin and his allies know they cannot defeat us on the field of battle or in a genuine battle of ideas," he declared in August 2007. "But they can provoke the reaction we've seen in Iraq: a misguided invasion of a Muslim country that sparks new insurgencies." He went on to link this strategy explicitly to the politics of fear and the state of exception it had inspired, vowing to end torture, end military commissions, close Guantánamo, and otherwise bring American policies more in tune with "who we are."

But the reality of his years in office have turned out to be more complicated. Guantánamo remains open. The military commissions go on. Torture goes unpunished. And while he struggled to bring Americans home from the shooting wars in Iraq and Afghanistan, he sent drones to kill thousands, including many civilians. Americans, believing themselves to stand proudly for the rule of law and human rights, have become for the rest of the world a symbol of something quite opposite: a society that imprisons people indefinitely without trial, kills thousands without due process, and leaves unpunished lawbreaking approved by its highest officials. The country has entered a twilight world when it comes to the law and is unlikely soon to emerge from it. This includes an enduring corruption of language, beginning with the president's paradoxical claim that he "prohibited" torture and his ongoing refusal to take responsibility for the "secret" but quite public deaths of people whose names appear on "kill lists" compiled by U.S. intelligence agencies. Though Obama struggled to "end the dumb wars" and otherwise focus the worldwide campaign, the political engine of the war on terror roars on. The worldwide insurgency has become politically self-sustaining.

Even as "core" al Qaeda has been battered and reduced, al Qaedism, the ideology, has thrived. Al Qaeda increasingly has *become* al Qaedism, a set of beliefs promoted by various organizations all partly powered by the outrage of young Muslims over Western imperialism, torture, drone attacks, and what they see as the oppression at the heart of the war on terror. Al Qaedism, or "viral al Qaeda," an ideology carried full-blown on hundreds of websites and Internet chat rooms, means young Muslims need not travel to Pakistan for training before an attack. All of it—ideology, tradecraft, bomb-making skills—can be accessed through a computer at home or in an Internet café. The only necessary outside ingredient is willing young men and women and these, thanks in part to the political responses of the United States over the last decade and a half, are in plentiful supply. This very plentitude means the odds against those charged with stopping attacks grow ever longer. Back in 2011 John Miller, then a high official of the Office of the Director of National Intelligence and a former reporter who had interviewed both Osama bin Laden and Ayman al-Zawahiri, noted that successful lone-wolf attacks were increasingly likely:

> In the [immediate] post 9/11 world, we had an average of about four plots targeting U.S. soil, or emanating on U.S. soil, a year. In 2008–2009, that jumps to nine and then ten. In 2011, we are already on a pace to pass that.
>
> Something has happened, a better maturation of ideology, a better way to get the message out, that has caused those plots to be coming at us literally at a rate or a pace of almost one a month. And when you deal in that kind of volume, you have a special challenge. Number one, we are operating at nearly 100 percent in interdicting all of them and shutting them down. But the odds of being able to maintain that batting average, as the numbers go up, those [odds] go down.

Miller was speaking a year and a half before the two pressure-cooker bombs went off near the finish line of the Boston Marathon. Today that "better maturation of ideology, better way to get the message out" and the rapidly growing number of possible adherents, especially of the Islamic State, make successful attacks—not a spectacular like 9/11, the planning and organizing for which is easier to detect, but a small, lone-wolf bombing or assault on a soft target—much more difficult to flag and prevent. In December 2015 a Muslim couple attacked a holiday party in San Bernardino,

California, killing fourteen people and dramatically demonstrating the power of a lone-wolf attack to terrify the country, especially during a political campaign. More than ever, the politics of fear and the media complex battening on it stands as a kind of enormous amplifier, ensuring the ongoing power of such an attack to spread fear, disrupt society, and provoke a self-defeating response. In the wake of each attack the politics of fear reignites, the escalatory spiral takes another turn.

Meantime young Muslims in ever greater numbers come streaming to the battlefields of the Middle East in order to devote their lives to righting wrongs against Muslims. Increasingly their destination is the training camps and battlefields of the "new Caliphate." In a powerful offensive in winter and spring 2014 the Islamic State, the successor of al Qaeda in Iraq, managed to occupy a good deal of Sunni Iraq, seizing first Fallujah and much of Anbar province and then Mosul, Iraq's second largest city. Though they are harsh fundamentalists in ideology, the Islamic State fighters were welcomed by significant numbers of Sunnis, who had been alienated and antagonized by former Iraqi prime minister Nouri al-Maliki's continuing Shia-dominating policies of disenfranchisement and repression, policies in effect foreshadowed by the Americans immediately after their invasion, when they purged Baathists from the Sunni-dominated government and dissolved the Iraqi army. Like the United States early in the occupation, Maliki had adopted policies that were a political godsend to al Qaeda, jailing and suppressing Sunnis and in other ways exacerbating the sectarian tensions and resentments that al Qaeda in Iraq had worked so hard to ignite.

A decade ago the Islamic State did not exist. Now, having risen amid the chaos of the American invasion, it stands as a second global terrorist network in competition with al Qaeda, governing more than five million people, claiming "provinces" from Algeria to Pakistan, and working to expand a network of affiliated organizations throughout the Middle East, North Africa, and South

Asia. But it is more than a competitor: Abu Bakr al-Baghdadi, the Islamic State's self-proclaimed Caliph, is in many ways Osama bin Laden's "true successor," assuming his mantle as the inspiration of global jihad and embodying a dream that bin Laden believed could only be realized in a distant future: the restoration of the Caliphate. Seizing on the opportunity presented by the American occupation, the organization that became the Islamic State formed itself out of the Islamists and Baathists; many of its key figures, including Baghdadi himself and his two senior deputies, both of them former senior officers in Saddam's army, got their start in the "jihad university" of Camp Bucca, the American detention center in southern Iraq. Perhaps a thousand or more of its key officials are former Baathist officers in Saddam's security services. Using plans which originated in those security services, they constructed an underground insurgent organization that, beginning with three spectacular suicide bombings in August 2003, proved to be the most savage and effective in opposing the occupation and sowing the seeds of sectarian civil war. Now, after various iterations over a dozen years the descendant of this organization governs territory roughly the size of Great Britain, collecting taxes, administering justice, drawing on revenues of billions of dollars a year, and waging war using tanks, artillery, and armored personnel carriers. Though it still uses terrorism with great effectiveness and unprecedented violence it is much more than "a terrorist organization, pure and simple," in President Obama's ill-chosen words. It is for all practical purposes indeed a state.

By the summer of 2014, the Islamic State was fighting to con-solidate and expand its territory by staging car bombings and other attacks against Shia in Baghdad and working to spread sectarian conflict by launching suicide attacks against Shia in Saudi Arabia and the Gulf states. For this task it is perfectly situated, for Iraq happens to sit squarely upon the major sectarian borderline divid-ing the Middle East. In provoking sectarian conflict within Iraq, the predecessors of the Islamic State were helping to create a vortex that has increasingly engulfed the entire region, drawing Sunnis from North Africa to the Gulf eager to defend the Caliphate.

The United States has been the cooperative and largely unwitting partner in all this. Even as the United States launches thousands of air strikes and drone attacks against Islamic State targets, tens of thousands of foreign fighters from throughout the Islamic world and the West flow into its ranks, drawn by the greatest cause for "holy warriors" since the mujahideen confronted the Soviets in their occupation of Afghanistan more than three decades ago. The American air attacks, though nowhere near frequent or effective enough to "degrade and ultimately destroy" the Islamic State, President Obama's stated objective, have served as a boon to its recruiting, to the point that Islamic State spokesmen have begged prospective recruits from some countries to stay at home and advance the struggle there.

All signs suggest that one of the Islamic State's goals is once again to "force America to abandon its war against Islam by proxy and force it to attack directly." The words are drawn from Abu Bakr Naji's *The Management of Savagery*, a work that, posted online in 2004, stands as a kind of map for achieving the Caliphate and sees the current critical stage as one of "vexation and exhaustion" in which the United States will be worn down by constant wars, wars that because of Western society's advanced "effeminacy" the country will find itself unable to sustain. Indeed, Osama bin Laden himself sketched out this strategy of bleeding the superpower as early as 2004:

> All that we have mentioned has made it easy to provoke and bait this administration. All we have to do is to send two mujahideen to the furthest point East to raise a cloth on which is written al Qaeda, in order to make the generals race there to cause America to suffer human, economic and political losses without achieving for it

anything of note . . . so we are continuing this policy of bleeding America to the point of bankruptcy.

After a decade and a half of war, the United States finds itself caught, in Zawahiri's phrase, "between two fires," between a war-weary people at home and an enemy abroad eager to provoke yet another conflict. The result is a self-proclaimed war to "degrade and ultimately destroy" the Islamic State consisting of a handful of air strikes a day to support an Iraqi army that the secretary of defense admits "shows no will to fight"—and whose activities do little more than promote Islamic State recruiting.

WHO WE ARE

How do we begin to escape the spiral of escalation and the state of exception itself? As Giorgio Agamben wrote, the state of exception exists "at the limit between politics and law . . . an 'ambiguous, uncertain, borderline fringe, at the intersection of the legal and the political.'" We find ourselves here in the realm of politics. The road toward restoring justice and escaping our state of exception runs first of all through politics, and education.

Look again to the lands of the "apostate regimes"—Egypt, Saudi Arabia—critical American allies that al Qaeda had originally hoped, by attacking their sponsor, to overthrow. In this region, where torture had underpinned the power of every national security state, the notorious images of America's state of exception, and especially those from Abu Ghraib, provoked a debate about torture and human rights that had been impossible before. Egyptians, forbidden by their autocratic, U.S.-supported government to talk about Egyptian torture, found themselves free to discuss, analyze, and condemn American torture, and thereby initiate a discussion of human rights and dignity that was a motivating element in the early upheavals of what came to be called the Arab Spring. "Because the torture and abuse depicted was so widely seen as directed towards the Arab or Muslim man," writes human rights specialist Shadi Mokhtari, "many felt a profound sense of personal violation."

> As they grappled to formulate a response, they often found themselves evoking human rights. . . . Instead of viewing human rights as a Western imposition, increasingly it became a language that Arab populations embraced. . . . It did not take long however for the focus to turn inward to the Arab world's own "Guantánamos," "Abu Ghraibs," and widespread practice of torture.

Ironies proliferate: Osama bin Laden had hoped, by provoking American invasions of Muslim countries, to incite Muslim anger that would lead to an upsurge in recruits willing to attack those U.S.-supported "apostate regimes" supported by the United States and eventually to replace them by a fundamentalist Islamic Caliphate. Though he succeeded beyond his dreams in provoking those invasions the brutal scenes of American repression of Muslims at Guantánamo and Abu Ghraib that followed set off a human rights debate, a debate that helped lead to a popular and *democratic* uprising that unseated the Mubarak regime and led, briefly, to the kind of elected moderate Islamic regime that al Qaeda militants most despise and fear. The violent unseating of this regime and its replacement by another autocratic military leader, seeming as it does to foreclose perhaps for many years any political progress in Egypt short of armed revolution or coup d'état, comes now as a boon to the jihadists, reinforcing the message that vanguard violence is the only way to achieve true political change.

Not the least of these intertwining ironies, as Mokhtari points out elsewhere, is that at the moment that "Arabs found the language of human rights gave expression to their immense sense of indignation," Americans were discovering that in their own country "the space for invoking human rights on moral grounds alone has virtually disappeared." President Obama, struggling early on to gain support for closing Guantánamo, felt compelled to argue that Americans must close the prison and prohibit torture not because it is right but because it will "make them safer." Even so, as Mokhtari points out, the president found himself pursuing these policies, insofar as he has pursued them, "not because of public opinion but in spite of it."

One might add, if not in mitigation then perhaps in explanation of these shaming words, the grim distinction that in Egypt, Egyptians tortured Egyptians while at those black sites Americans tortured ... others. When Egyptians, especially young Egyptians, think of torture, they fear it as potential victims. When Americans now think of torture, many of them think of it as vital self-protection, agreeing with our former vice president that "no moral value ... obliges public servants ever to sacrifice innocent lives to spare a captured terrorist from unpleasant things." Torture is presented as a shield to protect us from the dangerous other, not as a violation of our own values or even as a threat which could leave us all, as Americans, exposed to violence and violation or worse.

That is in part why the road to justice must run not primarily through the courts but through politics, through the kind of unblinkered, nonpartisan investigation and definitive judgment that only a publicly appointed Truth Commission could produce. The barrier to accountability, and thus to escaping our state of exception, is first of all a political one. Torture must be removed as a critical symbol of the politics of fear. The priority is destroying not the torturers but the idea of torture as necessary and vital and its consequent role as a symbol of ultimate commitment in the war on terror. Nothing has done more to nourish this idea—and with it the widespread belief that it is impossible to protect the country while also following the law—than the Myth of the Ticking Bomb.

TICKING BOMB

Here is what the president knows. A crude nuclear weapon is planted somewhere in the Bay Area. It is set to go off within a few hours. He has set all his considerable federal, state, and local resources—intelligence agencies, military, police and fire departments—to finding the weapon. But they have not found it. A man has been taken into custody. Unimpeachable intelligence sources have told the president that the man *knows*. After several hours of extensive interrogation, the man has freely admitted he knows, has offered verifiable facts that only someone intimately connected to the plot could know. But when asked to give the location of the bomb, he insistently repeats only these words: "Soon you will know. Soon everyone—all who survive—will know." What should the president do?

This is the dreaded ticking bomb scenario, fount of a thousand television dramas—most famously of *24*, a program that could well have been titled *The Ticking Bomb*—and a million law school and political science discussions. It is frankly fantastical in its assumptions: How could any president ever have such nearly perfect but achingly imperfect knowledge? When torture supporters insist that we entertain it they are insisting we talk about hypotheticals instead of discussing the scores of real cases in which the government actually made the decision to torture. One reason, of course, is the circumstances of those actual cases differ dramatically from the imaginary case I have just described, particularly when it comes to knowledge. As the CIA inspector general put it starkly in 2004:

> The Agency's intelligence on Al-Qa'ida was limited prior to the initiation of the . . . Interrogation Program. The Agency lacked adequate linguists or subject matter experts and had very little hard knowledge of what particular Al-Qa'ida leaders—who later became detainees—knew. This lack of knowledge led analysts to speculate

about what a detainee "should know," [versus] information the an-
alyst could objectively demonstrate the detainee did know. . . . When
a detainee did not respond to a question posed to him, the assump-
tion at Headquarters was that the detainee was holding back and
knew more; consequently, Headquarters recommended resumption
of [enhanced interrogation techniques].

Here there is no all-knowing interrogator, omniscient but for
one small piece of critical information. Torture often commences
when the prisoner knows very little but that minuscule bit leads interrogators to believe he must know much more. Consider the case
of Jean Améry, a resistance fighter in Belgium during World War
II, who was given a stark choice when arrested by the police: Either
cooperate and tell us *everything* or be sent to Gestapo interrogators
at the notorious Breendonk fortress. Améry writes:

I would [have been] most pleased to avoid Breendonk, with which I
was quite familiar, and give the evidence desired of me. Except that
I unfortunately knew nothing, or almost nothing. Accomplices? I
could name only their aliases. Hiding places? . . . The exact addresses
were never entrusted to me. For these men, however, that was far too
familiar twaddle. . . . They laughed contemptuously. And suddenly I
felt—the first blow. . . .
    The first blow brings home to the prisoner that he is helpless,
and thus it already contains in the bud everything that is to come. . . .
They are permitted to punch me in the face, the victim feels in numb
surprise and concludes in just as numb certainty: they will do with
me what they want.

When we compare these realities from the CIA and the Gestapo to the ticking bomb fantasy, what stands out is the reversal
in the assumption of knowledge, how the ticking bomb turns on its
head what we know to be epistemological reality. The ticking bomb

scenario posits perfect knowledge on the part of the interrogators and the president who will order them to torture, perfect apart from one small, vital piece. The reality is that it is the tortured prisoner alone—whether it be Jean Améry or Abu Zubaydah—who truly knows what he knows, and it is he who is faced with the task, often insurmountable, of convincing the almost entirely ignorant interrogator of what he does not. Like Saddam Hussein faced with American certainty that he was harboring weapons of mass destruction, the prisoner must prove a negative, must prove that what the Americans were certain is there is in fact not there. The reality is that there is no ticking bomb, no certain knowledge on the part of interrogators of a particular weapon about to explode, but a general fear of what might happen and a conviction that anyone who *might* know anything important, like Zubaydah, whether it be about attacks or about the mundane operations of the group, must be made to tell all he knows, *whatever it is*.

Of course at bottom the Myth of the Ticking Bomb does not sketch any recognizable reality; it is a kind of philosopher's trick, a sophomorically clever attempt to slash a rhetorical hole in the lining of our ethical world. It aims to demolish the wall of absolutism surrounding torture and to make the decision of whether to torture one of contingency and degree, not principle. It aims to take the staunch Kantian, who believes torture is always wrong, and by means of an alluring fantasy force him to become a consequentialist, who will willingly trade one act of torture for the prospect of saving hundreds or thousands of lives. And then of course the rhetorician pounces: "So you *would* torture under certain conditions?" And now that we have established the principle, to paraphrase George Bernard Shaw's quip about prostitution, it only remains to haggle about the price.

What matters about the ticking bomb scenario is not the likelihood it will happen in reality—that is vanishingly low—but its potency as an image of commitment and an emblem of the politics of fear. What matters is its inherent drama and the fact that it has captured, by means of *24* and its cultural ancestors, the imagination of the public.

We should—we must—disarm the ticking bomb. It is time to admit clearly that in the event of such a bizarre eventuality any president, any leader, would do what the situation requires, would be bound by his or her judgment of what the country's immediate welfare demands. In such a situation any leader in fact becomes a consequentialist: must become one, as Machiavelli recognized five centuries ago. Some writers have even suggested that such an exception be written into the law, that the president, under certain exigent conditions, should be granted the legal right to use cruel, inhuman, and degrading treatment to acquire information that could prevent an imminent attack. This is what might be called the paradox of the exception: Do we legislate the exception? Do we gain or lose by trying to legislate emergency procedures? By making them legal in certain situations, do we make it more likely they will be used? Or, by writing them into the law, do we bring them under the prudent rule of societal consent and regulation, perhaps by requiring court approval of some kind or by setting down very narrow conditions? It is a paradox contained in the various proposals for an "emergency constitution" and, in homologous form, in the notorious idea of instituting torture warrants to be signed by a judge.

The proposal for special legislation to provide for the ticking bomb seems to rely on an acceptance, as does the ticking bomb fantasy itself, of the most egregious illusion of all: that torture remains uniquely successful in extracting information from prisoners. The hard-won experience of the past decade, and the measured judgment of many experienced interrogators, several of whom have spoken out, argue persuasively against this. When Lieutenant General John Kimmons, then army deputy chief of staff for intelligence, introduced the new *Army Field Manual for Human Intelligence Collection*

Operations in 2006, reporters asked him whether by prohibiting torture the manual didn't "limit the ability of interrogators to get information that could be very useful." "I am absolutely convinced," General Kimmons replied, "that the answer to your . . . question is no. No good intelligence is going to come from abusive practices. I think history tells us that. I think the empirical evidence of the last five years, hard years, tells us that."

It is good to be reminded that among other things the last decade offers a terrible experiment in torture and what it can and cannot do. We need such conclusions based on actual evidence, conclusions like that of the Senate Select Committee on Intelligence's Report on Torture, which after five years of study of six million documents concluded starkly on its first page that the "CIA's use of its enhanced interrogation techniques was not an effective means of acquiring intelligence." Why, nevertheless, does the magic effectiveness of torture, and the ticking bomb fantasy in which it is embodied, remain a persistent myth? Much popular culture built on the ticking bomb satisfies because it delivers to the fearful a calming fantasy of unlimited power and unconquerable will on the part of those charged with protecting them. In *Dirty Harry* (1971), Clint Eastwood played a rogue cop rebelling against the red tape of the police department. In *24*, Kiefer Sutherland plays a covert agent working at the orders of the president himself. In both cases, the fantasy is one of real-world toughness and common sense backed by untrammeled power sweeping away unworldly liberal strictures, and saving thereby untold numbers of innocent lives. The heroism of both consists in their willingness to act alone and to overcome moral constraints, to smash any taboo, to *do anything*, in order to protect us. Torture—lurid, morbid, darkly alluring—is a suitably dramatic touchstone of their commitment.

More than anything else, the ticking bomb is a political manifestation of a certain migrant fear. The proposed legislation to let the president use cruel, inhuman, and degrading treatment in such circumstances in effect acknowledges the source of its appeal, and the need to reassure the public that those charged with protecting them are willing to do whatever it takes and are provided with all the powers necessary to keep them safe. For if such an unlikely situation were ever to arise the real pressure to use these techniques would come not from professional interrogators but from political advisers who fear the political costs if it were revealed in the wake of such a catastrophe that the president had not done "everything within his power" to avert it. In the end torture, like much else in the state of exception, is an artifact not of our security but of our politics and our fears.

FOREVER WAR

Whenever we delve deeply into the problem of our endless state of exception we sooner or later find nestled like a Russian doll within it the problem of our endless war on terror. From its inception the war on terror has been not one thing but many, a strange hybrid beast of the imagination, part conventional war, part counterinsurgency, part quiet worldwide counterterror campaign. Under Bush, even as shooting wars in Afghanistan and Iraq deteriorated into stalemated counterinsurgencies, the quiet war of intelligence agents and special operators fighting "on the dark side" eventually moved away from secret kidnapping, detention, and torture toward "cleaner" unmanned aerial vehicles. Under Obama the beast further evolved, mutated, gradually simplified. Even as U.S. involvement in shooting wars waned, in the twilight behind them the quiet war on terror ground on, a twenty-four-hour counterterror campaign of drone strikes and special operations raids, secret, migratory, centered now in Pakistan and Yemen but inching its way into Africa. And as the tide of overt war ebbed, the contradictions of the forever war, like detritus left glistening on the beach, were laid bare.

During his second term, President Obama has been pondering these contradictions and, as is his wont, has increasingly begun putting his ponderings before the public, launching a call, during a speech at the National Defense University in May 2013, for "a larger discussion . . . about a comprehensive counterterrorism strategy." After defending his administration's reliance on drones he acknowledged that, "for all the focus on the use of force, force alone cannot make us safe." Neither drones nor special operators, he conceded, kill ideas:

> *We cannot use force everywhere that a radical ideology takes root. And in the absence of a strategy that reduces the wellspring of extremism, a perpetual war through drones or special forces or troop deployments will prove self-defeating and alter our country in troubling ways.*

Force alone will not only prove ineffective but will end by altering *us*. The danger lies not only in failing to defeat the enemy but in damaging ourselves through perpetual war. How can we avoid this, in Obama's view? First, the country must somehow move to stanch that "wellspring of extremism" by "addressing the underlying grievances and conflicts that feed extremism, from North Africa to South Asia." The president called, more than two years after the Arab Spring, for "supporting transitions to democracy in places like Egypt and Tunisia and Libya, because the peaceful realization of individual aspirations will serve as a rebuke to violent extremism." He urged supporting "the opposition in Syria, while isolating extremist elements, because the end of a tyrant must not give way to the tyranny of terrorism." And then, coming to grips with the threat of perpetual war, Obama vowed to "engage Congress about the existing Authorization for the Use of Military Force, or AUMF, to determine how we can continue to fight terrorism without keeping America on a perpetual wartime footing." He went on:

> *The AUMF is now nearly twelve years old. The Afghan War is coming to an end. Core al Qaeda is a shell of its former self. Groups like [al Qaeda in the Arabian Peninsula] must be dealt with, but in the years to come, not every collection of thugs that labels themselves al Qaeda will pose a credible threat to the United States.*

In the face of the unremitting shouts of danger that are the ground bass of the war on terror, President Obama pleaded for distinction to be made, for discrimination, for parsing which threats were credible and which were not. In the face of the angry clamor of the politics of fear, he asked for a reasonable calculation of risk. And beside this plea for action taken only after calm thinking he placed its alternative: action taken out of fear. Which is to say, not action but *re*action—and, at the end of the day, compulsion.

> *Unless we discipline our thinking, our definitions, our actions, we may be drawn into more wars we don't need to fight or continue to grant presidents unbound powers more suited for traditional armed conflicts between nation states.*

The language is striking: a failure to "discipline our thinking, our definitions, our actions" will mean we are fated to be "*drawn into more wars we don't need to fight.*" *More* wars because, in Obama's view, the country had already fought wars it didn't need to fight, most obviously in Iraq. In the absence of clear thinking and discipline, the *politics* of the broader war on terror will compel us to fight when prudence and wisdom should dictate otherwise. "We must define the nature and scope of this struggle," Obama declared, "or else it will define us." And that, the implication seemed clear, was precisely what had been happening. The struggle was *already* defining us. And the president who had been leading that struggle, the man whom the struggle was defining, was pleading with the country to come together and help him, and us, find a way out. He was pleading with us to help him escape.

It would be hard to imagine a more eloquent warning of the danger of endless war, and it would be impossible to cite a more telling example of the contradictory policy impulses that haunt the president's approach to the forever war, in which he prosecutes it and criticizes his own prosecution of it at almost the same time. In order to define the struggle and prevent its defining us, the president proposed extending Congress's oversight of "lethal actions outside of warzones," including drone strikes. He called for an increase in foreign aid. He pleaded for a new effort to close Guantánamo. And he pledged he would soon be "engaging Congress and the American people in efforts to refine and ultimately repeal the AUMF's mandate." Set against his broader argument to "define the struggle" this last was crucial: the war would no longer define us because together the president and Congress would fashion an end to it. We need no longer fear the president's "unbound powers" because we together would act to limit them. The course ahead was clear, the vow unambiguous.

And in the wake of this eloquence and determination . . . nothing. The CIA resisted, successfully, several efforts to increase oversight of the drone program. Instead of increasing foreign aid, as the president had demanded, his administration slightly reduced it. And most striking, the president took nearly two years to "engage" with Congress or the American people on the Authorization for Use of Military Force, years during which the Egyptian experiment in democracy collapsed in a military coup, the Libyan revolution foundered in violence and anarchy, and the Islamic State rose amid the chaos of Syria's civil war and the repression of Iraq's Sunnis. In the event, the administration proposed a new authorization only in February 2015, eight months into its new campaign to "degrade and ultimately destroy" the Islamic State.

Why did Obama's eloquent warning produce not the promised effort "to refine and ultimately repeal the AUMF's mandate" but, for the better part of two years, only silence? Perhaps because his voice, heard only faintly and intermittently against the enormous grinding roar of a national security bureaucracy engaged in a permanent war on terror, was an exceedingly lonely one. That roar was well represented by the assistant secretary of defense for special operations and low-intensity conflict, who, days before the president spoke, told the Senate Armed Services Committee that the war on terror was "going to go on for quite a while . . . beyond the second term of the president . . . at least ten to twenty years." "Welcome," as one commentator put it, "to America's Thirty Years War." Indeed it might go on longer, with its geographic scope no more limited than its duration. Pressed by incredulous senators, Pentagon officials declared that the authorization gave them power to target terrorist threats "from Boston to the FATA" (Pakistan's Federally Administered Tribal Areas) and would cover fighting in Syria and "boots on the ground in the Congo."

Striking as it was to see Pentagon officials assert that the authorization had given them the power to use force anywhere in the world into the indefinite future, it was more striking to watch duly elected senators express shock and surprise at the scope of a war that many of them had voted into existence, as if they stood powerless in the face of the monster they had created. This authority, noted Senator John McCain, "has grown way out of proportion and is no longer applicable to the conditions that prevailed, that motivated the United States Congress to pass the authorization" back in 2001. Senator McCain found it "well, disturbing" that the officials would "come here and say we don't need to change it or revise or update it." Senator Angus King spoke more bluntly: "You guys have essentially rewritten the Constitution here," he declared to the Pentagon officials. "Under your reading we've granted unbelievable powers to the president and it's a very dangerous precedent." Dangerous perhaps, but to senators quite understandable: "I don't blame you," as McCain said, "because basically you've got carte blanche as to what you are doing around the world."

It made perfect sense, in other words, that Pentagon officials would prefer no change to a war authority that is interpreted to give them power to operate anywhere in the world far into the indefinite future. Senators express shock at this expansive interpretation of the military's powers even as they profess themselves powerless to limit them. The president who the following week asserted we must "define the nature and scope of this struggle or else it will define us" and who vowed to "engage Congress and the American people" to "refine and ultimately repeal" the authorization in fact did nothing. More than a year would pass before his counterterrorism adviser could be heard, in July 2014, calling for "a potentially narrowed version" of the AUMF that would "allow us to go after and address emerging terrorist threats that may not come under this current 2001 authority." Instead of repealing the authorization, in other words, his administration was now suggesting expanding it. Instead of taking action that would allow the country to get off its "permanent war footing," the administration was suggesting asking Congress to bless its perpetuation.

In the event no legislation was brought forward until February 2015, nearly two years after the president's speech and five months after he had announced a new campaign of air strikes and military trainers to "degrade and ultimately destroy" the Islamic State. The sixty-word authorization from September 2001 still serves as the legal foundation on which the state of exception rests. Those sixty words, despite complaints from president and Congress alike that they are dated and inadequate, go on supplying the oxygen that allows the state of exception to breathe, authorizing a war on unbounded battlefields around the world against enemies who are not even named—the Pentagon's list of al Qaeda's "associated forces" remains classified—but many of whom did not yet exist when the authorization was voted into law. As for those "nations, organizations, or persons" who "planned, authorized, committed or aided the terrorist attacks that occurred on September 11, 2001" against whom the Congress authorized the president "to use all necessary and appropriate force," it has long been clear that officials would consider not even their complete destruction a fulfillment of the authorization and thus an ending to the war. As far back as December 2011, U.S. counterterrorism and intelligence officials announced to *The Washington Post* that "the organization that brought us 9/11" had been rendered "operationally ineffective," with "the leadership ranks of the main al-Qaeda terrorist network . . . reduced to just two figures whose demise would mean the group's defeat." Asked what survives of al Qaeda's leadership beyond these, the official's reply was stark: "Not very much." Lest this success be taken as a sign the war might be nearing its successful end, U.S. officials "stressed that al-Qaeda's influence extends far beyond its operational reach, meaning that the terrorist group will remain a major security threat for years."

To which one might reasonably ask: How many years? Given that his national security officials hold "a broad consensus that [counterterrorism] operations are likely to be extended at least another decade," according to *The Washington Post*, and that in any event "no clear end is in sight . . . The United States has reached only the midpoint of what was once known as the global war on terrorism," Obama's silence following his National Defense University speech seems less of a mystery. Just who beyond the president himself, at least in one of his guises, and the odd speechwriter have any interest "to define the scope and nature of this struggle" before "it defines us"? After all, "engaging" Congress on narrowing or repealing the authorization would present the president with a political Gordian knot. Republicans, many of whom demand a stronger military response to the Islamic State, mostly prefer to broaden the authorization. Democrats, concerned about the endlessly expanding scope of the war, mostly prefer to narrow or repeal it. The president's eventual attempt to thread the needle by proposing an authorization limited to three years that would forbid "enduring offensive ground combat operations" against the Islamic State "or associated persons or forces" pleased neither. Republicans chafed at the three-year limit and the apparent bar on sending in ground troops. Democrats espied in that vague word "enduring" a loophole through which ground forces might be redeployed to Iraq or even Syria. Pleasing no one, the proposal was dead on arrival.

No matter; its failure left what seemed to many in the national security bureaucracy a more palatable alternative: the mostly free hand provided by the administration's spacious interpretation of the present authorization, however ancient it may be, which sees the war as a matter of decades, not years. The National Security Strategy, unveiled in February 2015, speaks of "a generational struggle" under way in the Middle East "in the aftermath of the 2003 Iraq war and the 2011 Arab uprisings" and it has become increasingly clear since Obama's cautionary speech that the American national security elite has come to see the war on terror in precisely such "generational" terms. General Martin Dempsey, then chairman of the Joint Chiefs of Staff, speaks of "this threat" of terrorism as "probably a 30-year issue." Senator McCain sees "a generational fight for civilization against brutal enemies." CIA director John Brennan also speaks in millennial terms: "It's a long war, unfortunately," he said. "But it's been a war that has been in existence for millennia." Though the National Security Strategy in its stated vow that "the United States—not our adversaries—will define the nature and scope of this struggle, lest it define us" echoes Obama's warning, the nation's leaders, in shaping "a comprehensive counterterrorism strategy," seem to have drawn from the president's words a quite different lesson. In defining the war on terror as boundless, apocalyptic, and unceasing, we have indeed let it define us, as ideological crusaders caught in an endless war.

SENSE OF AN ENDING

Behind the hyped-up ideological fervor, the war on terror goes poorly indeed. During 2014, according to U.S. government figures, 32,727 people died in terrorist attacks worldwide. In 2002, the first full year of President Bush's war on terror, 725 were killed. In other words, during the dozen years that the United States has been fighting its war on terror deaths from terrorism have grown by more than 4,000 percent. As recently as 2010, Barack Obama's first full year as president, 13,186 were killed. In 2014 alone the number of deaths grew by 83 percent over the year before and the number of attacks grew by 39 percent. The number of terrorist groups committing attacks also grew dramatically—thirty-three more in 2014—as did their collective membership, notably that of the Islamic State, which is estimated by the State Department to number as many as 31,500. According to a RAND study, between 2010 and 2013 the number of Salafi jihadist groups grew by 58 percent and the number of jihadists more than doubled. The answer to Rumsfeld's question of whether we are "capturing, killing or deterring and dissuading more terrorists every day than the *madrassas* and the radical clerics are recruiting, training and deploying against us" would seem to be a resounding no. The real question is whether in the war on terror the United States has managed to conjure a terrorist-creating machine.

Terror, as always, is opportunistic, preying on instability, often on the very instability the war on terror created. Sixty-three percent of the 13,463 attacks came in Iraq, Syria, Pakistan, Afghanistan, Nigeria, and India. Two invasions a dozen years ago and their follow-on effects in neighboring states have become prodigious terrorist-generating engines that show no signs of slowing. The 2003 invasion of Iraq has helped produce what increasingly looks like a failed state straddling the major line dividing Shia and Sunni in the Middle East, adding enormous centrifugal force to a sectarian conflict raging throughout the region. The century-old Sykes-Picot order is tottering: in 2014, in an operation touted as "The Breaking of the Borders" the black-hooded militants of the Islamic State obliterated with great fanfare the border the diplomats had secretly drawn during World War I to divide the new nations of Iraq and Syria. Now intractable wars have engulfed not only those two states but Yemen and, increasingly, Libya. In at least three of these conflicts the hand of the United States has been strong; in none has it been stabilizing.

If any law governs the grand strategy of the war on terror, it is the law of unintended consequences. More than a dozen years on that law continues its rule. Cloaked in intermittent secrecy and obscured by a fog of millenarian ideology, propelled more by the force of its own inertia than by a persuasive strategy of achievable goals, the war on terror grinds on. In Afghanistan, though the high tide of American involvement is long past, an increasingly defensive war against a resurgent Taliban sputters ahead. In Iraq, four years after the last American soldier left, a few thousand have returned to advise the hollowed-out Iraqi army in its campaign against the Islamic State, adding, to the open-ended drone campaigns in Pakistan, Yemen, Somalia, and now Libya, an open-ended bombing and drone war in Iraq and Syria.

Amid the rising chaos born of the war on terror it is important to point out the number of Americans who died in terrorist attacks in 2014: twenty-four. Not one of those deaths came in the United States. This is four fewer than the twenty-eight Americans who on average have died each year from terrorism since September 11. Amid all the carnage the number of Americans killed each year by terrorists is fewer than the number of Americans killed by lightning. During the darkest moments of the Iraq War President Bush was given to argue that we must "fight them over there so we don't have to fight them here." Can one argue convincingly that tens of thousands must die from terror around the world each year for Americans to live in safety? If one cannot, it would seem at least to raise the question, quite as fundamental as Rumsfeld's, whether much of the worldwide apparatus of the war on terror, the multiple wars overt and covert and the state of exception of torture and detention and surveillance that shadows them, has been self-defeating, producing an immense amount of instability and chaos and, as its most significant achievement beyond these, its own perpetuation.

Must that achievement go uncontested? Though the number of terrorist attacks has risen dramatically, almost all of those attacks are directed not at Americans but at one "near enemy" or another, part of a sharply rising struggle within the Muslim world itself. True, the threat of terror within the United States has not gone away. Another attack could come at any time. Indeed, as we have seen it is quite possible that the damage done to the central organization of al Qaeda and the rise of the Islamic State makes the success of a lone-wolf attack more likely. San Bernardino showed how easy it is for such an attack, especially if directed at a "soft target," to succeed. But can the possibility of such an attack and the efforts organized to prevent it be called, in any reasonable sense, a war? Is this not a containable threat? Will not terrorism of some kind always be with us? Could not our intelligence and law enforcement organizations, dramatically expanded and empowered as they have been since September 11, once again be given primary responsibility for preventing terrorist attacks? And when necessary would not the president's own inherent powers to defend the nation and its Constitution, his so-called Article II powers, serve to respond militarily to specific threats?

Given the numbers such a suggestion might seem impracticable, even reckless. There is, after all, the Islamic State to confront, a terror state that boasts tens of thousands of fighters. But is the essential problem here really one of terrorism? Behind the air strikes and the fighting in cities and towns of Iraq and Syria, beneath the armed struggles that ebb and flow, lie intractable political conflicts about voice and representation that go back a century and more. Contemplating the collapse of the traditional Middle East order in the wake of the Iraq War, one thinks of Hitler's misbegotten prophecy about the Soviet Union: "We have only to kick in the door and the whole rotten structure will come crashing down." In invading Iraq and wresting power away from the Sunni minority there the hapless United States kicked in the door and the whole rotten structure of the post–World War I Sykes-Picot order began to come crashing down, setting in train a complex regional struggle that may well go on for decades. Today in Iraq and Syria two confessional bloodbaths—two chronic Yugoslavias—rage and bleed side by side, complete with ethnic cleansing, mass murder, foreign fighters, and with the Islamic State forming a kind of vortex of instability straddling their common border. On one side American warplanes and drones support an Iraqi government with its Iranian-trained militias, on the other they oppose a Syrian government allied with Iranian-backed fighters. Hundreds of thousands have died, millions have been left homeless. No end is in sight.

The bloody apocalyptic whirlpool of Iraq and Syria has become, as then Secretary of State Warren Christopher once said of Yugoslavia, the "problem from hell." But again, is it really a problem of terrorism? On both sides of that imposed border, states that were artificially created threaten to violently break apart along sectarian and ethnic lines. Though the Islamic State descends fairly directly from the terrorist group founded by Abu Musab al-Zarqawi early in the American occupation, a dozen years, seven incarnations, and four leaders later it has evolved into something quite different. The Islamic State may still dispatch suicide bombers into Baghdad and other cities but now it also dispatches tanks and armored personnel carriers into battle in the struggle to occupy cities and towns. The Islamic State wages conventional military campaigns, governs millions of people. Though governments may go on classing it as a terrorist group, the Islamic State is surely something more: pseudo-state, proto-state, para-state maybe, but in any event closer to the state it claims to be. And its existence is inextricable from the complex foreign policy conundrum represented by the deteriorating states of Iraq and Syria at the heart of an increasingly unstable and sectarian Middle East.

It goes without saying that the United States, which has been the status quo power "east of Suez" since 1945, will use all the tools of state power to confront and manage this conundrum, including diplomacy, economic pressure, and, when it deems necessary, military force—though, regarding this last, perhaps it would be the beginning of strategic wisdom to recognize as a major lesson of the last dozen years that liberal applications of violence by the imperial superpower, given the ideology of the multinational jihadist insurgency, risk counterproductive and uncontrollable effects. If the region has indeed entered an "era of persistent conflict," as it seems to have done, if the Islamic State is only the vanguard of an ongoing jihadist insurgency within the Muslim world, as it seems to be, then what is needed from the United States is a broader approach born of statesmanship, patience, and judgment, a disciplined and minimalist conception of its true national interests, a recognition that its ability to manage that conflict without worsening it is distinctly limited, and a consequent determination to make sparing use of its military power, and only on those limited occasions when it might actually be expected to do some good. Subsuming a campaign of aerial bombardment intended to help "degrade and ultimately destroy" the Islamic State in an ill-defined, ramshackle, and far-flung war on terror of fourteen years' standing contributes neither to effective policy nor to meaningful oversight. Bombing the Islamic State because it seems the next logical step in a self-perpetuating war on terror is to adopt a tactic, which itself has had mixed results at best, in the absence of a strategy.

It might be the beginning of the end of the confusion obscuring American policy in the war on terror if President Obama took steps to do what he proposed in May 2013: engage "Congress and the

American people in efforts to refine and ultimately repeal the [present] AUMF's mandate." A true "engagement" with Congress and the public might begin with the president setting out clearly and specifically where, in the administration's view, the United States must currently be free to deploy military force, for what purpose, and for how long. It might continue with an open debate, with hard questions asked about whether a campaign of air strikes is really the best way to contain the Islamic State and its spreading ideology. And it might end with replacing the open-ended and obsolete 2001 authorization, as well as the 2002 authorization for the Iraq War, with one that approves the use of force, were Congress so convinced, as it sets out clearly what American bombing is intended to achieve, against whom it is directed and where and for how long, and suggesting how one might know when those goals had been met. Such a new authorization, in other words, would govern not only the present use of force but envision its ending. The terms of the authorization might flow from broader strategic concepts like containment and deterrence that have served the country well in protracted conflicts in the past, replacing "degrade and destroy" with "contain and deter" as the broader goal of U.S. policy. What the authorization would not do is approve an open-ended use of military force against scores of unnamed terrorist groups around the world.

The practical consequences of such a shift, were it actually held to, could be dramatic. In effect, it might begin to return military force to the president's toolkit to be used only in defending the country from truly imminent attack. It could also begin to contain the war on terror's present amoebalike sprawl. In order to mount a military attack under the president's Article II powers the administration would presumably have to have clear evidence of an imminent threat to the homeland. No more use of drones to decimate distant terrorist organizations by killing low-level militants. No more targeting unidentified militants simply because their behavior conforms to a pre-defined "signature" of terrorist activity. No more repeated attacks on distant groups unless they pose an imminent and demonstrable threat to American lives. The expanding war on terror embodied in unceasing drone and special operations campaigns in a half dozen countries would come to an end.

Even suggesting such a radical transition raises many hard questions. One of the hardest is how to redefine the paramilitary role that the intelligence agencies have taken on since 9/11, so that military tasks that had been limited by the new authorization would not simply be shifted to practitioners on "the dark side." On its face such redefinition would be simple, for it lies within the prerogative of the president himself: he need only issue a new Memorandum of Notification, or Finding, to in effect replace the fourteen-page document that President Bush signed on September 17, 2001. But the institutional struggles involved in limiting the CIA's vastly expanded role, and its greatly strengthened political power, would be brutal and the implications could be grave. Indeed, given that at any time a successful Islamic terrorist attack on American soil could bring on a surge of the politics of fear at home, the political risks for any leader even beginning to undertake a transition out of the war on terror would be great indeed, so great that insofar as such a change would be sure to be portrayed as a return to the pre-9/11 world, and to the dreaded law-enforcement model, it will likely remain a political nonstarter. For a president there are worse things than being at war. As far back as President Bush's second term, Pentagon officials recognized that the term "war on terror" was unhelpful in dealing with local populations in Muslim countries, who regarded it as a war against Islam. Officials proposed replacing the time-honored global war on terror—known in the acronym-addicted Department of Defense as GWOT—with GSAVE, the Global Struggle Against Violent Extremism. The effort began with a change in documents and stationery but was finally halted when President Bush, no matter what memos he received, went on using the war on terror as his rallying cry. For his part, President Obama tends to avoid the phrase, which led his political adversaries to claim his preference showed his lack of seriousness about national security. "It's one thing to adopt the euphemisms that suggest we're no longer at war," said Dick Cheney in May 2009. "Just remember it is a serious step to begin unraveling some of the very policies that have kept our people safe since 9/11." Such statements of course are meant not only as a critique of present policy but a predicate of blame for what tragedy might strike in the future, and they make any decision to appear to let up in prosecuting the war, let alone to declare it at an end, politically perilous.

EXCEPTIONAL BECOMES NORMAL

After all his warnings about defining the war lest it define us, President Obama finds himself alighting on the status quo as the least unattractive option. We go on with our endless war and our unending state of exception. The president has mostly stripped away the politically costly "boots on the ground" conventional wars in favor of his "light footprint," a far-flung anti-terror campaign built of drone strikes and Special Operations Forces raids, to which the air campaign in Iraq and Syria has now been added. Even as the president denounces the specter of "perpetual war," the war machinery whirs along around him and his administration makes plans for precisely that. There is, for example, the "disposition matrix," which, *The Washington Post* told us in late 2012, "the Obama administration has been secretly developing [as] a new blueprint for pursuing terrorists, a next-generation targeting list" and high-tech database that "goes beyond existing kill lists," and to which "the government expects to continue adding names . . . for years." The disposition matrix is a perfect symbol of that "other Obama," the one who, though troubled by the prospect of perpetual war, is troubled more by what seem to be the risks of truly ending it. Bemoan as he might the perpetual war, he has determined to armor himself against the politics of fear, and the result has been a state of exception regularized, legitimized, normalized.

One can't help but be reminded of another forever war, the endless shape-shifting struggle fought within the covers of the novel *Nineteen Eighty-Four* between the superpowers of Oceania, Eurasia, and East Asia in what was then a distant future. Of this endless struggle, Orwell wrote,

> *If we judge it by the standards of previous wars, it is merely an imposture like the battle between certain ruminant animals whose horns are set at such an angle that they are incapable of hurting one another. But though it is unreal, it is not meaningless. It helps to preserve the special mental atmosphere that a hierarchical society needs.*

The war on terror is not an imposture. We have seen tanks, artillery, infantry divisions. Though these have largely departed the scene, we know that beyond our ken drones are striking and special operators are raiding. People are dying. But alongside this invisible war stand the ghostly political benefits that Orwell has in mind. War produces fear. But so too does the rhetoric of war. As terrorism's ultimate product is not death or mayhem but fear, the rich political benefits of that most lucrative of political emotions will ultimately be shared, between the terrorists who create it and the political leaders who conduct the fight against them and who, more often than not, attempt to exploit that fear to their own advantage.

For the politician, however, the benefits can be fleeting indeed. We should recall here the true purpose of the "politics of the worst": to instigate "an escalatory spiral," one whose momentum is controlled by the terrorists, not by those who seek to destroy them. To the political leader, this spiral may seem to offer power and political leverage but in the end it may well escape control, for it is governed by reaction, not wise and considered action. As we have seen, such a spiral may lead to policies that, however powerful and dramatic they seem, corrupt our values and undermine our interests. Writing of *Nineteen Eighty-Four*, the literary critic Irving Howe remarked that

> The book appalls us because its terror, far from being inherent in the human condition, is particular to our century. What haunts us is the sickening awareness that in 1984, Orwell has seized upon those elements of our public life that, given courage and intelligence, were avoidable.

Certainly we are not living in anything like the totalitarian state painted so vividly in *Nineteen Eighty-Four*, but we do find ourselves in a parallel situation particular to our new century: under the influence of a worldwide war on terror unbounded in space and time, trapped in a state of exception the end of which we cannot see. And surely those scenes from the black sites are, as Howe said of the world of *Nineteen Eighty-Four*, "elements of our public life that, given courage and intelligence, were avoidable." What it took to avoid them at the time was, indeed, courage and intelligence. We did not get these from our leaders.

The politics of fear was used to great advantage during the Bush years, and its influence remains strongly with us. In the event of another devastating attack it may well grow stronger. Perhaps, with diligence and wise policy and a good bit of luck, we will be able to avoid this. I hope so. For when I hear the former vice president speak of the necessity of torture and criticize as foolish and reckless those who renounce its use, I hear the distant stirrings of that whirlwind.

In the end it is the power of the politics of fear that keeps us imprisoned in the state of exception. It is easier to let stand or expand a fourteen-year-old authorization for the use of military force than it is to repeal it. In the end it is impossible to legislate courage and intelligence in our public life. But only with these can we avoid being swept deeper into that cycle of fear if and when the next attack comes. Meanwhile the one element that since ancient Rome all states of exception have shared—that they come to an end—remains wanting in ours. In this forever war, what was the exceptional has become the normal. The improvisations of panic are the reality of our daily lives.

AFTERWORD

Nothing has changed.
The body shudders as it shuddered
Before the founding of Rome and after,
In the twentieth century before and after Christ.
Tortures are as they were, it's just the earth that's grown smaller,
And whatever happens seems right on the other side of the wall.

—"Tortures," by Wisława Szymborska (1986)

Nearly fifteen years after the attacks of September 11, the question is whether nothing has changed or everything has. We remain in a state of exception that has acquired the character of the barely noticed day-to-day. Indefinite detention, extrajudicial killing, warrantless surveillance, and other practices once unthinkable remain quietly accepted weapons in an endless war. As candidates fight to gain the White House, the cycle of the politics of fear accelerates. "We're already in World War III," one candidate declared after two gunmen in San Bernardino, California, killed fourteen people. "Radical Islamic jihadists everyday are trying to . . . destroy our way of life." A second demanded we "carpet bomb them into oblivion" until we "see if sand can glow in the dark." A third—the leading candidate—demanded torture. "Would I bring back waterboarding?" he shouted to the jubilant cheers of the crowd. "You bet your ass I would. . . . It works. And even if it doesn't work they deserve it anyway for what they do to us." Thousands roared their approval.

The dynamic of the politics of fear embodies itself more vividly in each successive news cycle. Each attack heightens the fevered demand for action. Each act of violence brings calls for greater violence in response: carpet bombing, invasion, torture. The politics of fear, set off by a relatively modest attack, leads quickly toward the escalatory spiral. Standing between that spiral and us is the current president, who insists, in a voice that seems to grow ever fainter, that terrorists, however frightening, do "not represent an existential threat." Could that voice prevail in the face of a larger death toll—a lone-wolf attack that killed thirty? Or a Paris-style commando assault that killed a hundred? The political pressure to respond would be irresistible.

The country is already bombing the Islamic State; what comes next? One recalls that the main goal of jihadist forces, as set out in Abu Bakr Naji's tract, *The Management of Savagery,* is to "Force America to abandon its war against Islam by proxy and force it to attack directly." Drawing American troops in their thousands to fight again on Muslim land is the ultimate strategic goal of both the Islamic State and al Qaeda. The cycle of fear, revivified by even the smallest attacks, forces American politics inexorably in that direction. What would be the consequence of a successful bombing that killed scores or even hundreds of Americans weeks before the election? Could such an attack ensure the election of the hardest of hard-liners? Could the jihadists by their actions determine who is elected America's president? Why not? The cycle of fear puts our politics in their hands.

· · · · ·

What of the flip side of the forever war, the unending state of exception? After all the revelations about torture, is it conceivable that a new president might reinstitute it? The tumultuous reception of the voluminous executive summary of the Senate Select Committee on Intelligence torture report in December 2014, with former CIA officials vigorously denouncing its findings and insisting that torture was necessary to save "thousands of lives," and Republican lawmakers cheering them on, showed vividly that a decade of controversy has made torture a bitterly partisan issue. The Senate report is the most thorough study of CIA torture ever compiled, and its 549-page executive summary is singularly damning, depicting in stomach-turning detail a netherworld of brutal black sites where "individuals were so sensory deprived, i.e., constant white noise, no talking, everyone in the dark, with the guards wearing a light on their head when they collected and escorted a detainee to an interrogation cell, detainees constantly being shackled to the wall or floor, and the starkness of each cell (concrete and bars)." The horrors depicted on page after page are revolting, and yet the executive summary's release provoked a clamor that included scores of voices raised in support of torture, including many who denounced the report by insisting torture "saved thousands of lives"—even as we read in the report itself how the CIA lawyers suggested, before the program came into being, precisely this argument as the "necessity" defense to shield it from legal scrutiny. In a sense, nearly a decade after the last prisoner was waterboarded, we remain trapped within the torture program itself.

How to escape back to legality? Certainly not by "looking forward and not back." Rendering justice implies looking backward. But the political costs of the sort of justice provided even by a Truth Commission, let alone prosecution of interrogators and public officials, has proven far too great for a society living under the politics of fear. Prosecutions, if they ever come, will not come for many years. A return to legality will proceed only in fits and starts, and only after the politics of fear loosens its grip on the public—when, and if, it does. For the state of exception to come to an end, so must the conflict that has been its lifeblood. "This war, like all wars, must end"— so declared the president in May 2013. In the years since, the war has expanded, creeping beyond Pakistan and Afghanistan and Yemen and Somalia back to Iraq and now to Syria and perhaps Libya. The tools of the war are not George W. Bush's infantry divisions and "shock and awe" bombing campaigns but instead the signature "light footprint" perfected by Barack Obama: drone attacks, Special Operations raids, bombing campaigns. Military advisers have returned to Iraq, and special operators are at work in Syria. The wars of September 11 go on.

What can move this "multigenerational struggle" toward its end? The beginning of an end, as discussed above, might be the replacement of the two obsolete Authorizations for Use of Military Force, one voted a few days after September 11, the second passed the following fall to approve the Iraq War, with more restrictive provisions that would allow for the use of force against specific enemies in specific countries for a stated length of time. If indeed it is in the national interest of the United States to conduct sustained hostilities with the Islamic State, then the administration should persuade Congress explicitly to approve such use of force and the same should be true of other descendant organizations of al Qaeda. A new authorization should include the organizations to be targeted, the geographic boundaries of the struggle, and its duration. A sunset clause should require not necessarily the conclusion of the war but a new effort by the administration, or a succeeding one, to persuade Congress and the public that the hostilities must be continued. In the case of terrorist organizations that do not normally threaten the United States directly, the president's Article II powers should be sufficient to allow him to act to protect the country in case of a specific threat.

It is the job of the president to devise policy that promotes the national interest and it is within that broader conception that the use of military force should play its part. During the war on terror organized violence has too often come to serve as a stand-in for the nation's broader foreign policy across the Middle East, South Asia, and the Horn of Africa. Too often violent tactics, including killing terrorists, have supplanted strategic policies that should make use of all the constituents of national power to reduce long-term support for them and their organizations. Comparing the world of today with that of 2001, the self-defeating consequences of American military violence stand out with stark clarity.

In the Middle East, the imperial order presided over by Great Britain and France after World War I and by the United States after World War II is collapsing. Iraq and Syria have imploded and the Islamic State's triumphant bulldozing of the Sykes-Picot border between them in June 2014 only added characteristically flamboyant ceremony to a reality already well established: the borders drawn by France and British diplomats a century ago, and many of the confected states within them, are vanishing. Regime change across the region had brought not stability and democratic accountability but strengthened sectarian identities and badly weakened states. As historian Robert Kaplan writes,

> *The fall of Saddam Hussein in Iraq, Muammar al-Qaddafi in Libya, and the reduction of Bashar al-Assad's regime in Syria to that of an embattled statelet has ended the era of post-colonial strongmen, whose rule was organically connected to the legacy of imperialism. After all, those dictators ruled according to the borders erected by the Europeans. And because those imperial borders did not often configure with ethnic or sectarian ones, those dictatorial regimes required secular identities in order to span communal divides. All this has been brutally swept away.*

American policymakers face a conundrum: How to remain the status quo power in a region in which the status quo is being destroyed? The United States of a different era might have stepped in and tried to prop up tottering rulers in the interest of the status quo. But the U.S. intervention in Iraq, a promised cakewalk that turned into a grinding and seemingly endless counterinsurgency, had destroyed the patience of the American public for full-on intervention. Instead, Americans, exhausted by one unfinished war in Iraq and a second in Afghanistan, went on to elect a president who denounced "dumb wars" and promised to end them, and then mostly stood back and watched as the region-wide order they had presided over for seven decades fell to pieces. It marked, claims Kaplan, "the end of America's great power role in organizing and stabilizing the region." If this proves true, the irony is that that role came to an end only after the Bush administration's audacious and wrongheaded attempt to "organize and stabilize" the Middle East through creative destabilization.

In any event that role, and the imperial order it sustained, will not soon return. What will replace it? Drones and Special Operations Forces cannot substitute for active statesmanship and diplomacy. Too often since September 11 they have served as stopgaps when foreign policy conundrums seemed insoluble. Thus it has been in Afghanistan, when the problem of Pakistan, a supposed American ally that actively sheltered both the Taliban and al Qaeda, has proved intransigent, and thus it has been in Iraq and Syria, where damnably complex political problems involving multifaceted sectarian antagonisms have resisted the efforts of American diplomacy.

Resolving the conflict in Syria is certainly not a matter of drones and air strikes. A solution, or at least a more stable status quo, will likely emerge only as part of a new geopolitical order in the Middle East. What should that order look like? To answer that question one must begin with another: What are America's interests in the Middle East? The Carter Doctrine warned that any "attempt by an outside force to gain control of the Persian Gulf region will be regarded as an assault on the vital interests of the United States" and will be "repelled by any means necessary." But this dates from 1980, after the Soviets had invaded Afghanistan. Today American troops garrison that country and the Soviet Union no longer exists. The region is threatened not by "outside forces" but by its own chaotic internal struggles. Is it truly in America's vital interest to attempt to dominate and guide these? More likely, in the years ahead the United States will increasingly exchange its traditional imperial role for that of offshore balancer, working with and through proxies on the ground and the larger states of the region, including not just its longtime allies in Saudi Arabia and Turkey but strategic competitors like Iran. No return to stability in Syria, or in Iraq, is possible without the cooperation, tacit or explicit, of the Islamic Republic of Iran. This is a geopolitical fact born of the Bush administration's decision to invade Iraq and deliver power to the Shia majority, and it is no accident that such tacit cooperation is already taking shape, as American air strikes support the efforts of Iranian-led Shia militias in their battles against the Islamic State.

Crafting a new regional framework that on the one hand will help Saudi Arabia and other traditional Sunni allies push back against Iranian ambitions and on the other will create space for working out perhaps tacit agreements to bring a new stable status quo in Syria and Iraq will be the challenge of American diplomacy in the coming decade. These are damnable political problems, and immensely complicated; but drones and Special Operations Forces are not the solution. Statecraft must be. That political problems must be recognized and dealt with as such is not only the wise course. It is the necessary one, not least because Americans, given the experience of the last dozen years, are unlikely soon again to countenance a large-scale use of force in the Middle East or South Asia. Barack Obama owes his rise to this reluctance: as a political phenomenon he was a creation of the failed war in Iraq. That he represents a pervasive opinion not only among the broader public was reinforced by Obama's first secretary of defense and George W. Bush's last, Robert Gates, who remarked in early 2011 that "any future defense secretary who advises the president to again send a big American land army into Asia or the Middle East or Africa should 'have his head examined.'"

Obama's counterterror light footprint of drones and special operators was in part an answer to this political fact, for it helped make it possible to wind down the shooting wars and place the forever war firmly in the background of most Americans' daily concerns. In the shadows, though, the war has thrived, fed on itself. The time has long passed when we must act to bring it to an end. It is not only a matter of national interest but of moral imperative, for only with the forever war's ending can the state of exception come to an end. As I have argued in these pages, the forever war and the state of exception are two sides of the same coin. Joining them together is a deep belief in American exceptionalism, in the role of the United States as a crusading country in which goodness and right naturally inhere—and to which the rules apply only when they seem to be in the American self-interest. No matter how often or how egregiously we violate those rules, after all, it won't alter "who we are."

At no time more than the last decade and a half have the paradoxes of these deeply held beliefs been on more vivid display. It is not only that the United States has believed itself free to invade a sovereign country—to fight a war of choice—against the will of the international community. It has seen its justification, here as so often, in its own professed good intentions. The crude practicalities of national interest must be gilded with missionary zeal. As the aftermath of the Iraq War has shown, it is Americans more than others who seem to find themselves blinded by these attitudes. It is why Obama's admonition to "look forward, not backward" strikes precisely the wrong note. Only by looking backward with a clear gaze, only by retracing the road that led us here—paved as it was, as it always is, with good intentions—can we hope to understand our current pass. Only by looking backward can we hope to move fully into a future free of the state of exception and the moral entanglements of American exceptionalism.

· · · · ·

When in the late 1970s I first came to take an interest in human rights, it was the time of the dirty wars in South and Central America, of death squads and paramilitaries, clandestine torture chambers and secret cemeteries for the disappeared. The task of those working for the advancement of human rights, it was thought, was to reveal these atrocities, to bring them to the light of day where the public would be forced to gaze on them in appalled horror and demand they be stopped. Revelation of this wrongdoing would lead inexorably to credible investigation and then expiation in the form of indictments and truth commissions and, perhaps, trials and prison sentences. Even a bloody military-imposed state of emergency had to come to an end. Even if the moral reckoning took a long time, the reckoning would come.

Perhaps such a moment will come in the United States but there are as yet few signs of it. The policies that President George W. Bush developed and ordered in the wake of the attacks of September 11, 2001, and that President Barack Obama perpetuated and normalized after 2008, have attained a quiet acceptance. In a political landscape still shadowed by the politics of fear, Barack Obama has made himself the president of the state of exception. It would be comforting to write that this peculiar dynamic is partly owed to ignorance. If only the American public *knew*. But in fact the public does know. Widespread warrantless surveillance, Guantánamo, assassination by drone, the use of torture: all have been extensively investigated and hotly debated. Human Rights Watch, the American Civil Liberties Union, Human Rights First, and many other organizations have acquired and made public tens of thousands of documents and compiled definitive reports based on what they reveal. Since the photographs of Abu Ghraib were broadcast in the spring of 2004, legions of articles and books on torture have been published. And what has been the result? Of our two mainstream political parties, one has developed and promulgated a clear position on what it insists on calling "enhanced interrogation techniques": it is for them. If the last decade has proved anything, it is that there is plenty of room in the American political empyrean for one president who ordered the use of waterboarding and goes on vigorously defending it and a second who denounced it but does nothing to punish its use.

So the emphasis on knowledge and proof that greeted me as a college student coming upon the human rights realm has been shown to be, in the United States in the state of exception, at the least problematic. The idea that the job of human rights workers and journalists and their colleagues was to tear off the veil concealing the horror and that good citizens, once convinced by real evidence that those controlling their government are committing human rights abuses, would exert growing political pressure to stop them, seems to have been proved wrong. What if you tear off the veil and no one gasps, no one cringes, no one even blinks? What if, apart from a handful, the public mostly yawns and turns the channel?

The poet is certainly right when she tells us that "the body shudders as it shuddered / Before the founding of Rome and after." When it comes to the fundamentals of blood and bone nothing has changed. We have seen enough proof of this in the accounts of Abu Zubaydah and others. But what about those watching? Have we changed? Or is it that the romance of human rights has been shown to be just that? I had assumed, as a young man, that when I gazed south toward the death squads that I was looking at the workings of a different political culture, that though the American intelligence services had engineered coups and helped their allies in designing regimes of torture, nothing like that could ever be officially approved as the stated policy of the U.S. government, let alone countenanced by the American people. Americans, who mostly remain blissfully unaware of the outside world and the darker acts performed by their government to maintain the country's power, evidence on occasion a strong moral streak, most recently after the Watergate revelations of the mid-1970s and the Church Committee unveiling of the CIA's "dirty tricks" that followed.

These attitudes were worse than naive. In the main, societies convulsed by terror leave their moral convictions behind. People who commit terrorist acts do it to produce fear. Fear empowers not just terrorists but those who rise to lead the fight against them, which is why terror so often brings in its wake counterterror and why counterterror is so often embodied in the use of torture. This dynamic, which appeared with terrible clarity in Latin America during the era of the dirty wars, was recognizable in U.S. policy in the wake of the September 11 attacks. Its inertial force was powerful enough to shatter certain taboos and though the urgency has lessened and Americans have turned their eyes to other things, those taboos have not been restored. Instead, the country, under a new Democratic president, its first African American president—who never could have come to office were it not for the unpopularity of the wartime president who came before him—has settled into a quietly lethal mode of combat that relies on methods that would have been inconceivable a decade and a half ago.

Perhaps there will be a turning away from these methods—perhaps after enough time has elapsed and the fear, and the political advantages incumbent on its manipulation, have eased, there will come a questioning, and a reconsideration of some of the darker decisions taken during this last dark decade. Must not our state of exception, like all such states before it, come to an end? How can it not? On the other hand, perhaps the poet is right, perhaps it is "just the earth that's grown smaller / and whatever happens seems right on the other side of the wall." As I write, I see no sense of an ending. But I am looking—and will go on looking—hard.

—*Mark Danner*
Grizzly Peak, Berkeley
January 2016

ACKNOWLEDGMENTS

The foregoing pages, I am aware, raise more questions than they answer. This is no accident. They had their origins in a welcome invitation from John Hennessy, president of Stanford University, to come to his campus and deliver the Tanner Lectures on Human Values. The intent was to say what was vital, and provocative, on these complicated matters within the attention span of an interested audience on succeeding afternoons. The original lectures have been extensively revised but that purpose remains: to provoke debate and perhaps to help move us in some small way toward the reckoning that must come.

I wish to thank President Hennessy and the Tanner Foundation for their kind invitation, and to thank many others at Stanford for their gracious welcome. These include Provost John Etchemendy, Professors Debra Satz and Joshua Cohen, and Joan Berry. I am grateful to my respondents, Stephen Holmes, Steven Kleinman, Eric Posner, and Elaine Scarry, for their incisive and provocative comments on the lectures, and to the many Stanford students, graduate and undergraduate, who took part in the vigorous discussions that followed. Warm thanks also to my indispensable agent and friend, Joy Harris, who faithfully journeyed west to attend the lectures, and to Alice Mayhew and her colleagues at Simon & Schuster for their patience, skill, and support in preparing this book for publication. I thank Jonathan Cobb, Robert B. Silvers, and Gerald Marzorati for kindly reading and commenting on the text, and Michael Pollan and Robert Hass for invaluable encouragement on Inspiration Point and on the circuit. And I offer loving thanks to my wife, Michelle, and our children, Grace and Truman, for their patience and their faith.

Finally, I wish to thank Robert J. Cox, former editor of the *Buenos Aires Herald*. It has been many years since he and I have spoken more than a few words but I have never forgotten the lessons he taught and I still draw daily on the hope he instilled. In that spirit, and with deep gratitude, I dedicate this book to him.

NOTES

1   *"or else it will define us"*: Remarks by President Obama at the National Defense University, Fort McNair, Washington, D.C., May 23, 2013.

1   *"America must move off a permanent war footing"*: President Barack Obama's State of the Union Address, January 28, 2014.

4   *twenty-four in 2014*: Twenty-four is the State Department's official count for 2014. See Micah Zenko, "Terrorism Is Booming Almost Everywhere but the United States," *Foreign Policy*, June 19, 2015. Others insist on even lower numbers. See, for example, the comments of CNN national security analyst and terrorism expert Peter Bergen: "There are seventeen Americans who have been killed by jihadi terrorist attacks since 9/11. More people die in their bathtubs every year." Peter Bergen, *Fresh Air*, National Public Radio, July 28, 2011. *The New York Times* puts the number of Americans killed by "self-proclaimed jihadists" since 9/11 at 26, compared to 48 by "extremists who are not Muslim." Scott Shane, "Homegrown Extremists Tied to Deadlier Toll than Jihadists in U.S. Since 9/11," *New York Times*, June 24, 2015, and "Deadly Attacks Since 9/11," New America Foundation, http://securitydata.newamerica.net /extremists/deadly-attacks.html, accessed June 25, 2015.

4   *the United States' military spending . . . nearly doubled*: Dylan Matthews, "Defense Spending in the U.S., in Four Charts," *Washington Post*, August 28, 2012.

4   *its intelligence budget . . . more than doubled*: We know this only

thanks to documents made public by Edward Snowden. Ewen MacAskill and Jonathan Watts, "US Intelligence Spending Has Doubled Since 9/11, Top Secret Budget Reveals," *The Guardian,* August 29, 2013.

4   *so-called third war:* Micah Zenko, "The Long Third War," *Foreign Policy,* October 30, 2012.

4   *"degrade and ultimately destroy":* President Obama, "We Will Degrade and Ultimately Destroy ISIL," The White House, September 10, 2014.

4   *"successfully pursued in Yemen and Somalia for years":* Ibid.

5   *hastening a vast flow of foreign fighters into its ranks:* "The Islamic State jihadist organization has recruited more than 6,000 new fighters since America began targeting the group with air strikes last month, according to the U.K.-based Syrian Observatory for Human Rights." "Islamic State Recruitment Soaring in Wake of U.S. Bombing," *Ha'aretz,* September 19, 2014.

5   *"given a one-way ticket to Guantanamo":* The speaker is Marco Rubio, though all candidates for the Republican presidential nomination evince a similar enthusiasm for making use of the Cuban prison camp. Sahil Kapur and John McCormick, "In 2016, Marco Rubio Is Both Sunny and Ominous," *Bloomberg News,* January 8, 2016.

6   *the number of deaths from terrorism . . . has soared: Country Reports on Terrorism: 2014,* U.S. Department of State, Bureau of Counterterrorism (June 2015).

6   *unofficial estimates are much higher:* See, for example, Patrick Cockburn, "Gulf State Donors Bankroll Salaries of Up to 100,000 ISIS Fighters," *Counterpunch,* February 24, 2015.

7   *established under his sole command enduring secret bureaucracies:* For a succinct summary of the construction and elaboration of the post–World War II "emergency state," see Garry Wills, *Bomb Power: The Modern Presidency and the National Security State* (New York: Penguin, 2011).

8   *"interrogation techniques . . . that are safe, legal and effective"*: Charlie
     Savage, "Election to Decide Future Interrogation Methods in
     Terrorism Cases," *New York Times,* September 27, 2012.

8   *leading Republican candidates for president in 2016 seem mostly to*
     have embraced the same position, some of them vehemently: The most
     vehement is Donald Trump: "Would I approve waterboarding?
     You bet your ass I would—in a heartbeat. And I would approve
     more that. Don't kid yourself, folks. It works, okay? It works.
     Only a stupid person would say it doesn't work." Jenna John-
     son, "Donald Trump on Waterboarding: 'If it doesn't work,
     they deserve it anyway,'" *Washington Post,* November 23, 2015.
     Though Trump has spoken out most strongly in favor of tor-
     ture, most if not all of the Republican candidates hold similar
     views. See Michael Crowley, "On torture, Cruz stands alone,"
     Politico, January 21, 2016.

9   *United Nations' Convention Against Torture:* The Convention Against
     Torture and Other Cruel, Inhuman and Degrading Treatment
     or Punishment was signed by President Reagan in 1988 and rat-
     ified by the United States Senate in 1994. The "federal statutes
     that until quite recently had been used to prosecute [torture] as
     a crime" are Title 18, Part I, Chapter 113C, of the U.S. Code, sec-
     tions 2340, 2340A, and 2340B. They define torture and provide
     for harsh punishment for anyone who commits it, including up
     to twenty years of prison or, in cases where the victim died, even
     the death penalty.

10   *"crudely written email threat"*: Hailey Branson-Potts, Stephen
     Ceasar, and Howard Blume, "L.A. Schools to Reopen Wednes-
     day; Threat Against Schools Was 'Not Credible,' Officials Say,"
     Los Angeles Times, December 15, 2015.

11   *into what has become a forever war:* I first used the phrase "for-
     ever war" more than a decade ago to describe our endless war
     on terror in a long cover essay on bin Laden and al Qaeda, "Is
     He Winning? Taking Stock of the Forever War," *New York Times*

Magazine, September 11, 2005. The phrase has also been used by former *New York Times* reporter Dexter Filkins as the title of his 2008 book on the Iraq occupation, *The Forever War.* In 2014, I learned from a student about the existence of Joe Haldeman's remarkable science fiction classic, *The Forever War,* originally published in 1974.

11 *"hopefully, we don't do it again in the future"*: Press Conference by the President, The White House, August 1, 2014.

12 *"indispensable nation"*: The phrase seems to have been first used in public to describe the United States by Madeleine Albright when she was U.S. ambassador to the United Nations. It was coined by James Chace and Sidney Blumenthal. As Blumenthal wrote, "We were able to describe the concept of the United States as the guarantor of stability as the sole superpower within the framework of multinational institutions, but I was intent on boiling it down to a phrase. Finally, together, we hit on it: 'indispensable nation.' Eureka! I passed it on first to Madeleine Albright, at the time the United Nations ambassador, and then to the president." See Sidney Blumenthal, "James Chace, 1931–2004," *The American Prospect,* October 19, 2004.

PART ONE
Bush: Imposing the Exception

13 *"our first responsibility is to live by them"*: "Transcript of President Bush's Address," CNN.com, September 21, 2001. Bush's speech was to a joint session of Congress on September 20, 2001.

16 *"constitutional dictatorship"*: Clinton Rossiter, *Constitutional Dictatorship: Crisis Government in the Modern Democracies* (New York: Transaction, 2002 [Princeton University Press, 1948]).

16 *"9/11 constitution" or an "Emergency Constitution"*: See, for example, Bruce Ackerman, *Before the Next Attack: Preserving Civil Liberties in an Age of Terrorism* (New Haven: Yale University Press,

2007), Introduction and *passim*. See also Cass R. Sunstein, "The 9/11 Constitution," *The New Republic*, January 16, 2006.

16 *"at the intersection of the legal and the political"*: Giorgio Agamben, *State of Exception* (Chicago: University of Chicago Press, 2005), p. 1. The second phrase Agamben quotes from François Saint-Bonnet, *L'état d'exception* (Paris: Presses Universitaires de France, 2001).

17 *little sense of an ending:* For a brilliant exploration of this expression, see Frank Kermode, *The Sense of an Ending: Studies in the Theory of Fiction* (New York: Oxford University Press, 2000 [1967]).

17 *"every terrorist group of global reach has been found, stopped and defeated"*: "Transcript of President Bush's Address," CNN.com, September 21, 2001.

18 *his predecessor had the power to order it:* Here is the passage from President Obama's Nobel Peace Prize speech: "Where force is necessary, we have a moral and strategic interest in binding ourselves to certain rules of conduct. And even as we confront a vicious adversary that abides by no rules, I believe the United States of America must remain a standard bearer in the conduct of war. That is what makes us different from those whom we fight. That is a source of our strength. That is why I prohibited torture." "This paragraph is pleasant on the surface," Barry Eisler, a former CIA covert operator and now a novelist and blogger, writes, "and poisonous underneath. . . . *Torture is illegal in America.* The law, not the president, is what prohibits torture. What would you make of it if the president said, 'That is why I prohibited murder.'" Barry Eisler, "It's Good to Be the King," *The Heart of the Matter* (blog), December 17, 2009.

18 *"any future acts of terrorism or aggression against the United States"*: The version the Congress declined to accept would have authorized the president to use force to deter *any attacks at all*, without limiting the authorization to those who had planned, committed, or aided the September 11, 2001, attacks.

19 *"including tools we had never before used"*: John Rizzo, *Company Man: Thirty Years of Controversy and Crisis in the CIA* (New York: Scribner, 2014), p. 174.

19 *a vast collection of metadata*: Kurt Eichenwald, *500 Days: Secrets and Lies in the Terror War* (New York: Touchstone, 2013), pp. 100, 104–6.

20 *did not constitute torture*: David Cole, ed., *The Torture Memos: Rationalizing the Unthinkable* (New York: New Press, 2009), pp. 14, 279, and *passim*.

22 *the so-called preventive paradigm*: See David Cole and Jules Lobel, *Less Safe, Less Free: Why America Is Losing the War on Terror* (New York: New Press, 2007), pp. 23–70.

24 *"I woke up, naked, strapped to a bed, in a very white room"*: This and other firsthand accounts of torture are drawn from "ICRC Report on the Treatment of Fourteen 'High Value Detainees' in CIA Custody," which I published on *The New York Review of Books* website in April 2009. It can be accessed at http://assets.ny books.com/media/doc/2010/04/22/icrc-report.pdf. It should be noted that the firsthand accounts echo one another to a precise degree, though the detainees were permitted no contact among them. They also echo in all relevant details the accounts gathered in the executive summary of *The Senate Intelligence Committee Report on Torture* released in December 2014. See *The Senate Intelligence Committee Report on Torture: Committee Study of the Central Intelligence Agency's Detention and Interrogation Program* (Brooklyn: Melville House, 2014). For more information on the Red Cross report, see my "US Torture: Voices from the Black Sites," *New York Review of Books*, April 9, 2009.

25 *"He's where he belongs"*: "George W. Bush: Remarks at a Republican Luncheon in Greenwich, Connecticut," The American Presidency Project, April 9, 2002.

25 *"I think that's well established"*: "DoD News Briefing—With Secretary Rumsfeld and General Myers," April 1, 2002, http://www

.globalsecurity.org/military/library/news/2002/04/mil-020401
-dod02.htm.

27 *"alternative set of procedures"*: The phrase is George W. Bush's. See
"President Discusses Creation of Military Commissions to Try
Suspected Terrorists." The East Room, The White House, Sep-
tember 6, 2006.

27 *"indefinite not only in the temporal sense but in its very nature"*: Agamben, *State of Exception*, pp. 3–4.

27 *copied directly from techniques developed by the Soviets:* See Mark
Danner, "Into the Light? Torture, Power, and Us," in *Stripping
Bare the Body: Politics Violence War* (New York: Nation Books,
2009), pp. 521–44.

28 *"one of bin Laden's most trusted lieutenants"*: See Condoleezza Rice,
No Higher Honor: A Memoir of My Years in Washington (New York:
Crown, 2011), p. 117.

28 *nor was he a member of al Qaeda or "formally" identified with it at
all:* In documents filed in U.S. District Court in Washington
in September 2009, the Justice Department conceded that the
government was no longer contending that Zubaydah was a
"'member' of al-Qaeda in the sense of having sworn *bavat* (alle-
giance) or having otherwise satisfied any formal criteria that either [Zubaydah] or al-Qaeda may have considered necessary for
inclusion in al-Qaeda. . . . Rather, [the government's] detention
of [Zubaydah] is based on conduct and actions that establish
[Zubaydah] was 'part of' hostile forces and 'substantially supported' those forces."

Earlier, at his Combatant Status Review Tribunal at Guantánamo, Zubaydah noted that his interrogators had "told me
sorry we discover that you are not number three [in al Qaeda],
not a partner, even not a fighter." See, for example, Jason Leo-
pold, "Government Recants Major Terror Claims Against 'High-
Value' Detainee Abu Zubaydah," *TruthOut*, March 30, 2010; and
Andy Worthington, "Abu Zubaydah: Tortured for Nothing,"

Commentaries: The Future of Freedom Foundation, April 5, 2010. See also Barton Gellman, "The Shadow War, in a Surprising New Light," *Washington Post*, June 20, 2006.

28 *"'No, no. We have plans for you'"*: CIA-Abu Zubaydah. Interview with John Kiriakou," pp. 8–9, an unedited, rough, and undated transcript of a video interview conducted by Brian Ross of ABC News, apparently in December 2007, and available at abcnews .go.com. Quotation edited slightly for clarity.

29 *Traditional interrogation, he and his colleagues contend, was working:* Ali Soufan, with Daniel Freedman, *The Black Banners: The Inside Story of 9/11 and the War Against al-Qaeda* (New York: W. W. Norton, 2011), pp. 375–76.

30 *"what the individual might or should know":* Inspector General, Central Intelligence Agency, *Special Review: Counterterrorism and Detention Activities (September 2001–October 2003)*, May 7, 2004, pp. 104–5.

30 *"Headquarters recommended resumption of [enhanced interrogation techniques]":* Ibid., p. 83.

30 *demolish at any moment the building above:* Richard A. Clarke, *Against All Enemies: Inside America's War on Terror* (New York: Free Press, 2004), pp. 1–34.

31 *"every threat directed at the United States":* Jack Goldsmith, *The Terror Presidency: Law and Judgment Inside the Bush Administration* (New York: W. W. Norton, 2007), p. 71.

31 *"scared to death about what it portended":* Ibid., p. 72.

31 *must stop every shot to escape instant defeat:* Ibid., pp. 72–73.

32 *"All that fed the fear and urgency":* Robert M. Gates, *Duty: Memoirs of a Secretary at War* (New York: Alfred A. Knopf, 2014), p. 93.

32 *"didn't tell the president or the White House of a threat and it became true":* Quoted in Peter L. Bergen, *The Longest War: The Conflict Between America and Al Qaeda* (New York: Free Press, 2011), pp. 95–96.

32 *"just about anything anybody said might be a threat":* Elisabeth Bumiller, *Condoleezza Rice: An American Life* (New York: Random House, 2007), p. 168, quoted in Bergen, *The Longest War*, p. 95.

32 *"any obstacle . . . to accomplishing those objectives had to be overcome"*: Gates, *Duty*, p. 93.

33 *put into effect during one of the president and vice president's weekly lunches:* Barton Gellman, *Angler: The Cheney Vice Presidency* (New York: Penguin, 2008), pp. 162–68.

34 *"attack on America to take place on their watch"*: Gates, *Duty*, p. 93.

34 *"and it's going to happen soon!"*: Lawrence Wright, *The Looming Tower: Al-Qaeda and the Road to 9/11* (New York: Alfred A. Knopf, 2006), p. 389. Clarke finally did get his meeting—on September 4, 2001.

35 *"including recent surveillance of federal buildings in New York"*: The briefing, in Crawford, Texas, was held on August 6, 2001. "Politics: Bin Laden Determined to Strike in US," *CNN Politics*, April 10, 2004, http://edition.cnn.com/2004/ALLPOLITICS /04/10/august6.memo/index.html. This was reportedly only the last in a series of Presidential Daily Briefs, dating back to early May, that had carried specific warnings of "imminent" attacks planned for within the United States. Kurt Eichenwald, "The Deafness Before the Storm," *New York Times*, September 10, 2012.

35 *"You've covered your ass, now"*: Ron Suskind, *The One Percent Doctrine: Deep Inside America's Pursuit of Its Enemies Since 9/11* (New York: Simon & Schuster, 2006), p. 2.

35 *heightened alert . . . before the millennium celebrations:* See, for example, "Late 1999–Early 2000: 'Wall' Procedures Altered for Expected Millennium Attacks" and subsequent entries in the "Complete 9/11 Timeline: Millennium Bomb Plots," *History Commons*, www.historycommons.org.

36 *had then failed, by accident or design, to "hand off" to the bureau:* Wright, *The Looming Tower*, especially pp. 354–55. Wright suggests that the CIA's failure to alert the FBI to the presence of the two men in the United States, rather than a regrettable bureaucratic oversight, was part of a deliberate attempt to

"turn" the two men, using, as agent—since the CIA was barred from doing this within the United States—a figure linked to the Saudi consulate, Omar al-Bayoumi, who brought the men to San Diego, found them housing, and helped them in various ways. Perhaps CIA officials, Wright speculates, "decided that Saudi intelligence would have a better chance of recruiting these men than the Americans. That would leave no CIA fingerprints on the operation as well." A recent report quoting former FBI agent Mark Rossini, who was detailed to the CIA's Counterterrorism Center before the attacks, adds much weight to these suspicions. Rossini recounts his attempts and those of an FBI colleague, some of them in writing, to warn others at the FBI that one of the eventual hijackers was in the country. These attempts were actively thwarted by officers and executives in the CIA. In the time since 9/11, this incident, cataclysmic in its implications, has been repeatedly covered up by government redaction of key passages in various reports and inquiries. Jeff Stein, "FBI Agent: The CIA Could Have Stopped 9/11," *Newsweek,* June 19, 2015.

36 *"Would they still have been able to . . . crash it into the Pentagon?"*: FBI agent Mark Rossini's answer to this "what would have happened" scenario is actually quite definite and clear: "There would not have been a 9/11 if" his colleague's report "on [Flight 77 hijacker Khalid] al-Mihdhar was sent. Period. End of story." Stein, "FBI Agent: The CIA Could Have Stopped 9/11."

37 *they exhorted the White House not to be "fooled"*: Eichenwald, "The Deafness Before the Storm."

37 *"taking a plane and crashing into the World Trade Center"*: Wright, *The Looming Tower,* p. 396.

37 *not a paucity of available legal powers*: Ibid., page 381; and Oren Gross and Fionnuala Ni Aolain, *Law in Times of Crisis: Emergency Powers in Theory and Practice* (Cambridge, U.K.: Cambridge University Press, 2006), p. 230.

38 *bitterly criticized . . . for failing to send the suspect to Guantánamo:* See, for example, Stephanie Condon, "GOP Mass. Senate Candidate Scott Brown: Send Abdulmutallab to Gitmo," CBS News, January 5, 2010.

38 *"We did not have a terrorist attack on our country during President Bush's term":* "Giuliani: No Terror Attacks in U.S. Under Bush: Former NYC Mayor Neglects to Mention 9/11 and Shoe Bomber Attacks," Associated Press, January 9, 2010. See also Kevin Zieber, "Fox Has No Memory of Any 'Successful Terror Attack Since 9-11,'" *Media Matters,* September 17, 2012.

38 *"inherited the most tragic attack on our soil in our nation's history":* See "Mary Matalin: Bush 'Inherited' 9/11 Attacks," *Huffington Post,* January 18, 2016. (emphasis added)

39 *"After 9/11 the gloves came off":* Testimony of Cofer Black, Senate Intelligence Committee, September 26, 2002.

40 *"to erode the authority . . . the president needs to be effective":* Richard W. Stevenson, "Cheney Says 9/11 Changed the Rules," *New York Times,* December 21, 2005.

41 *"and thereby protecting America":* Richard L. Berke, "Bush Adviser Suggests War as Campaign Theme," *New York Times,* January 19, 2002.

42 *"in history's unmarked grave of discarded lies":* "Text: President Bush Addresses the Nation," *Washington Post,* September 20, 2001.

42 *"to answer these attacks and rid the world of evil":* "Text: Bush Remarks at Prayer Service," *Washington Post,* September 14, 2001.

43 *"U.S. government reflexively inclined toward Cold War–style responses":* Report of the Defense Science Board Task Force on Strategic Communications, Office of the Under Secretary of Defense for Acquisition, Technology and Logistics, September 2004, pp. 42–43.

43 *"we'll get hit again and that we'll be hit in a way that will be devastating":* Dana Milbank and Spencer S. Hsu, "Cheney: Kerry Victory Is Risky," *Washington Post,* September 8, 2004.

44 *"on the dark side," as Vice President Cheney put it:* See "The Vice

President appears on *Meet the Press* with Tim Russert," The White House, September 16, 2001.

45 *to grant them the prestige of declaring war on them:* As Obama defense official Rosa Brooks writes, "The decision to view this as an armed conflict was a policy choice, not a decision somehow dictated by the law. Indeed, from an historical perspective it was in some ways a rather odd choice: As my Georgetown colleague Laura Donohue has noted, most governments have historically been quite reluctant to place attacks by insurgent groups or terror groups under the rubric of armed conflict, for fear of legitimizing these groups. Why give mass murderers such a soap box to stand upon? Calling Al Qaeda a combatant in war against the United States gave Al Qaeda a certain international prestige, and arguably helped it gain new recruits and funding." Rosa Brooks, "Cross-Border Targeted Killings: 'Lawful but Awful'?," *Harvard Journal of Law and Public Policy,* Vol. 38, 2014.

45 *"protection of the laws of war":* Michael Howard, "What's in a Name? How to Fight Terrorism," *Foreign Affairs,* January/February 2002.

47 *"work through, sort of, the dark side":* The full quotation, which the vice president uttered five days after September 11, is: "We also have to work, though, sort of the dark side, if you will. We've got to spend time in the shadows in the intelligence world. A lot of what needs to be done here will have to be done quietly, without any discussion, using sources and methods that are available to our intelligence agencies, if we're going to be successful. That's the world these folks operate in, and so it's going to be vital for us to use any means at our disposal, basically, to achieve our objective." See *Meet the Press,* NBC News, September 16, 2001.

48 *"someone with no interrogation or terrorism experience had been sent by the CIA on this mission":* Soufan with Freedman, *The Black Banners,* pp. 394–96. Here the bracketed words indicate redactions by the CIA.

49   *"attacks on U.S. supermarkets and shopping malls"*: Mark Hosenball, "How Good Is Abu Zubaydah's Information?," *Newsweek*, Web Exclusive, April 27, 2002.

49   *"as were the claims that he wasn't cooperating"*: Soufan with Freedman, *The Black Banners*, p. 411.

49   *"a kind of travel agent"*: Bergen, *The Longest War*, pp. 110–13.

49   *"even the terrorist group's number three or four in command"*: Soufan with Freedman, *The Black Banners*, p. 380.

49   *"No Sir, Mr. President," Tenet replied*: Suskind, *The One Percent Doctrine*, p. 100.

50   *"primary purpose of making room for cruelty"*: Quoted in Gellman, *Angler*, p. 176. Mora protested that the treatment of Qahtani "constituted, at a minimum, cruel and unusual treatment and, at worst, torture." Gellman, *Angler*, p. 188.

50   *"That's the point"*: Barrister and author Philippe Sands asked Undersecretary Feith whether the Geneva decision was taken to ensure that limits on interrogation should not apply to detainees in Guantánamo and elsewhere and Feith frankly admitted, "That's the point." Philippe Sands, *Torture Team: Rumsfeld's Memo and the Betrayal of American Values* (New York: Palgrave, 2008), p. 35.

51   *ambitious young professionals breaking new legal ground*: Office of Professional Responsibility, Department of Justice, *Investigation into the Office of Legal Counsel's Memoranda Concerning Issues Relating to the Central Intelligence Agency's Use of "Enhanced Interrogation Techniques" on Suspected Terrorists*, July 29, 2009, p. 45.

52   *"immediate needs more than the information he is protecting"*: Central Intelligence Agency, *Background Paper on CIA's Combined Use of Interrogation Techniques*, December 30, 2004.

52   *"time was running out"*: Rice, *No Higher Honor*, pp. 117–18.

52   *"the United States must now act as if it was a certainty"*: Suskind, *The One Percent Doctrine*, p. 62.

53   *at its height held more than eighty thousand prisoners*: Katherine

Shrader, "U.S. Has Detained 83,000 in War on Terror," *Washington Post*, November 26, 2005. "To put that in context," Shrader writes, "the capacity of the Washington Redskins FedEx Field, the NFL's largest, is 91,704. The second largest, Giants Stadium, holds 80,242."

53 *"a real erring on the conservative side"*: "Interview: Chris Mackey and Chris Miller discuss their book, *The Interrogators*," *Fresh Air*, National Public Radio, July 20, 2004. The name Chris Mackey is a pseudonym.

53 *"why the prisoner had been detained in the first place"*: Declaration of *Colonel Lawrence B. Wilkerson in Adel Hassan Hamad v. George W. Bush, Donald Rumsfeld, Jay Hood, and Brice Gyurisko*, U.S. District Court for the District of Columbia, CV 05-1009 JDB, March 24, 2010.

54 *"to less actionable intelligence"*: Maj. Gen. George R. Fay, *AF 15-6 Investigation of the Abu Ghraib Detention Facility and 205th Military Intelligence Brigade (The Fay Report)*, p. 37.

56 *these local apostate regimes would eventually crumble*: For a succinct account of al Qaeda's ideology and strategy, see Michael Scott Doran, "Somebody Else's Civil War," *Foreign Affairs*, January/ February 2002.

57 *as Michael Scott Doran has put it*: Ibid.

57 *leading to an endless, grinding conflict*: Many analysts have pointed out that provocation is the signal attribute of al Qaeda's strategy, for example, Lawrence Wright: "[Osama bin Laden's] goal, for at least five years, had been to goad America into invading Afghanistan, an ambition that had caused him to continually raise the stakes—the simultaneous bombings of the United States Embassies in Kenya and Tanzania, in August 1998, followed by the attack on an American warship in the harbor of Aden, Yemen, in October, 2000. Neither of those actions had led the United States to send troops to Afghanistan. After the attacks on New York and Washington, however, it was clear that

there would be an overwhelming response." Lawrence Wright, "The Master Plan," *The New Yorker,* September 11, 2006.

57 *a grand reenactment of the destruction of the Soviet Union a dozen years before:* For a much fuller treatment of this argument, see my essay "Is He Winning? Taking Stock of the Forever War," *New York Times Magazine,* September 11, 2005.

57 *a bloody quagmire:* On the other hand, as Lawrence Wright notes, al Qaeda, and bin Laden himself, seemed to have been initially ambivalent about an Iraq invasion: "The invasion of Iraq posed a dilemma for Al Qaeda. Iraq is a largely Shiite nation, and Al Qaeda is composed of Sunnis who believe that the Shia are heretics. Shortly before the invasion, in March, 2003, bin Laden issued his own list of targets, which included Jordan, Morocco, Nigeria, Pakistan, Saudi Arabia, and Yemen—not Afghanistan or Iraq. Presumably, he regarded the chances of a Taliban resurgence as remote; moreover, he was aware that an Iraqi insurgency could ignite an Islamic civil war and lead to ethnic cleansing of the Sunni minority." Wright, "The Master Plan."

57 *"awaken the inattentive" Muslims:* Zarqawi Letter: "February 2004 Coalition Provisional Authority English translation of terrorist Musab al Zarqawi letter obtained by United States Government in Iraq," U.S. Department of State Archive.

58 *"the capabilities of the kingdom of Satan that is waging war on us":* See "Letter from al-Zawahiri to al-Zarqawi," GlobalSecurity.org, dated July 9, 2005.

58 *"they wanted to humiliate us":* Bob Woodward, *State of Denial: Bush at War, Part III* (New York: Simon & Schuster, 2007), p. 428.

59 *"to fly airplanes into buildings in New York and Washington":* Dana Milbank, "Patience on Iraq Policies Urged," *Washington Post,* August 26, 2003.

59 *"a favorable solution of the Arab-Israeli problem":* See my essay "The Struggles of Democracy and Empire," published in *The New York*

Times, October 9, 2002. Here is the broader context: "In promoting the Iraq expedition as a necessary response to an immediate terrorist threat, however, [Bush officials] have failed to prepare the American public for what looks to be a long and costly engagement in the Middle East. Much of the confusion surrounding the Iraq debate thus far is owed to the chasm between the justifications proffered and the more elaborate geopolitical enterprise motivating many in the Bush administration.

"The first phase of the war on terror saw the overthrow of the Taliban in Afghanistan and the escape of the leaders of Al Qaeda. The second sent American troops to the Philippines, Georgia and Yemen for counterinsurgency missions against parts of the Qaeda network. The third phase, now about to unfold in the Persian Gulf, envisions the remaking of the Middle East.

"Behind the notion that an American intervention will make of Iraq 'the first Arab democracy,' as Deputy Defense Secretary Paul Wolfowitz put it, lies a project of great ambition. It envisions a post–Saddam Hussein Iraq—secular, middle-class, urbanized, rich with oil—that will replace the autocracy of Saudi Arabia as the key American ally in the Persian Gulf, allowing the withdrawal of United States troops from the kingdom. The presence of a victorious American Army in Iraq would then serve as a powerful boost to moderate elements in neighboring Iran, hastening that critical country's evolution away from the mullahs and toward a more moderate course. Such an evolution in Tehran would lead to a withdrawal of Iranian support for Hezbollah and other radical groups, thereby isolating Syria and reducing pressure on Israel. This undercutting of radicals on Israel's northern borders and within the West Bank and Gaza would spell the definitive end of Yasir Arafat and lead eventually to a favorable solution of the Arab-Israeli problem.

"This is a vision of great sweep and imagination: comprehensive, prophetic, evangelical. In its ambitions it is wholly foreign to the modesty of containment, the ideology of a status-quo power that lay at the heart of American strategy for half a century. It means to remake the world, to offer to a political threat a political answer. It represents a great step on the road toward President Bush's ultimate vision of 'freedom's triumph over all its age-old foes.'" I noted that "by invading and occupying Iraq and using it as a base to remake the region, the United States risks revitalizing the political project embodied by Osama bin Laden." *New York Times,* October 9, 2002. See also Danner, *Stripping Bare the Body.*

59 *"creative chaos" or "creative instability":* Both terms were widely used in neoconservative think tank circles around the time of the launching of the Iraq War and its aftermath. See for example Mahdi Darius Nazemroaya, "Plans for Redrawing the Middle East: The Project for a 'New Middle East,'" Global Research, November 18, 2006. Also Joshua Micah Marshall, "Practice to Deceive: Chaos in the Middle East is not the Bush hawks' nightmare scenario—it's their plan," *Washington Monthly,* April 2003.

60 *"bringing in its wake popular, democratic, America-supporting regimes":* For the "Democratic Tsunami" proposition, see, for example, Joshua Muravchik, "Democracy's Quiet Victory," *New York Times,* August 19, 2002.

61 *codified their "combined use of interrogation techniques":* See "CIA Memo: Background Paper on CIA's Combined Use of Interrogation Techniques," dated December 30, 2004, and addressed to Daniel B. Levin in the Department of Justice, accessed at The Torture Database. www.thetorturedatabase.org.

62 *"scars . . . were visible on both wrists as well as on both ankles":* "ICRC Report on the Treatment of Fourteen 'High Value Detainees' in CIA Custody," p. 35.

62 *"which break and exude watery serum":* Lawrence E. Hinkle Jr. and

Harold G. Wolff, "Communist Interrogation and Indoctrination of 'Enemies of the State,'" *A.M.A. Archives of Neurology and Psychiatry* 76, no. 2 (August 1956): 134.

63 *measure the swelling in his remaining leg using a tape measure:* "ICRC Report on the Treatment of Fourteen 'High Value Detainees' in CIA Custody," February 2007, p. 22.

63 *"the basic KGB technique . . . sleep deprivation, stress positions, cold":* The words are Tom Malinowski's of Human Rights Watch, quoted in Gellman, *Angler,* p. 188.

63 *"illegal exploitation . . . of prisoners over the last 50 years":* "Executive Summary and Conclusions," *Inquiry into the Treatment of Detainees in U.S. Custody,* Senate Armed Services Committee, December 2008, p. xiii (my emphasis).

64 *legal, subtle, and, by all accounts immensely effective:* Robert Destro et al., *Educing Information: Interrogation, Science and Art* (CreateSpace, 2006), pp. 244–45.

65 *"or not presented at all":* Suskind, *The One Percent Doctrine,* pp. 225–26.

65 *no record of anyone ever discussing "what we should do":* Philip Zelikow, "Legal Policy for a Twilight War," *Houston Journal of International Law* 30, no. 1 (2007): 92. See also Philip Zelikow, "Codes of Conduct for a Twilight War," *Houston Law Review* 49, no. 1 (2012): 24: "None of the policy or moral issues connected with these choices appear to have been analyzed in any noticeable way."

65 *"physical torment to break prisoners and make them talk":* "Statement of Philip Zelikow," United States Senate Committee on the Judiciary, Subcommittee on Administrative Oversight and the Courts, May 13, 2009, pp. 4–5.

67 *"used in the military training of thousands of U.S. soldiers":* Rice, *No Higher Honor,* p. 117.

68 *the decision of the president . . . was foreordained. He approved:* Zelikow, "Codes of Conduct for a Twilight War."

69   *"Committees continued to be aware of and approve CIA's actions":* Inspector General, Central Intelligence Agency, *Special Review: Counterterrorism and Detention Activities (September 2001–October 2003),* May 7, 2004, p. 23.

70   *"History will not judge this kindly":* Jan Crawford Greenburg, Howard L. Rosenberg, and Ariane de Vogue, "Sources: Top Bush Advisors Approved 'Enhanced Interrogation,'" ABC News, April 9, 2008. According to this account, the meetings were chaired by National Security Adviser Rice and included Vice President Cheney, Secretary of State Powell, Secretary of Defense Rumsfeld, and CIA Director Tenet, in addition to Attorney General Ashcroft.

71   *"obviously that would be prohibited by the statute":* Office of Professional Responsibility, Department of Justice, *Investigation into the Office of Legal Counsel's Memoranda Concerning Issues Relating to the Central Intelligence Agency's Use of "Enhanced Interrogation Techniques" on Suspected Terrorists,* July 29, 2009, pp. 53–54.

71   *"the CIA program, either singly or in combination, constituted torture":* "ICRC Report on the Treatment of Fourteen 'High Value Detainees' in CIA Custody," p. 26.

71   *waterboarding as "simply a controlled acute episode":* Cole, ed., *The Torture Memos,* p. 118.

73   *"puts ye unhappy wretch into the agonies of death":* Cecil Roth, *The Spanish Inquisition* (London: W. W. Norton, 1996 [1937]).

73   *waterboarding prisoners first appeared . . . in a report in* The New York Times: See James Risen, David Johnston, and Neil A. Lewis, "The Struggle for Iraq: Detainees; Harsh C.I.A. Methods Cited in Top Qaeda Interrogations," *New York Times,* May 13, 2004.

73   The Washington Post *had run a lengthy report . . . on "stress and duress" techniques:* Dana Priest and Barton Gellman, "U.S. Decries Abuse but Defends Interrogations," *Washington Post,* December 26, 2002.

73 The New York Times *had followed with its own report several months later:* Raymond Bonner, Don Van Natta Jr., and Amy Waldman, "Questioning Terror Suspects in a Dark and Surreal World," *New York Times,* March 9, 2003.

75 *"hallucinations of dogs mauling and killing his sons and family":* The Senate Intelligence Committee Report on Torture, p. 109.

75 *force-fed rectally "without documented medical necessity":* The Senate Intelligence Committee Report on Torture, p. 4.

75 *"impeding a proper legal analysis of the CIA's Detention and Interrogation Program":* The Senate Intelligence Committee Report on Torture, p. 4.

75 *the acts likely constituted torture, even under Yoo's exceedingly narrow definition:* "The Justice Department's Office of Legal Counsel found that the [enhanced interrogation] methods wouldn't breach the law because those applying them didn't have the specific intent of inflicting severe pain or suffering. The Senate report, however, concluded that the Justice Department's legal analyses were based on flawed information provided by the CIA, which prevented a proper evaluation of the program's legality." Ali Watkins, Jonathan S. Landay, and Marisa Taylor, "CIA's Use of Harsh Interrogation Went Beyond Legal Authority, Senate Report Says," McClatchyDC.com, April 11, 2014.

75 *a general "drifting downward" into greater cruelty:* This phenomenon can be seen in many of the various plotlines that comprise the post-9/11 torture narrative. As a former interrogator writes, "The rules of engagement at Abu Ghraib may have had nothing to do with the sadistic behavior that took place in the high-security cellblock known as Tier 1A. But both represented the gravitational laws that govern human behavior when one group of people is given complete control over another in a prison. Every impulse tugs downward. We had seen it in our unit in Afghanistan. The prohibition on the use of stress positions early in the war gave way to policies allowing their use to punish prisoners

for disrespectful behavior." Chris Mackey and Greg Miller, *The Interrogators: Task Force 500 and America's Secret War Against Al Qaeda* (New York: Back Bay, 2005), p. 471.

76 *"a detainee can eventually call the interrogator's bluff"*: See *Testimony of Ali Soufan,* Senate Judiciary Committee, May 9, 2009.

77 *"it depends on why the President thinks he needs to do that"*: Nat Hentoff, "Don't Ask, Don't Tell," *The Village Voice,* January 24, 2006.

78 *they had all read Voltaire on torture and tolerance and limited power:* Voltaire, *Treatise on Tolerance and Other Writings* (Cambridge, U.K.: Cambridge University Press, 2000 [1763]); and also "Torture," in Voltaire, *Philosophical Dictionary, Part V,* in William F. Fleming (trans.), *The Works of Voltaire: A Contemporary Version, Volume VII* (Berkeley: University of California Press, 1901 [1764]).

78 *"when the president does it, that means that it's not illegal"*: Former President Nixon uttered this opinion in his interviews with David Frost, recorded in March and April 1977.

78 *in black sites in Thailand, Poland and other undisclosed locations:* "Mr Husayn submits that, having been seized in Pakistan in March 2002 and subsequently transferred to a secret CIA detention facility in Thailand, he was brought to Poland on 5 December 2002 where he was held in a secret CIA detention facility until 22 September 2003. He was then taken to Guantanamo Bay and consecutively to several secret detention facilities in a number of countries before eventually being transferred back to Guantanamo Bay." "Poland Failed Its Obligation Under Article 38 of the European Convention on Human Rights," *eTurboNews,* June 24, 2014.

78 *a historic White House speech revealing and defending his "alternative set of procedures"*: "President Discusses Creation of Military Commissions to Try Suspected Terrorists," East Room, The White House, September 6, 2006.

79 *released to the public the full texts of the torture memos:* Cole, ed., *The Torture Memos.*

80 *"the radical clerics are recruiting, training and deploying against us?":* See "Rumsfeld's War-on-Terror Memo," *USA Today,* May 20, 2005.

81 *"states and non-state entities that pose no direct or imminent threat to the United States":* Jeffrey Record, *Bounding the Global War on Terrorism* (Carlisle, PA: Strategic Studies Institute, 2003), quoted in David Kilcullen, *Counterinsurgency* (New York: Oxford University Press, 2010), pp. 212–13.

81 *"overstretch, exhaustion of popular will, and ultimate failure":* Kilcullen, *Counterinsurgency,* p. 213.

82 *"and if they pull out, they lose everything":* "Al Zawahiri: U.S. Faltering in Afghanistan—CIA Analyzing al Qaeda Videotape That Appeared on Al Jazeera," CNN Online, November 9, 2004, quoted in David Kilcullen, "Blood Year: Terror and the Islamic State," *Quarterly Essay,* 2015.

83 *"invaded and under attack—to broad public support":* Report of the Defense Science Board Task Force on Strategic Communication, Office of the Under Secretary of Defense, September 2004, p. 40.

PART TWO
Obama: Normalizing the Exception

85 *"Turns out I'm really good at killing people":* Mark Halperin and John Heilemann, *Double Down: Game Change 2012* (New York: Penguin, 2013), p. 55. President Obama was speaking to White House staff the day a CIA-directed U.S. drone strike killed the American Muslim preacher Anwar al-Awlaki in Yemen.

85 *"This war, like all wars, must end":* Remarks by the President at the National Defense University, Fort McNair, Washington, D.C., May 23, 2013.

87 *"the complete restoration of the status quo ante bellum":* Rossiter, *Constitutional Dictatorship,* p. 7. The italics are Rossiter's.

89 *"justice is not arbitrary"*: Remarks of Senator Obama, "The War We Need to Win," Washington, D.C., August 1, 2007.

89 *ordering that the offshore prison itself be closed within one year*: Scott Shane, Mark Mazzetti, and Helene Cooper, "Obama Reverses Key Bush Security Policies," *New York Times,* January 22, 2009.

90 *"legal black hole"*: The phrase is Lord Steyn's, a judicial member of the House of Lords. See Johan Steyn, "Guantanamo Bay: The legal black hole," Twenty-Seventh F. A. Mann Lecture, November 25, 2003.

90 *to govern and manage their indefinite detention*: Peter Finn and Anne E. Kornblut, "Obama Creates Indefinite Detention System for Prisoners at Guantánamo Bay," *Washington Post,* March 8, 2011.

92 *One thing that was* not *allowed to be brought in? The memo itself:* Carroll Bogert, "There's Something You Need to See at Guantánamo Bay," *Politico,* January 22, 2014. Bogert is deputy executive director for external relations at Human Rights Watch.

94 *"in ways that were hard if not impossible to unravel"*: Jack Goldsmith, "The Cheney Fallacy," *The New Republic,* May 18, 2009.

94 *"approving others, and acquiescing in yet others"*: As Goldsmith persuasively argued, in some ways Obama has proved closer to the Bush of his second term than either president was to the early, post-9/11 Bush. Goldsmith, "The Cheney Fallacy."

94 *it largely did the same for his surveillance program two years later*: "Bush Signs Controversial Wiretap Bill, Calls for Permanent Fix," CNN.com, August 5, 2007.

94 *albeit a strikingly ineffective one, for their detention*: Linda Greenhouse, "Justices, 5–3, Broadly Reject Bush Plan to Try Detainees," *New York Times,* June 30, 2006; and Greenhouse, "Justices, 5–4, Back Detainee Appeals for Guantánamo," *New York Times,* June 13, 2008.

95 *"the emergence of a cross-party and cross-branch consensus"*: Robert M. Chesney, "Beyond the Battlefield, Beyond Al Qaeda: The Destabilizing Legal Architecture of Counterterrorism," *Michigan Law Review,* November 2013, p. 167 and *passim*.

95 *grounded only in his predecessor's inherent powers as "unitary execu-tive"*: the "unitary executive" is a theory of American constitu-tional law in which the president is believed to hold the power to control the entire executive branch. Its exponents were widely represented within the George W. Bush administration. See for example Cass Sunstein, "What the 'Unitary Executive' Debate Is and Is Not About," The University of Chicago Law School Fac-ulty Blog, August 6, 2007.

96 *the power of secrecy, including the state secrets privilege:* According to the ACLU explanation, "the state secrets privilege, when prop-erly invoked, permits the government to block the release of any information in a lawsuit that, if disclosed, would cause harm to national security." The Obama administration increasingly followed the Bush administration in using the privilege to per-suade courts to dismiss lawsuits at the onset. See "Background on the State Secrets Privilege," www.aclu.org.

97 *in including in its secret list of adversaries al Qaeda's "associated forces":* On the problem of "associated forces," a phrase not contained in the 2001 authorization and first employed by the Obama administration, see, for example, Rosa Brooks: "The threat has metastasized: even as U.S. military action has decimated 'Al Qaeda Central' and the network of Taliban leaders most active in 2001, new extremist groups have evolved, some inspired by or affiliated with Al Qaeda and the Taliban, others linked merely by a similar extremist ideology and a similar willingness to use violence against civilian targets to achieve their ends. In the last few years, U.S. drone strikes outside of hot battlefields have consequently targeted not only the remnants of 'core' Al Qaeda and the Taliban, but also known or suspected members of other organizations—including Somalia's al Shabaab—as well as vari-ous individuals identified by U.S. intelligence only as 'militants,' 'foreign fighters,' and 'unknown extremists.'

"For the moment, leave aside the question of whether the

expanding range of groups targeted by the United States all pose a threat (or the same degree of threat) to the United States. Maybe all these groups and individuals pose a threat to the United States, and maybe they don't—but on its face, the 2001 AUMF simply does not appear to cover groups and individuals that were unconnected to the September 11 attacks and are not planning or carrying out future terrorist attacks against the United States.

"The Obama administration has countered this argument by asserting that insofar as Congress intended the AUMF to be the functional equivalent of a declaration of war, the AUMF must be read to include the implied law of war-based authority to target groups that are 'associates' of Al Qaeda or the Taliban. However, it is far from clear that Congress intended to authorize the use of force outside of traditional territorial battlefields against mere 'associates' of those responsible for the September 11 attacks, particularly when many of those associated groups did not exist in 2001. It is also not clear how the executive branch defines 'associates' of Al Qaeda." Brooks, "Cross-Border Targeted Killings: 'Lawful but Awful'?," p. 237.

98 *"So if we choose to call this a war, it will be endless"*: Bruce Ackerman, "The Emergency Constitution," *Yale Faculty Scholarship Series* (121), January 1, 2004, http://digitalcommons.law.yale.edu/fss_papers/121.

99 *Obama tells us as a matter of course that al Qaeda has been "decimated"*: See, for example, "Obama: Al Qaeda Has Been Decimated," YouTube, November 1, 2012.

99 *grounding his authority on the 2001 Authorization for Use of Military Force:* Daniel Klaidman, *Kill or Capture: The War on Terror and the Soul of the Obama Presidency* (New York: Houghton, 2012), pp. 59–60.

99 *retains the power to send in U.S. military forces anywhere, from Yemen to the Congo:* Rosa Brooks, "The War Professor: Can Obama

Finally Make the Legal Case for His War on Terror?," *Foreign Policy*, May 23, 2013.

99   *"a virtually open-ended ability to use lethal force, anywhere, any time"*: Brooks, "Cross-Border Targeted Killings: 'Lawful but Awful'?," p. 242.

100 *the indefinite detention of those in Guantánamo:* Michael Hirsh and James Oliphant, "Obama Will Never End the War on Terror," *National Journal*, February 27, 2014.

101 *"without a major-casualty attack on the U.S.":* Jim Vandehei, John F. Harris, and Mike Allen, "Cheney Warns of New Attacks," *Politico*, February 5, 2009.

101 *"If you turn them loose and they go kill more Americans, who's responsible for that?":* Ibid.

102 *had become a plan to "put terrorists in our neighborhoods":* See for example Mark Mazzetti and Scott Shane, "Where Will Detainees from Guantanamo Go?" *New York Times*, January 23, 2009.

102 *"They weren't breathing down our necks pushing the vote or demanding unified action":* Peter Finn and Anne F. Kornblut, "Guantánamo Bay: Why Obama Hasn't Fulfilled His Promise to Close the Facility," *Washington Post*, April 24, 2011. See also, for a broader account of the Guantánamo story, Klaidman, *Kill or Capture*, pp. 93–117 and *passim*.

103 *"they will be an albatross around our efforts to combat terrorism in the future":* "Remarks by the President on National Security," National Archives, Washington, D.C., May 21, 2009.

103 *"would be cause for great danger and regret in the years to come":* Remarks by Richard B. Cheney, American Enterprise Institute, May 21, 2009.

105 *"this was a time for reflection, not retribution":* Carrie Johnson and Julie Tate, "New Interrogation Details Emerge as Administration Releases Justice Department Memos," *Washington Post*, April 17, 2009.

106 *"spend all their time looking over their shoulders":* David Johnston

and Charlie Savage, "Obama Reluctant to Look into Bush Programs," *New York Times,* January 11, 2009.

107   *"the military becomes more stealthy, agile and lethal in its ability to capture or kill terrorists":* See "Obama's Speech at Woodrow Wilson Center," Council on Foreign Relations, August 1, 2007.

107   *"who acted in good faith . . . regarding the interrogation of detainees":* "Statement of Attorney General Eric Holder on Closure of Investigation of Certain Detainees," Department of Justice, August 30, 2012.

108   *declined to bring any prosecutions against interrogators or those who directed them:* Adam Serwer, "Investigation of Bush-era Torture Concludes with No Charges," *Mother Jones,* August 31, 2012.

109   *"we honor those ideals by upholding them not just when it is easy, but when it is hard":* See "Remarks by the President at the Acceptance of the Nobel Peace Prize," The White House, December 10, 2009.

109   *"using international* fora, *judicial processes and terrorism": The National Defense Strategy of the United States of America* (March 2005), p. 5, http://www.globalsecurity.org/military/library/policy/dod/nds-usa_mar2005_ib.htm.

109   *embedding American power in the North Atlantic Treaty Organization, the United Nations, and other multilateral institutions:* For a useful history of this well-known story, see Walter Isaacson, *The Wise Men: Six Friends and the World They Made* (New York: Simon & Schuster, 2013). Also see my essay "Marooned in the Cold War" in *Stripping Bare the Body,* pp. 333–61.

112   *"that the CIA considered to be virtually inevitable":* Gellman, *Angler,* p. 177.

112   *"US officials who tortured to obtain information that saved many lives":* See *The Senate Intelligence Committee Report on Torture,* pp. 179–80.

113   *that the torture program, yes, "saved thousands of lives":* George J. Tenet, Porter J. Goss, Michael V. Hayden, et al., "Ex-CIA Directors: Interrogations Saved Lives," *Wall Street Journal,* December 10, 2014.

113 *it contains an appendix that would seem in some cases to permit forced isolation, stress positions, and other questionable techniques:* Jeff Kaye, "UN Review Cites Torture and 'Ill Treatment' in US Army Field Manual's Appendix M," *Shadowproof,* November 28, 2014.

114 *explicitly shielded members of the Bush administration from prosecution:* For a thorough treatment of these provisions, see Elizabeth Holtzman with Cynthia L. Cooper, *Cheating Justice: How Bush and Cheney Attacked the Rule of Law and Plotted to Avoid Prosecution—And What We Can Do About It* (New York: Beacon, 2012), pp. 90–100.

114 *"they complied with the law, including international treaty obligations such as the United Nations Convention Against Torture":* Dick Cheney with Liz Cheney, *In My Time: A Personal and Political Memoir* (New York: Threshold, 2011), pp. 358–61.

114 *he replied without hesitation, "Damn right!":* George W. Bush, *Decision Points* (New York: Crown, 2010), p. 170.

115 *"take out" certain al Qaeda and Taliban figures:* Mark Mazzetti, *The Way of the Knife: The CIA, a Secret Army, and a War at the Ends of the Earth* (New York: Penguin, 2013).

115 *striking Pakistan with Hellfire missiles on average every three days and killing that year alone perhaps a thousand people:* Mazzetti, *The Way of the Knife,* p. 228.

116 *"They tried to minimize collateral damage, especially women and children":* Tara Mckelvey, "Inside the Killing Machine," *Newsweek,* February 13, 2011.

116 *perhaps as many as one in four of these were civilians:* There are no official figures on drone strikes and the casualties resulting from them. A number of reputable organizations, including *The Long War Journal,* the Bureau of Investigative Journalism, and the New America Foundation, track the number of strikes and the number of casualties, using various methods. As of mid-June 2015, *The Long War Journal* estimated that in Pakistan the United States had launched 386 drone strikes, killing 2,930, of

whom 158 were civilians. The Bureau for Investigative Journalism estimated that the United States had launched 419 drone strikes, killing from 2,467 to 3,976, of whom 423 to 965 were civilians. The New America Foundation estimated the United States had launched 399 strikes, killing 2,242 to 3,623, of whom 260 to 309 were civilians.

116 *as many as eleven hundred people, of whom a hundred or so have been civilians:* As of mid-June 2015, *The Long War Journal* estimated that in Yemen the United States had launched 115 drone strikes, killing 677, of whom 115 were civilians. The Bureau for Investigative Journalism estimated that the United States had launched 98 to 118 drone strikes, killing between 456 and 676, of whom 65 to 97 were civilians. The New America Foundation estimated the United States had launched 126 strikes, killing between 854 to 1,114, of whom 87 to 93 were civilians.

117 *"He didn't like the idea of kill 'em and sort it out later":* Klaidman, *Kill or Capture,* p. 43.

117 *have killed as many as five thousand people, according to credible sources:* Senator Lindsey Graham, a longtime member of the Armed Services Committee, asserted publicly in early 2013 that "We've killed 4,700. Sometimes you hit innocent people, and I hate that, but we're at war, and we've taken out some very senior members of Al Qaeda." "Sen. Graham Says U.S. Drones Have Killed Nearly 5,000 People," *The Arab American News,* February 22, 2013.

117 *at least one in ten of these have been noncombatants:* "Covert War on Terror—The Data," Bureau of Investigative Journalism. The bureau estimated as of January 21, 2016, that drones had killed a minimum of 2,494 people in Pakistan of whom at least 423 had been civilians.

117 *Obama embraced drones . . . as a stopgap measure when a planned counterinsurgency campaign in Afghanistan proved too open-ended and expensive:* Lloyd C. Gardner, *Killing Machine: The American Presidency*

in the Age of Drone Warfare (New York: New Press, 2013), especially pp. 32–65.

118 *during the first two years of the Obama administration one struck every four days:* Peter Bergen, "Warrior in Chief," *New York Times,* April 26, 2012.

118 *JSOC, whose numbers have more than doubled since the start of the war on terror, to nearly seventy thousand:* "The total number of special operations forces was once planned to reach 72,000, but budget constraints have capped the number at 69,700. The Special Operations Command budget for the next year is $7.7 billion, a 10 percent increase." Rowan Scarborough, "Obama Runs Special Forces into the Ground: Global Demand Drains Readiness even as U.S. Wars Wind Down," *Washington Times,* March 11, 2014.

118 *their primary focus is on conducting black ops raids and kill/capture missions in Pakistan, Afghanistan, and Yemen and various other nations in the Middle East and Central Asia:* Nick Turse, *The Changing Face of Empire: Special Ops, Drones, Spies, Proxy Fighters, Secret Bases, and Cyberwarfare* (New York: Haymarket, 2012), p. 15.

118 *"something just short of war, every day of the year":* David E. Sanger, *Confront and Conceal: Obama's Secret Wars and Surprising Use of American Power* (New York: Crown, 2012), p. 244.

119 *half of the strikes over that period . . . struck members of groups other than al Qaeda:* Jonathan S. Landay, "Obama's Drone War Kills 'Others,' Not Just al Qaida Leaders," *McClatchy Newspapers,* April 9, 2013.

119 *"we can't capture the individual before they move forward on some sort of operational plot against the United States":* "Obama Reflects on Drone Warfare," *CNN Security Clearance,* September 5, 2012.

119 *"patterns of merely suspicious activity by a group of [unidentified] men":* Peter Bergen writes: "To the extent that targets of drone attacks can be ascertained, under Bush, al Qaeda members accounted for 25% of all drone targets compared to 40% for Taliban targets.

Under Obama, only 8% of targets were al Qaeda compared to just over 50% for Taliban targets.

"And while under Bush, about a third of all drone strikes killed a militant leader, compared to less than 13% since President Obama took office. . . . While Bush sought to decapitate the leadership ranks of al Qaeda, Obama seems to be aiming also to collapse the entire network of allied groups, such as the Pakistani Taliban." Peter Bergen, "Drone Is Obama's Weapon of Choice," CNN.com, September 19, 2012.

119 *"it's hard to make the case that [they] threaten the United States in some way"*: Bergen is quoted in Greg Miller, "Increased U.S. Drone Strikes in Pakistan Killing Few High-Value Militants," *Washington Post*, February 21, 2011.

119 *"side payment strikes" that killed Pakistani Taliban as a favor to the Pakistani government*: Micah Zenko, "An Inconvenient Truth: Finally, Proof That the United States Has Lied in the Drone Wars," *Foreign Policy*, April 10, 2013.

119 *"It seems they really want to kill everyone, not just the leaders"*: Jane Perlez and Pir Zubair Shah, "Drones Batter Al Qaeda and Its Allies Within Pakistan," *New York Times*, April 4, 2010.

120 *"We must not create more enemies than we take off the battlefield"*: See "Remarks by the President at the United States Military Academy Commencement Ceremony," The White House, May 28, 2014.

120 *"clear evidence that a specific attack on U.S. persons and interests will take place in the immediate future"*: Rosa Brooks, "The Constitutional and Counterterrorism Implications of Targeted Killing: Testimony Before the Senate Judiciary Subcommittee on the Constitution, Civil Rights and Human Rights," April 21, 2013, p. 12.

120 *"a president doesn't have to deem the country under immediate threat of attack before acting on his or her own"*: Michael Hirsh and James Oliphant, "Obama Will Never End the War on Terror," *National Journal*, February 27, 2014.

121   *"there is now an intense anger and growing hatred of America"*: Quoted in Peter Bergen, "Obama's High-Stakes Drone War in Yemen," CNN.com, April 21, 2014.

121   *to attempt attacks of their own:* Both Zazi and Shahzad "said they were, in part, motivated by drone strikes in their ancestral home-lands." Klaidman, *Kill or Capture*, p. 119.

121   *drone strikes perpetuate many of the political sentiments at the root of the war on terror:* For American attitudes about drones, see Jaime Fuller, "Americans Are Fine with Drone Strikes. Everyone Else in the World? Not So Much," *Washington Post,* July 16, 2014, which includes Pew Research Center figures showing that while 52 percent of Americans approve of drone strikes, 90 percent of Jordanians, 87 percent of Egyptians, 84 percent of Palestinians, and 66 percent of Pakistanis disapprove. The numbers are com-parable for other Muslim countries.

121   *"spend more time thinking about their own safety than plotting against us"*: Remarks by the President at the National Defense Univer-sity, Fort McNair, Washington, D.C., May 23, 2013.

122   *"evidence suggests that the broader strategic struggle against terrorist en-tities is not succeeding"*: Recommendations and Report of the Task Force on US Drone Policy, Stimson Center (June 2014), p. 29.

123   *"their martyrdom would inject energy into the system and allow a new class of leaders to emerge"*: Kilcullen, *Counterinsurgency*, pp. 220–21.

123   *"the dramatic narrative since 9/11 has essentially borne out the entire radical Islamist bill of particulars"*: Report of the Defense Science Board Task Force on Strategic Communications, pp. 42–43.

124   *"The minute you stop mowing the grass is going to grow back"*: Greg Miller, "Plan for Hunting Terrorists Signals U.S. Intends to Keep Adding Names to Kill Lists," *Washington Post,* October 23, 2012.

125   *implying that if he became president he'd order more such attacks:* Rom-ney's full statement was: "I support that entirely, and feel the president was right up to the usage of that technology." Having

noted earlier that "we can't kill our way out of this mess," he went on to call for "a far more effective and comprehensive strategy"—focused on education and economic development—"to help move the world away from terror and Islamic extremism." It is a fair indication of President Obama's political strength on national security during his reelection campaign that not only was the word "drones" hardly uttered but that, when it finally was, the Republican challenger found himself vigorously supporting their use while reverting to faintly progressive-sounding calls for regional development.

125 *"based on information that is secret and has been collected and evaluated according to secret criteria by anonymous individuals in a secret procedure"*: Brooks, "Cross-Border Targeted Killings: 'Lawful but Awful'?," p. 244. It is worth quoting the passage in full: "I do not for one moment doubt the good faith of the U.S. government officials making the decisions on drone strikes. But at the end of the day, all that good faith notwithstanding, we now have a state of affairs in which our government—the government of a nation that was founded on the premise that all men are created equal, and endowed by their creator with certain unalienable rights, including the rights to life and liberty—is claiming for itself the unreviewable power to kill any person, anywhere on earth, at any time, based on information that is secret and has been collected and evaluated according to secret criteria by anonymous individuals in a secret procedure." See also Rosa Brooks, "Take Two Drones and Call Me in the Morning," *Foreign Policy*, September 12, 2012.

126 *by managing during his light footprint version of the war on terror to avoid taking prisoners*: See "Interrogation Techniques," a campaign policy paper written by former Bush and Reagan officials, which notes that "Governor Romney has recommended for years that a sounder policy outcome is the revival of the enhanced interrogation program" and urges him to "expressly

endorse such an outcome during the campaign," or risk "signaling to the bureaucracy that this is not a deeply-felt priority." See also Charlie Savage, "Election to Decide Future Interrogation Methods in Terrorism Cases," *New York Times,* September 27, 2012.

126 *Drones, they argued, had replaced the interrogation room:* Micah Zenko,"Kill > Capture," *Foreign Policy,* April 14, 2015.

127 *looked like a "military coup in a far-off banana republic":* Paul's remarks on the Boston "military coup" were widely quoted. See, for example, Kevin Robillard, "Ron Paul slams Boston 'Occupation,'" *Politico,* April 29, 2013.

128 *in Baghdad in 2003, "politically at least, we can't take those steps":* A full report on the bombing and this exchange can be found in Mark Danner, "Delusions in Baghdad," in *Stripping Bare the Body,* pp. 379–91.

130 *"this will begin to erode the willingness of a democratic public to continue the fight":* Michael Ignatieff, *The Lesser Evil: Political Ethics in an Age of Terror* (Princeton: Princeton University Press, 2005), pp. 61–62. (emphasis added)

131 *Little evidence exists that the Americans even understood the problem, let alone had a solution:* Certainly there were people within the American governmental bureaucracies who knew Iraq well, but there is little to suggest they had any influence on policy, which was closely held in the upper reaches of the White House and the Department of Defense. Knowledge of the country there was not extensive: "Bush is a man who has never shown much curiosity about the world. When he met with [Kanan] Makiya and two other Iraqis in January, I was told by someone not present, the exiles spent a good portion of the time explaining to the president that there are two kinds of Arabs in Iraq, Sunnis and Shiites. The very notion of an Iraqi opposition appeared to be new to him." George Packer, "Dreaming of Democracy," *New York Times Magazine,* March 2, 2003.

131 *"it will become possible to awaken the inattentive Sunnis as they feel im-minent danger and annihilating death"*: "Zarqawi Letter: February 2004 Coalition Provisional Authority English translation of ter-rorist Musab al Zarqawi letter obtained by United States Gov-ernment in Iraq," U.S. Department of State Archive.

132 *"so they'd go out of their way to provoke the most horrific violence against their own people"*: David Kilcullen, "Blood Year: Terror and the Islamic State," *Quarterly Essay* 58 (2015): 19.

134 *"the radical clerics are recruiting, training and deploying against us"*: "Rumsfeld's War-on-Terror Memo," *USA Today*, May 20, 2005.

134 *gain ground in the "battle of the story"*: For more on "the battle of the story"—the war of ideas between terrorist propaganda and that of those they target—see John Arquilla and David Ronfeldt, "Fight Networks with Networks," *RAND Review*, Fall 2001.

134 *"a misguided invasion of a Muslim country that sparks new insurgen-cies"*: See "Obama's Speech at the Woodrow Wilson Center," Au-gust 1, 2007.

136 *"But the odds of being able to maintain that batting average, as the num-bers go up, those [odds] go down"*: *Piers Morgan Tonight*, CNN, Sep-tember 6, 2011.

138 *Abu Bakr al-Baghdadi, the Islamic State's self-proclaimed Caliph, is in many ways Osama bin Laden's "true successor"*: Malise Ruthven, "In-side the Islamic State," *New York Review of Books*, July 9, 2015.

138 *Perhaps a thousand or more of its key officials are former Baathist offi-cers in Saddam's security services*: Charles B. Lister, *The Islamic State: A Brief Introduction* (Washington: Brookings Institution, 2015), p. 35.

138 *Using plans which originated in those security services*: Christoph Reu-ter, "The Terror Strategist: Secret Files Reveal the Structure of Islamic State," *Spiegel Online International*, April 18, 2015.

138 *the most savage and effective in opposing the occupation and sowing the seeds of sectarian civil war*: For a report on the Islamic State's roots in U.S.-occupied Iraq and one of the most thorough accounts

of the career of Abu Musab al-Zarqawi, see Joby Warrick, *Black Flags: The Rise of ISIS* (New York: Doubleday, 2015).

138 *much more than "a terrorist organization, pure and simple," in President Obama's ill-chosen words:* "Statement by the President on ISIL," The White House, September 10, 2014.

139 *"force America to abandon its war against Islam by proxy and force it to attack directly":* Abu Bakr Naji, *The Management of Savagery: The Most Critical Stage Through Which the Umma Will Pass* (Cambridge, Mass.: John M. Olin Institute for Strategic Studies, Harvard University, 2004), p. 10.

140 *"we are continuing this policy of bleeding America to the point of bankruptcy":* Bin Laden made the comments in a video broadcast by Al Jazeera in November 2004. Quoted in Kilcullen, *Counterinsurgency,* p. 213.

140 *to support an Iraqi army that the secretary of defense admits "shows no will to fight":* Greg Jaffe and Loveday Morris, "Defense Secretary Carter: Iraqis Lack 'Will to Fight' to Defeat Islamic State," *Washington Post,* May 24, 2015.

140 *"'ambiguous, uncertain, borderline fringe, at the intersection of the legal and the political'":* Agamben, *State of Exception,* p. 1. The second phrase Agamben quotes is from Saint-Bonnet.

141 *"to the Arab world's own 'Guantánamos,' 'Abu Ghraibs,' and widespread practice of torture":* Shadi Mokhtari, "Human Rights Irony for the US and Arab World," Al Jazeera, August 25, 2011.

142 *"the space for invoking human rights on moral grounds alone has virtually disappeared":* Ibid.

142 *"not because of public opinion but in spite of it":* Ibid.

142 *"no moral value . . . obliges public servants ever to sacrifice innocent lives to spare a captured terrorist from unpleasant things":* Remarks by Richard B. Cheney, American Enterprise Institute, May 21, 2009.

144 *"consequently, Headquarters recommended resumption of [enhanced interrogation techniques]":* Special Review: Counterterrorism and Detention Activities (September 2001–October 2003), May 7, 2004, p. 83.

144 *"concludes in just as numb certainty: they will do with me what they want"*: Jean Améry, *At the Mind's Limits: Contemplations by a Survivor of Auschwitz and Its Realities* (Bloomington: Indiana University Press, 1980 [1966]), pp. 26–27.

146 *the legal right to use cruel, inhuman, and degrading treatment to acquire information that could prevent an imminent attack*: Philip Heymann and Juliette Kayyem, *Protecting Liberty in an Age of Terror* (Cambridge, Mass.: MIT Press, 2005).

146 *in the notorious idea of instituting torture warrants to be signed by a judge*: Bruce Ackerman, *Before the Next Attack: Preserving Civil Liberty in an Age of Terrorism* (New Haven: Yale University Press, 2007); and Alan Dershowitz, "Tortured Reasoning," in Sanford Levinson, ed., *Torture: A Collection* (New York: Oxford University Press, 2006).

146 *experienced interrogators, several of whom have spoken out, argue persuasively against this*: See, for example, Matthew Alexander, *How to Break a Terrorist: The U.S. Interrogators Who Used Brains, Not Brutality, to Take Down the Deadliest Man in Iraq* (New York: St. Martin's, 2011); Soufan with Freedman, *The Black Banners*; and Glenn Carle, *The Interrogator: An Education* (New York: Nation Books, 2011).

147 *"the empirical evidence of the last five years, hard years, tells us that"*: "DoD News Briefing with Deputy Assistant Secretary Stimson and Lt. Gen. Kimmons from the Pentagon," September 6, 2006.

147 *"CIA's use of its enhanced interrogation techniques was not an effective means of acquiring intelligence"*: The Senate Intelligence Committee Report on Torture (Brooklyn: Melville House, 2014), p. 4.

150 *"continue to grant presidents unbound powers more suited for traditional armed conflicts between nation states"*: "Text of President Obama's May 23 speech on National Security," *Washington Post*, May 23, 2013.

151 *Instead of increasing foreign aid, as the president had demanded, his administration slightly reduced it*: Sarah Kreps, "Obama's Report Card on Drone Policy Reform," *The Hill*, May 19, 2014.

152   *"Welcome," as one commentator put it, "to America's Thirty Years War"*: Spencer Ackerman, *Wired*, quoted in Glenn Greenwald, *The Guardian*, May 17, 2013.

152   *would cover fighting in Syria and "boots on the ground in the Congo"*: See Spencer Ackerman, "Pentagon Spec Ops Chief Sees 10 to 20 More Years of War Against Al-Qaida," *Wired*, May 16, 2013.

153   *the administration was suggesting asking Congress to bless its perpetuation:* Josh Gerstein, "White House Wants New OK for 'Evolving' Terror Fight," *Washington Post*, July 26, 2014.

154   *the official's reply was stark: "Not very much"*: Greg Miller, "Al Qaeda Targets Dwindle as Group Shrinks," *Washington Post*, November 23, 2011.

154   *"The United States has reached only the midpoint of what was once known as the global war on terrorism"*: Greg Miller, "Plan for Hunting Terrorists Signals U.S. Intends to Keep Adding Names to Kill Lists," *Washington Post*, October 23, 2012.

155   *Pleasing no one, the proposal was dead on arrival:* Scott Wong, "GOP: Obama War Request Is Dead," *The Hill*, April 13, 2015.

155   *The National Security Strategy . . . speaks of "a generational struggle"*: The writers of the document describe "a struggle for power . . . underway among and within many states of the Middle East and North Africa. This is a generational struggle in the aftermath of the 2003 Iraq war and 2011 Arab uprisings, which will redefine the region as well as relationships among communities and between citizens and their governments. This process will continue to be combustible, especially in societies where religious extremists take root, or rulers reject democratic reforms, exploit their economies, and crush civil society." *National Security Strategy*, The White House, February 2015, p. 5.

155   *"this threat" of terrorism as "probably a 30-year issue"*: Micah Zenko, "Countering ISIS: The Pentagon Wants Perpetual Warfare," *Newsweek*, February 1, 2015.

155   *"a generational fight for civilization against brutal enemies"*: Micah

Zenko, "America's Virulent, Extremist Counterterrorism Ideology," *Foreign Policy*, May 21, 2015.

155   *"it's been a war that has been in existence for millennia"*: Paul R. Pillar, "The Endless War," *The National Interest*, February 6, 2013.

155   *"the United States . . . will define the nature and scope of this struggle"*: *National Security Strategy*, The White House, February 2015, p. 9.

156   *deaths from terrorism have grown by more than 4,000 percent:* These figures, collected in the Department of State's *Country Reports on Terrorism: 2014,* are drawn from Micah Zenko, "Terrorism Is Booming Almost Everywhere but in the United States," *Foreign Policy,* June 19, 2015.

156   *According to a RAND study . . . the number of jihadists more than doubled:* Seth G. Jones, *A Persistent Threat: The Evolution of al Qa'ida and Other Salafi Jihadists* (Santa Monica, Calif.: RAND, 2014), p. 26.

156   *"the* madrassas *and the radical clerics are recruiting, training and deploying against us":* "Rumsfeld's War-on-Terror Memo," *USA Today,* May 20, 2005.

158   *"fight them over there so we don't have to fight them here":* Though President Bush began using this rationale much more frequently after the Iraq War began to go badly, there are hints of it in statements he made before the invasion, for example, on February 14, 2003, when he said in a White House statement that "The strategy focuses on taking the fight against terrorists directly to them, isolating the terrorists from each other and potential allies, and disrupting plots before attacks occur." On October 25, 2014, he argued that "We are fighting these terrorists with our military in Afghanistan and Iraq and beyond so we do not have to face them in the streets of our own cities." By June 9, 2005, he was making the familiar declaration, "We're taking the fight to the terrorists abroad, so we don't have to face them here at home."

158   *part of a sharply rising struggle within the Muslim world itself:* As Anthony Cordesman writes, "for all the U.S. and other Western

fears of terrorism, RAND found that, 'Approximately 99 percent of the attacks by al Qaeda and its affiliates in 2013 were against "near enemy": largely other Muslims in the Middle East and North Africa.'" Anthony Cordesman, "The Imploding U.S. Strategy in the Islamic State War?," Center for Strategic and International Studies, October 23, 2014.

158 *law enforcement organizations . . . once again be given primary responsibility for preventing terrorist attacks:* See, for example, Jennifer Daskal and Stephen L. Vladeck, "Don't Expand the War on Terror," *New York Times,* May 15, 2013; and Jennifer Daskal and Stephen L. Vladeck, "After the AUMF," *Harvard National Security Journal* 5 (2014): 132–35.

159 *"and the whole rotten structure will come crashing down":* Hitler is quoted as saying this on June 22, 1941, while leaving for his new headquarters in East Prussia. See Stephen Van Evera, *Causes of War: Power and the Roots of Conflict* (Ithaca: Cornell University Press, 1999), p. 21.

160 *entered an "era of persistent conflict":* Michael R. Gordon, "After Hard-Won Lessons, Army Doctrine Revised," *New York Times,* February 8, 2008.

161 *suggesting how one might know when those goals had been met:* See, for example, Rosa Brooks, Sarah H. Cleveland, Walter Dellinger, et al., "Principles to Guide Congressional Authorization of the Continued Use of Force Against ISIL," https://www.justsecurity.org/wp =content/uploads/2014/11/ISIS-AUMF-Statement-FINAL.pdf.

161 *"contain and deter" as the broader goal of U.S. policy:* For an interesting discussion of containment and the war on terror, see Ian Shapiro, *Containment: Rebuilding a Strategy Against Global Terror* (Princeton: Princeton University Press, 2007). See also Steven Walt, "What Should We Do if the Islamic State Wins? Live with It," *Foreign Policy,* June 10, 2015. For an analysis of deterring terrorists, see David Ignatius, "A Hint of Deterrence in U.S. Drone-War Strategy," *Washington Post,* October 4, 2011.

163   *"unraveling some of the very policies that have kept our people safe since 9/11"*: Dick Cheney, Speech to the American Enterprise Institute, May 21, 2009.

163   *There is, for example, the "disposition matrix"*: Miller, "Plan for Hunting Terrorists Signals U.S. Intends to Keep Adding Names to Kill Lists."

164   *"preserve the special mental atmosphere that a hierarchical society needs"*: George Orwell, *Nineteen Eighty-Four* (New York: Signet, 1961 [1949]), p. 199.

164   *instigate "an escalatory spiral," one whose momentum is controlled by the terrorists, not by those who seek to destroy them*: Ignatieff, *The Lesser Evil*, pp. 61–62.

165   *"elements of our public life that, given courage and intelligence, were avoidable"*: Irving Howe, *Politics and the Novel* (New York: Ivan R. Dee, 2002), p. 236.

AFTERWORD

167   *"And whatever happens seems right on the other side of the wall"*: Wisława Szymborska, *View with a Grain of Sand: Selected Poems*. Translated by Stanisław Barańczak and Clare Cavanagh (New York: Houghton Mifflin Harcourt, 1995).

167   *"destroy our way of life"*: Reena Flores, "Chris Christie: 'We're Already in World War III,'" CBS News, December 16, 2015.

167   *"see if sand can glow in the dark"*: Matthew Patane, "Cruz: Carpet Bomb ISIS 'into Oblivion,'" *Des Moines Register*, December 5, 2015.

167   *"even if it doesn't work they deserve it anyway for what they do to us"*: "Trump: 'You Bet Your Ass' I'd Approve Waterboarding, 'If It Doesn't Work, They Deserve It Anyway,'" *RealClearPolitics*, November 24, 2015.

168   *"and force it to attack directly"*: Abu Bakr Naji, *The Management of Savagery*, p. 10.

169 *"the starkness of each cell (concrete and bars)"*: See The Senate Intelligence Committee Report on Torture, p. 60.

172 *"the end of America's great power role in organizing and stabilizing the region"*: Robert D. Kaplan, "The Ruins of Empire in the Middle East," *Foreign Policy,* May 25, 2015.

173 *"should 'have his head examined'"*: Thom Shanker, "Warning Against Wars Like Iraq and Afghanistan," *New York Times,* February 25, 2011. Gates was quoting Gen. Douglas MacArthur.

BIBLIOGRAPHY

Ackerman, Bruce. *Before the Next Attack: Preserving Civil Liberty in an Age of Terrorism.* New Haven: Yale University Press, 2007.

Agamben, Giorgio. *State of Exception*, translated by Kevin Attell. Chicago: University of Chicago Press, 2005.

Ajami, Fouad. *The Arab Predicament: Arab Political Thought and Practice Since 1967.* Cambridge, U.K.: Cambridge University Press, 1981.

———. *The Dream Palace of the Arabs: A Generation's Odyssey.* New York: Vintage, 1998.

———. *The Foreigner's Gift: The Americans, the Arabs, and the Iraqis in Iraq.* New York: Free Press, 2006.

———. *The Vanished Imam: Musa al Sadr and the Shia of Lebanon.* Ithaca, N.Y.: Cornell University Press, 1986.

Alexander, Matthew. *How to Break a Terrorist: The U.S. Interrogators Who Used Brains, Not Brutality, to Take Down the Deadliest Man in Iraq.* New York: St. Martin's, 2011.

Allison, Graham. *Nuclear Terrorism: The Ultimate Preventable Catastrophe*. New York: Henry Holt, 2004.

Améry, Jean. *At the Mind's Limits: Contemplations by a Survivor of Auschwitz and Its Realities*. Bloomington: Indiana University Press, 1980.

Arquilla, John, and David Ronfeldt. *Networks and Netwars: The Future of Terror, Crime, and Militancy*. Santa Monica: RAND, 2001.

Aussaresses, Gen. Paul. *The Battle of the Casbah: Terrorism and Counter-Terrorism in Algeria, 1955–1957*. New York: Enigma, 2002.

Bacevich, Andrew J. *The Imperial Tense: Prospects and Problems of American Empire*. Chicago: Ivan R. Dee, 2003.

———. *The Limits of Power: The End of American Exceptionalism*. New York: Metropolitan, 2008.

Baer, Robert. *See No Evil: The True Story of a Ground Soldier in the CIA's War on Terrorism*. New York: Three Rivers, 2002.

———. *Sleeping with the Devil: How Washington Sold Our Soul for Saudi Crude*. New York: Three Rivers, 2003.

Baker, James A. III, and Lee H. Hamilton. *The Iraq Study Group Report: The Way Forward—A New Approach*. New York: Vintage, 2006.

Baker, Peter. *Days of Fire: Bush and Cheney in the White House*. New York: Doubleday, 2013.

Bell, J. Bowyer. *The Dynamics of the Armed Struggle*. Portland: Frank Cass, 1998.

Benjamin, Daniel, and Steven Simon. *The Age of Sacred Terror*. New York: Random House, 2002.

Bergen, Peter L. *The Longest War: The Enduring Conflict Between America and Al-Qaeda*. New York: Free Press, 2011.

———. *The Osama bin Laden I Know: An Oral History of al Qaeda's Leader*. New York: Free Press, 2006.

Berman, Paul. *Terror and Liberalism*. New York: W. W. Norton, 2003.

Blix, Hans. *Disarming Iraq: The Search for Weapons of Mass Destruction*. New York: Pantheon, 2004.

Bobbit, Philip. *Terror and Consent: The Wars of the 21st Century*. New York: Alfred A. Knopf, 2008.

Bremer, L. Paul. *My Year in Iraq: The Struggle to Build a Future of Hope*. New York: Simon & Schuster, 2006.

Brisard, Jean-Charles. *Zarqawi: The New Face of al-Qaeda*. New York: Other Press, 2005.

Bumiller, Elisabeth. *Condoleezza Rice: An American Life*. New York: Random House, 2007.

Bush, George W. *Decision Points*. New York: Crown, 2010.

Carle, Glenn. *The Interrogator: An Education*. New York: Nation Books, 2011.

Carr, Matthew. *Unknown Soldiers: How Terrorism Transformed the Modern World*. London: Profile, 2006.

Chandrasekaran, Rajiv. *Imperial Life in the Emerald City: Inside Iraq's Green Zone*. New York: Alfred A. Knopf, 2006.

Cheney, Dick, with Liz Cheney. *In My Time: A Personal and Political Memoir*. New York: Threshold, 2011.

Clarke, Richard A. *Against All Enemies: Inside America's War on Terror*. New York: Free Press, 2004.

Cockburn, Patrick. *The Occupation: War and Resistance in Iraq*. London: Verso, 2006.

Cole, David, and Jules Lobel. *Less Safe, Less Free: Why America Is Losing the War on Terror*. New York: New Press, 2007.

Cole, David, ed. *The Torture Memos*. New York: New Press, 2009.

Coll, Steve. *Ghost Wars: The Secret History of the CIA, Afghanistan, and bin Laden, from the Soviet Invasion to September 11, 2001*. New York: Penguin, 2004.

Conroy, John. *Unspeakable Acts, Ordinary People: The Dynamics of Torture: An Examination of the Practice of Torture in Three Democracies*. Berkeley: University of California Press, 2000.

Cordesman, Anthony H. *The Iraq War: Strategy, Tactics, and Military Lessons*. Washington: CSIS, 2003.

Cronin, Isaac, ed. *Confronting Fear: A History of Terrorism*. New York: Thunder's Mouth, 2002.

Daalder, Ivo H., and James M. Lindsay. *America Unbound: The Bush Revolution in Foreign Policy*. Washington: Brookings Institution, 2003.

Danner, Mark. *The Secret Way to War: The Downing Street Memo and the Iraq War's Buried History*. New York: New York Review Books, 2006.

———. *Stripping Bare the Body: Politics Violence War*. New York: Nation Books, 2009.

———. *Torture and Truth: America, Abu Ghraib and the War on Terror*. New York: New York Review Books, 2004.

Devji, Faisal. *Landscapes of the Jihad: Militancy Morality Modernity*. Ithaca, N.Y.: Cornell University Press, 2005.

Diamond, Larry. *Squandered Victory: The American Occupation and the Bungled Effort to Bring Democracy to Iraq*. New York: Times Books, 2005.

Dodge, Toby. *Inventing Iraq: The Failure of Nation Building and a History Denied*. New York: Columbia University Press, 2003.

Eichenwald, Kurt. *500 Days: Secrets and Lies in the Terror Wars*. New York: Touchstone, 2012.

Fallows, James. *Blind into Baghdad: America's War in Iraq*. New York: Vintage, 2006.

Friedman, George. *America's Secret War: Inside the Hidden Worldwide Struggle Between America and Its Enemies*. New York: Broadway, 2004.

Fromkin, David. *A Peace to End All Peace: The Fall of the Ottoman Empire and the Creation of the Modern Middle East*. New York: Henry Holt, 1989.

Frum, David, and Richard Perle. *An End to Evil: How to Win the War on Terror*. New York: Random House, 2003.

Gaddis, John Lewis. *Strategies of Containment: A Critical Appraisal of American National Security Policy During the Cold War.* Oxford: Oxford University Press, 2005.

Galbraith, Peter W. *The End of Iraq: How American Incompetence Created a War Without End.* New York: Simon & Schuster, 2006.

Gardner, Lloyd C. *Killing Machine: The American Presidency in the Age of Drone Warfare.* New York: New Press, 2013.

Gates, Robert M. *Duty: Memoirs of a Secretary at War.* New York: Alfred A. Knopf, 2014.

Gellman, Barton. *Angler: The Cheney Vice Presidency.* New York: Penguin, 2008.

Goldsmith, Jack. *The Terror Presidency: Law and Judgment Inside the Bush Administration.* New York: W. W. Norton, 2007.

Gordon, Michael R., and Gen. Bernard E. Trainor. *Cobra II: The Inside Story of the Invasion and Occupation of Iraq.* New York: Pantheon, 2006.

Gray, John R. *Al Qaeda and What It Means to Be Modern.* New York: New Press, 2003.

Greenberg, Karen J., and Joshua Dratel, eds. *The Torture Papers: The Road to Abu Ghraib.* New York: Cambridge University Press, 2005.

Greenwald, Glenn. *No Place to Hide: Edward Snowden, the NSA, and the U.S. Surveillance State.* New York: Metropolitan, 2014.

Gross, Oren, and Fionnuala Ní Aoláin. *Law in Times of Crisis: Emergency Powers in Theory and Practice.* Cambridge, U.K.: Cambridge University Press, 2006.

Gunaratna, Rohan. *Inside Al Qaeda: Global Network of Terror.* New York: Columbia University Press, 2002.

Halperin, Mark, and John Heilemann. *Double Down: Game Change 2012.* New York: Penguin, 2013.

Hashim, Ahmed S. *Insurgency and Counter-Insurgency in Iraq.* Ithaca, N.Y.: Cornell University Press, 2006.

Hersh, Seymour M. *Chain of Command: The Road from 9/11 to Abu Ghraib.* New York: HarperCollins, 2004.

Heymann, Philip, and Juliette Kayyem. *Protecting Liberty in an Age of Terror.* Cambridge, Mass.: MIT Press, 2005.

Hoffman, Bruce. *Inside Terrorism.* New York: Columbia University Press, 1998.

Hoge, James F. Jr., and Gideon Rose, eds. *Understanding the War on Terror.* New York: Council on Foreign Relations, 2005.

Holtzman, Elizabeth, and Cynthia L. Cooper. *Cheating Justice: How Bush and Cheney Attacked the Rule of Law and Plotted to Avoid Prosecution— And What We Can Do About It.* New York: Beacon, 2012.

Ignatieff, Michael. *The Lesser Evil: Political Ethics in An Age of Terror.* Princeton: Princeton University Press, 2005.

International Committee of the Red Cross, Delegates of. *ICRC Report on the Treatment of Fourteen "High Value Detainees" in CIA Custody.* February 2007.

———. *Report of the International Committee of the Red Cross (ICRC) on the Treatment by the Coalition Forces of Prisoners of War and Other Protected*

Persons by the Geneva Conventions in Iraq During Arrest, Internment and Interrogation. February 2004.

Kennan, George F. *American Diplomacy.* Chicago: University of Chicago Press, 1984.

Kepel, Gilles. *Bad Moon Rising: A Chronicle of the Middle East Today.* London: Saqi, 2003.

———. *Jihad: The Trail of Political Islam.* Cambridge, Mass.: Belknap Press, 2002.

———. *The War for Muslim Minds: Islam and the West.* Cambridge, Mass.: Belknap Press, 2004.

Kilcullen, David. *Counterinsurgency.* New York: Oxford University Press, 2010.

Kissinger, Henry. *Diplomacy.* New York: Touchstone, 1994.

Klaidman, Daniel. *Kill or Capture: The War on Terror and the Soul of the Obama Presidency.* New York: Houghton, 2012.

Korb, Lawrence J. *A New National Security Strategy in an Age of Terrorists, Tyrants, and Weapons of Mass Destruction: Three Options Presented as Presidential Speeches.* New York: Council on Foreign Relations, 2003.

Laqueur, Walter. *Guerrilla: A Historical and Critical Study.* Boston: Little, Brown, 1976.

———. *No End to War: Terrorism in the Twenty-First Century.* New York: Continuum, 2003.

Laqueur, Walter, ed. *Voices of Terror: Manifestos, Writings and Manuals of al Qaeda, Hamas, and Other Terrorists from Around the World and Throughout the Ages*. New York: Reed, 2004.

Lawrence, Bruce, ed. *Messages to the World: The Statements of Osama bin Laden*. London: Verso, 2005.

Levinson, Sanford, ed. *Torture: A Collection*. New York: Oxford University Press, 2006.

Lewis, Bernard. *The Crisis of Islam: Holy War and Unholy Terror*. New York: Modern Library, 2003.

———. *From Babel to Dragomans: Interpreting the Middle East*. Oxford: Oxford University Press, 2004.

———. *The Middle East: A Brief History of the Last 2,000 Years*. New York: Touchstone, 1997.

———. *What Went Wrong? Western Impact and Middle Eastern Response*. Oxford: Oxford University Press, 2002.

Lister, Charles B. *The Islamic State: A Brief Introduction*. Washington: Brookings Institution, 2015.

Luttwak, Edward. *Coup d'État: A Practical Handbook*. Cambridge, Mass.: Harvard University Press, 1979.

———. *Strategy: The Logic of War and Peace*. Cambridge, Mass.: Belknap Press, 2001.

Makiya, Kanan. *Republic of Fear: The Politics of Modern Iraq*. Berkeley: University of California Press, 1998.

Mann, James. *Rise of the Vulcans: The History of Bush's War Cabinet.* New York: Viking, 2004.

Marr, Phebe. *The Modern History of Iraq.* Boulder: Westview, 2004.

Mayer, Jane. *The Dark Side: The Inside Story of How the War on Terror Turned into a War on American Ideals.* New York: Doubleday, 2008.

Mazzetti, Mark. *The Way of the Knife: The CIA, a Secret Army, and a War at the Ends of the Earth.* New York: Penguin, 2013.

McCoy, Alfred W. *A Question of Torture: CIA Interrogation, from the Cold War to the War on Terror.* New York: Metropolitan Books, 2006.

Merry, Robert W. *Sands of Empire: Missionary Zeal, American Foreign Policy, and the Hazards of Global Ambition.* New York: Simon & Schuster, 2005.

Naji, Abu Bakr. *The Management of Savagery: The Most Critical Stage Through Which the Umma Will Pass.* Cambridge, Mass.: John M. Olin Institute for Strategic Studies, Harvard University.

Nakash, Yitzhak. *The Shi'is of Iraq.* Princeton: Princeton University Press, 2003.

Nance, Malcolm W. *The Terrorists of Iraq: Inside the Strategy and Tactics of the Iraq Insurgency.* Charleston: BookSurge, 2007.

Nasr, Vali. *The Shia Revival: How Conflicts Within Islam Will Shape the Future.* New York: W. W. Norton, 2006.

National Commission on Terrorist Attacks. *The 9/11 Commission Report: Final Report of the National Commission on Terrorist Attacks upon the United States.* New York: W. W. Norton, 2004.

Phillips, David L. *Losing Iraq: Inside the Postwar Reconstruction Fiasco.* New York: Westview, 2005.

Podhoretz, Norman. *World War IV: The Long Struggle Against Islamofascism.* New York: Doubleday, 2007.

Pollack, Kenneth M. *The Threatening Storm: The Case for Invading Iraq.* New York: Random House, 2002.

Posner, Gerald. *Secrets of the Kingdom: The Inside Story of the Saudi-U.S. Connection.* New York: Random House, 2005.

Reuters. *Afghanistan: Lifting the Veil.* Upper Saddle River, N.J.: Prentice Hall, 2002.

Rice, Condoleezza. *No Higher Honor: A Memoir of My Years in Washington.* New York: Crown, 2011.

Rich, Frank. *The Greatest Story Ever Sold: The Decline and Fall of Truth from 9/11 to Katrina.* New York: Penguin, 2006.

Ricks, Thomas E. *Fiasco: The American Military Adventure in Iraq.* New York: Penguin, 2006.

Rieff, David. *A Bed for the Night: Humanitarianism in Crisis.* New York: Simon & Schuster, 2002.

Risen, James. *State of War: The Secret History of the CIA and the Bush Administration.* New York: Free Press, 2006.

Riverbend. *Baghdad Burning: Girl Blog from Iraq.* New York: Feminist, 2005.

———. *Baghdad Burning II: More Girl Blog from Iraq*. New York: Feminist, 2006.

Rizzo, John. *Company Man: Thirty Years of Controversy and Crisis in the CIA*. New York: Scribner, 2014.

Robinson, Linda. *Tell Me How This Ends: General David Petraeus and the Search for a Way Out of Iraq*. New York: PublicAffairs, 2008.

Rosen, Nir. *In the Belly of the Green Bird: The Triumph of the Martyrs in Iraq*. New York: Free Press, 2006.

Rossiter, Clinton I. *Constitutional Dictatorship: Crisis Government in the Modern Democracies*. New York: Transaction, 2002 [Princeton University Press, 1948].

Roth, Cecil. *The Spanish Inquisition*. London: W. W. Norton, 1996 [1937].

Rothkopf, David. *Running the World: The Inside Story of the National Security Council and the Architects of American Power*. New York: PublicAffairs, 2004.

Roy, Oliver. *Globalized Islam: The Search for a New Ummah*. New York: Columbia University Press, 2004.

Sageman, Marc. *Understanding Terror Networks*. Philadelphia: University of Pennsylvania Press, 2004.

Saint-Bonnet, François. *L'état d'exception*. Paris: Press Universitaires de France, 2001.

Sands, Philippe. *Torture Team: Rumsfeld's Memo and the Betrayal of American Values*. New York: Palgrave, 2008.

Sanger, David. *Confront and Conceal: Obama's Secret Wars and Surprising Use of American Power.* New York: Crown, 2012.

Scheuer, Michael ("Anonymous"). *Through Our Enemies' Eyes: Osama bin Laden, Radical Islam, and the Future of America.* Washington: Brassey's, 2002.

Schlesinger, James R., Harold Brown, Tillie K. Fowler, and General Charles A. Horner (USAF-Ret.). *Final Report of the Independent Panel to Review DoD Detention Operations (The Schlesinger Report).* 2004.

Shapiro, Ian. *Containment: Rebuilding a Strategy Against Global Terror.* Princeton: Princeton University Press, 2007.

Sick, Gary. *All Fall Down: America's Tragic Encounter with Iran.* New York: Penguin, 1985.

Soufan, Ali, with Daniel Freedman. *The Black Banners: The Inside Story of 9/11 and the War Against al-Qaeda.* New York: W. W. Norton, 2011.

Stewart, Rory. *The Prince of the Marshes and Other Occupational Hazards of a Year in Iraq.* Orlando: Harcourt, 2006.

Suskind, Ron. *The One Percent Doctrine: Deep Inside America's Pursuits of Its Enemies Since 9/11.* New York: Simon & Schuster, 2006.

Szymborska, Wisława. *View with a Grain of Sand: Selected Poems.* Translated by Stanisław Barańczak and Clare Cavanagh. New York: Houghton Mifflin Harcourt, 1995.

Taber, Robert. *War of the Flea: The Classic Study of Guerrilla Warfare.* Washington: Potomac, 2002.

Taguba, Maj. Gen. Antonio M. *Article 15-6 Investigation of the 800th Military Police Brigade (The Taguba Report)*. 2004.

——. *Broken Laws, Broken Lives: Medical Evidence of Torture by US Personnel and Its Impact*. New York: Physicians for Human Rights, June 2008.

Telhami, Shibley. *The Stakes: American in the Middle East: The Consequences of Power and the Choice for Peace*. Boulder: Westview, 2002.

Timerman, Jacobo. *Prisoner Without a Name, Cell Without a Number*. New York: Vintage, 1988.

Turse, Nick. *The Changing Face of Empire: Special Ops, Drones, Spies, Proxy Fighters, Secret Bases, and Cyberwarfare*. New York: Haymarket, 2012.

Visser, Reidar, and Gareth Stansfield, eds. *An Iraq of Its Regions: Cornerstones of a Federal Democracy?* New York: Columbia University Press, 2008.

Voltaire. *Treatise on Tolerance and Other Writings*. Cambridge, U.K.: Cambridge University Press, 2000 [1763].

Voltaire, and William F. Fleming, trans. *The Works of Voltaire: A Contemporary Version, Volume VII*. Berkeley: University of California Press, 1901 [1764].

Whittaker, David J., ed. *The Terrorism Reader*. London: Routledge, 2001.

Woodward, Bob. *Bush at War*. New York: Simon & Schuster, 2002.

——. *Plan of Attack*. New York: Simon & Schuster, 2004.

——. *State of Denial: Bush at War, Part III*. New York: Simon & Schuster, 2006.

Wright, Lawrence. *The Looming Tower: Al-Qaeda and the Road to 9/11*. New York: Alfred A. Knopf, 2006.

Zizek, Slavoj. *Iraq: The Borrowed Kettle*. London: Verso, 2004.

INDEX

ABOUT THE AUTHOR

Mark Danner has written about foreign conflicts, human rights, and American politics for three decades, covering among other places Central America, Haiti, the Balkans, and the Middle East. He was for many years a staff writer at *The New Yorker* and is a regular contributor to *The New York Review of Books* and other publications. Among his books are *Stripping Bare the Body*, *Torture and Truth*, and *The Massacre at El Mozote*. Danner's writing has won many awards, including a National Magazine Award, three Overseas Press Awards, an Emmy, and a MacArthur Fellowship. He is currently Chancellor's Professor of Journalism and English at the University of California, Berkeley, and James Clarke Chace Professor of Foreign Affairs and the Humanities at Bard College. He and his wife, Michelle, and children, Grace and Truman, divide their time between New York and Berkeley, California.